THE SECRETS OF SILENCE

The Secrets of Silence

THE EVERYDAY POLICING OF BLACK WOMEN AND THEIR STORIES ABOUT VIOLENCE

SHANNON MALONE GONZALEZ

PRINCETON UNIVERSITY PRESS

PRINCETON & OXFORD

Published by Princeton University Press
41 William Street, Princeton, New Jersey 08540
99 Banbury Road, Oxford OX2 6JX

press.princeton.edu

All Rights Reserved

ISBN 9780691260433
ISBN (e-book) 9780691260471

Library of Congress Control Number: 2025932467

British Library Cataloging-in-Publication Data is available

Editorial: Rachael Levay and Tara Dugan
Production Editorial: Natalie Baan
Jacket Design: Chris Ferrante
Production: Erin Suydam
Publicity: William Pagdatoon
Copyeditor: Dana Henricks

This book has been composed in Arno

Printed in the United States of America

10 9 8 7 6 5 4 3 2 1

There's a saying in Mississippi where I'm from that my elders would often use: "Some lessons are bought, and some are taught." Whenever my grandmother saw me heading down a particular road that she or someone else had already been down; she'd let me know that this is where we might part ways. Standing beside me, she'd invite me to see that all lessons—whether bought or taught—carry a price. Someone paid for them. This is just the way things were. So, I could either buy mine with my own experiences, or I could listen to what she and those before me had learned from theirs. Either way, she made sure I understood that *understanding* comes from experience. No way around that. So, standing beside me, she'd first invite me to see the crossroads— the space between here and there where agency, however constrained, often resides. She'd then wait for me to see my choices. Did I want to buy a lesson? If so, she'd meet me on the other side. Or did I want to be taught a lesson? If so, I could walk back with her and listen to what she had to say. Waiting patiently, she never judged my choices, even when I could tell she wished I made different ones. She also didn't pretend to always know the outcome either, even though I could tell she was able to see way farther down the road than I. Many times, I'd take her hand, walk back with her, and listen to all the stories she would tell about others who had met a similar crossroad before and the many ways they fell, stumbled, got back up, danced, perished, sang, and made it through. Other times, I'd squeeze her hand tight before letting go to take my first steps down a path unknown. Yet, before I'd get too far, she'd run up to me and lean down over my shoulders. Whispering loudly in my ear so I and anyone else tuning in to the crossroads could hear, she'd declare: "She belongs to me." Then, she'd let me go.

I didn't understand back then why she would do that.

I do now.

Most importantly, she'd always meet me again—no matter how long it took—on the other side.

———

This book is dedicated to my grandmother, the fiercest and sweetest Amanda Ella, the one who teaches me and the one who catches me each and every time I pay full price for lessons. Thank you for always being a guiding light in the space between. See you on the other side of these chapters and pages dedicated to you, my daughters who also belong to you, and our ancestral mothers whose stories live on and continue to pave the way.

By and by.
Ashé

CONTENTS

THE SECRETS OF SILENCE

"when we gather"

"i was kinda scared to report it"

"he's just gonna be right back out there"

"what happens in our house"
"you don't call the police on your family"

"i wish i was taught to be okay in me"

Introduction

Sometimes, silence is loud.

A dry and raspy laugh. A pause followed by a long and exasperated exhale. *Can you still even call it a pause if she hesitated, sardonically laughed, waited, and sighed all before trying once more to explain her point?* Abena and I found it hard to meet in person.[1] We tried. But with our conflicting schedules, we quickly gave up and decided to speak late one evening over the phone after we had both put our kids to bed. A dark brown-skinned, black,[2] cisgender woman in her early thirties, Abena spent the first twenty minutes of our conversation proudly sharing how she lived in the exact same house in the working-poor neighborhood where she grew up.

It's changed, though. When she was a little girl, the area was mostly black folks; neighbors watched out for each other's kids, and houses cost "$20,000." Back then, the police didn't come quickly when called for help. Instead, Abena grew up watching officers heavily patrol the border between her neighborhood and the predominantly white and wealthier part of the city. Now, houses cost "6, 7, $800,000." Newcomers and coffee shops displaced her friends and neighbors. And the police—they were always around now, with Abena saying the cops were like, "Oh, now we have to protect our white people from the few black people that are left."

Gentrification upended Abena's social world. Her voice was low and seemingly far away over the phone as she described the many changes that came with the shift from historical divestment in her black neighborhood to police-assisted "revitalization" for her new white neighbors. But her laugh? It was loud, wry, and broken up by long sighs as she repeatedly pauses before trying once again to explain to me that there was absolutely no point in black women and girls speaking about violence—police or otherwise—because "nothing is going to happen anyway." She's shared her story before. She's learned her lesson. In our interview, she shared her stories and lessons with me, detailing exactly how she learned the hard way just what types of consequences lay on the other sides of violence disclosures folks weren't ready or willing to hear from black girls.

————

A high-pitched giggle. A pause? *Okay, a pause filled with nervous, high-pitched childlike giggles, sighs, and long looks out the back café window.* Joy and I were the only two visibly black people in the coffee shop, so we quickly found each other. Greeting one another with a hug, we stood in line and chatted while ordering our drinks. An upwardly mobile, light brown-skinned, black, cisgender woman with sandy hair in her early thirties, Joy hated the working-poor neighborhood in which she grew up, calling it a "terrible city." She's glad she made it out. She listed the many reasons why most folks don't. Even though she's now far away from the inner city where she spent most of her youth, she's carried the stories with her.

We found a table in the back corner of the sparsely populated café to guarantee she and I had some privacy. Before we could settle into our seats, Joy started in with a series of questions about the project, sharing details along the way about who she would and wouldn't allow to interview her. No one was in the back room with us. We were so far away from the front bar that we couldn't even smell the freshly roasted coffee. Even still—once Joy was satisfied with my answers—she leaned forward and waved her hand to gesture that it was time for me to join her. Hunched over the table with our heads almost touching, it was as if we were kids on the playground sharing secrets as she nervously giggled and admitted, "I got like three decades' worth of stories."

After announcing the arrival of stories amassed and untold over the course of her life, Joy leaned back in her chair, clasped her warm mug with both hands, and sighed as she looked out the window at some place far off in her memories. Although I couldn't go there with her, the slump in her shoulders and the tears forming on the outer edges of her eyes let me know that it was not easy for her to return. Yet, she did. And she described what it was like to grow up terrified of officers and her neighbors, anxious about neighborhood violence *and* the police. She knew as a child that "police officers can't protect me." In her city: "You'd rather get robbed by a criminal than get pulled over by police."

Even though she's now far away from the inner city where she grew up, it's still really difficult for her when she meets new people. It triggers old wounds around trust. It reminds her of how hard it was back then to distinguish between the danger from corrupt cops and those in her neighborhood engaged in illicit activities, questioning: "Who's the bad guy? Who's the good guy?" All she knew back then was that they all scared her. As a little girl, she didn't know how to figure out the difference. When we met, she still didn't.

———

The grating clink of a metal chair dragged across the concrete each time she shuffled. Her backpack rustling as she pulled it closer to her chest for comfort or more warmth. Not a pause, then. *A long ellipsis punctuated by fidgeting movements, shaky laughter, and anxious apologies.* It was November, and it was freezing. Yet, we still sat on the outside patio so Nema could have some privacy away from the crowd gathering in the heated café. She is an eighteen-year-old, dark brown-skinned, black, cisgender teenager with shoulder-length braids who didn't really have a strong opinion one way or the other about what it was like to grow up in a wealthy, mostly white suburb located outside a large metropolitan city. And stories? Nema anxiously laughed as she emphatically stated, "I really don't interact with the police as often," especially "as an individual who grew up in a middle-class suburban area." To further emphasize her point, Nema disclosed that prior to speaking with me, she "*really* had to reflect" on her experiences with police, stressing the "really" to let me know the memories did not come easy. Given as an apology, she then eagerly explained why she was excited to talk.

She was learning a lot about mass incarceration and policing in inner cities in one of her favorite college classes. From what they had covered so far that semester, she was curious and unsure why I would even do a project exclusively focused on black women and girls—especially including those from middle-class backgrounds like hers.

> I mean, I really don't feel like the situation affects [*pause*], well, let me stop—I feel like certain aspects of police brutality and interaction don't really apply to all black [people] or [*pause*] other people of color.

Starting, stopping, and abruptly changing directions several times while making this statement, Nema went on to specify who exactly was at risk of "certain aspects" of police violence. It's definitely not folks like her. Maybe? She's unsure.

Her cheery disposition gradually shifted as she began answering the interview questions and discussed dealing with the police. Remembering, the act of speaking aloud and listening to herself provide the details of her encounters conjured up new realizations about her own story. She fidgeted. The metal chair scraped the concrete. Squeezing her backpack closer to her chest, Nema worked through, in real time, her growing confusion about what happened during a recent police encounter, speaking to herself and me as she trailed off, "Well, he said he had a daughter too—."

———

Like most black women and girls in the United States, Abena's, Joy's, and Nema's experiences with officers wouldn't show up in any national databases tracking police violence.[3] Their police encounters wouldn't be covered in mainstream news reports or local news outlets.[4] Nor would their stories likely be shared and passed down in intergenerational talks in black families and communities.[5] For many, their experiences would be what black feminist activists and scholars have called out as "invisible"—or the countless instances of police violence against black women and girls that go unnamed and unrecognized.[6]

But, despite our absence from official and unofficial accounts, Abena, Joy, Nema, and other black women exist.[7] Our police encounters happen. Our lives matter. And so too do our stories.

One major contribution of this book is demonstrating how the policing of black women is inextricably tied to the policing of our stories. Released in 2015, the #SayHerName report directly challenged the erasure of black women's experiences, lifting up the names of Miriam Carey, Tarika Wilson, Janisha Fonville, and many others who were killed by the police.[8] The report also invited researchers, activists, and media to use gender expansive policing frames that account for the many ways black women and girls experience police violence. In Invisible No More, Andrea Ritchie further calls our attention to these harms, naming police sexual violence, neglect in a crisis, and psychological abuse as acts of police violence that policymakers and communities tend to minimize and ignore.[9] Yet, as black feminists arduously counter what Kimberlé Crenshaw calls out as the loud public silence around policing in black women's and girl's lives, the report also stresses that these absences are "not purely a matter of missing facts."[10] Indeed, the "missing-ness" of our stories from the facts and so many conversations on policing warns of deeper processes at work in our social worlds.

By trade, sociologists are obsessed with social processes like these. The entire field is dedicated to picking apart just exactly how inequality is reproduced in our day-to-day lives. And it is from people's stories—whether directly shared through narratives or filtered through other methods and measures— that we understand how the police are critical to reproducing the unequal social world that exists today. In every encounter, officers are on the front lines of deciding who is entitled to personhood, safety, and resources and who is relegated to the "invisible." However, as a discipline, we have been complicit in the loud public silence: Very little sociological attention has been paid to the social problem of police violence against black women and girls.[11] Even less has been given to the incessant social processes that render our stories so perpetually "missing."

Like many black feminists who come to research and write about violence, this "missing-ness" is not something that sits far away from me. Its personal, and I don't recall a time in my life when I didn't want to make sense of it or push through it. Yearning to deeply understand this seemingly ever-present process that makes our stories "missing," this book draws on a long lineage of black feminist sociology, which Zakiya Luna and Whitney Pirtle state is un-apologetically grounded in the belief that "no one in the Black community [is] disposable."[12] In firmly taking this stance, "black feminist sociology theorizes about the value of everyday life and all that it entails."[13] Thus, to understand "missing-ness" around policing as an everyday social process, I knew I needed to speak directly to black women about their encounters, and more, I needed to talk with them about their journeys to sharing their accounts with others. So, for four years, I sought out and listened to black women's stories: the ones that far too often don't find their way into the data, news headlines, and famil-ial talks stressing the importance of making it home. From 2017 to 2021, I in-terviewed sixty-two black women. I spoke with many others at anti–police violence protests and neighborhood events. I talked with those at school meet-ings and police-community forums. Throughout our interviews and conversa-tions, black women intimately described their lived experiences with officers. They also very, *very* cautiously shared their interactions with people in their lives who adopted similar practices of social control.

In *Arrested Justice*, Beth E. Richie explores these shared practices, offering the violence matrix as a way to see the connections between police violence and communal violence and interpersonal violence in our social worlds.[14] The violence matrix, more specifically, allows us to map black women's vulnerabili-ties across a continuum of harm, bringing into view physical assault, sexual harassment, exploitation, verbal harassment, and emotional manipulation from officers and others in their everyday lives. While Richie focuses on the experiences of poor black women, the black women I interviewed come from different social backgrounds. Yet, they also spoke to the violence matrix, to these various harms and connections, and more, how "missing-ness" occurred in any place where they experienced violence. It linked their public encounters with their private ones. It relegated their experiences to an individual issue rather than a systemic social problem. Thus, their stories make visible how policing moves across domains—linking the structural, institutional, and bureaucratic with the intimate and everyday through acts of violence as well as stories told, suppressed, and distorted about these harms.[15] Indeed, our absence is not just an issue of missing facts. It's about the stories we tell and the ways we decide each and every day who and what matters. It's about the ways we rely on social structures to recognize each other, relate to one another, and right ourselves in a crisis. And as Shatema Threadcraft argues, this process of determining what goes missing and what crystalizes into view is central to how we build and rebuild people and our social worlds.[16]

In sharing their stories, many for the first time, black women poignantly describe what it was like for them to confront and embody this systemic and intimate process of "missing-ness," which left them alone to address the violence in their lives. Thus, what started as an investigation into black women's "invisible" interactions with officers quickly expanded to the ways people in and out of uniform police black women and our stories about violence to relegate us to the outer edges of our social worlds. In spotlighting these connections, this book brings into view continuities in police practices and moments of collusion between officers and others in institutions, families, and communities. These moments reveal what I refer to as *everyday policing*—or how officers and others build and rebuild people and social worlds in public and intimate spaces by withholding recognition, asserting dominance, and enforcing their interests and realities. This social process effectively puts and keeps black women in their place—in their homes, their schools, their communities, and in political organizing.

This place is not new. Black feminist research, literature, and other writings on violence are dedicated to centering this place as a significant site of social inquiry and change. Working to understand the macro and micro ways black women are pushed, forced, and coerced into "knowing her place," black feminists highlight the violence that occurs here along with how testimonies and knowledge from "her place" are persistently dismissed. Some, like Crenshaw, refer to this place as the margins—a space etched out by multiple, interconnected structures of inequality.[17] Others like Patricia Hill Collins and Kristie

Dotson also understand this place as a space outside of mainstream recognition and categories that form the building blocks of what we claim to know about society and one another.[18] Still, others, like bell hooks, emphatically state that while this place materializes from multiple systems of domination, it also offers "to one the possibility of radical perspective from which to see and create, to imagine alternatives, new worlds."[19]

Thus, when I set out in 2017 to investigate what felt so stubbornly "invisible," it mandated centering her place—or taking seriously black women's everyday encounters along with our stories about violence that often lie on the outer edges of dominant policing frames and research. In this vein, Matthew Clair issues an invitation, asking sociologists to take seriously the intersectional subjectivities of people subjected to criminalization.[20] These subjectivities, Clair argues, carry "unique understandings and visions" about the social problem of policing and the carceral system as well as provide insights into what is needed for radical social change.[21] Many sociologists of policing and violence, such as Victor Rios and Nikki Jones, do this by focusing on the experiences and stories of those directly subjected to surveillance and punishments.[22] For example, Rios's Oakland-based ethnography traces the everyday experiences of black and Latino adolescent boys and, in the process, demonstrates how police practices extend way beyond the four walls of the department and are taken up by other authority figures in their lives.[23] From these youths' place, we see how criminalization connects their experiences with officers and others in schools and neighborhoods to create a complex web of youth social control. Similarly, Jones's ethnography of black girls in Philadelphia follows their day-to-day challenges surviving violence.[24] Complicating the code of the street, gendered norms steeped in respectability constrain their options for safety. From these girls' place, we see how they are forced to make strategic decisions between cultivating an image of a "good girl" or being seen as a "bad one" by those around them all while trying to defend themselves from violence.

My book joins scholars of policing and violence to show how practices of social control, as Uriel Serrano notes, move and seep into our lives, interweaving our public worlds with our private ones.[25] Through centering black women's place, each chapter focuses on what I came to conceptualize as *the space between*: defined as spaces where black women encounter and make meaning around our lived experiences of violence from officers and others outside of what is conventionally recognized and known about policing. As a liminal space,[26] the space between is where black women and girls have to quickly and slowly figure out what's happening to us when others inflict violence, along with deciding if we will name, share, report, or hide it. *Here*—black women in this study not only, as Eduardo Bonilla-Silva says, felt race, they embodied an emotional register that mapped onto the ways policing dynamically reproduced intersectional inequality in daily life.[27] As a literal space,[28] the space between materializes as a terrain spanning multiple contexts where officers and others target black women and girls, inflicting many unnamed and unrecognized acts of violence. *Here*—they were often left with sole responsibility for protecting themselves from harm that others minimized and ignored. Bridging the literal with the liminal in our social worlds, the black women I interviewed *felt* pathology, exclusion, apathy, idealization, and coercion, or what Audre Lorde describes as the master's tools carving out their place.[29] They *felt* the everyday policing of their personhood and stories, of the social process breaking and bending black lives and social relations into a complex web of social control. Thus, black women's experiences and searches for recognition shared in this book illuminate everyday policing as a social process that reproduces the margins in our social worlds, therein revealing how policing is just as much about silence as it is about violence.

Importantly, the black women I interviewed are not voiceless. However, as Gayatri Chakravorty Spivak reminds us, to speak is to be heard—or politically and social recognized.[30] Or, as Arundhati Roy puts it, "We know of course there's really no such thing as the 'voiceless.' There are only the deliberately silenced, or the preferably unheard."[31] Hence, silence exposes the links in the dynamic reproduction of inequitable social worlds between speakers and listeners—be they individuals, social groups, or institutions.[32] As an active social process, silence elucidates how certain people's experiences are made visible, legible, and important, while others are rendered invisible, illegible, and disposable. Thus, silence brings into focus who and what is policed. For example: How is it that police violence against one group is used to dismiss police violence against another? Why is it that speaking about one's experiences with officers in certain contexts is seen as a distraction or form of betrayal? How is it that many times black women's "invisible" encounters happened in broad daylight, or in homes surrounded by family, friends, and partners, or in public places while strangers, teachers, neighbors, and co-workers watched?

The Secrets of Silence theorizes this silence and how it operates—as deception, as disavowal, as gendered socialization, as social control, and as forms of self-protection. In doing so, this book shifts us away from relative comparisons to black men that often obscure black women's stories. Grounded in a diverse group of black women's experiences with police violence, I parse through how silence around violence constitutes a distinct vulnerability to harm. And ultimately, I define *silence as a matrix* that consists of politics, norms, and sanctions that make it difficult and dangerous for black women and girls to speak about and report violence. Within the silence matrix, politics are a collection of beliefs about vulnerabilities and violence that shape our ideas about protection and people's right to safety.[33] Norms are steeped in our politics and dictate our daily practices of protection, while sanctions reinforce them.[34] Everyday policing, then, is how officers and others use violence and the silence matrix as the master's tools to draw and redraw intersectional lines of exclusion and coercive inclusion in daily life, normalizing black women's place on the margins. In centering black women's experiences, this book contributes to research on contemporary policing as a racial project.[35] However, this book shows how policing is not just a racial project: It is an intersectional project that is just as much grounded in maintaining heteropatriarchal order as white supremacy. And, as Candice Merritt warns us not to forget, understanding black women's experiences of violence pushes us to examine black heteropatriarchy alongside white heteropatriarchy as interconnected systems of social control that put us "in our place."[36] Indeed, black women's persistent absence from the official and unofficial accounts is grounded in the symbiotic relationship between white heteropatriarchy and black heteropatriarchy—both of which make black women and girls vulnerable to violence and our stories "missing."

As a result of everyday policing, I met Joy and others like her: *black women who had been holding on tight to their stories since they were little girls.* Over coffee or over the phone, they would tell me that our interviews were the first time they had ever told anyone about their experiences. They traveled back in their memories. Or maybe their memories traveled forward with them. Either way, together, they described in vivid detail their encounters along with the emotional, psychological, and physical toll of police and other violence in their lives. Sitting across from them or on the other end of the telephone line, we shared quiet moments—*here*, in the space between—where they narrated some of their most intimate experiences even as they questioned throughout our interviews whether their stories would be recognized or deemed important.

Others I met were like Nema: *black women who made anxious apologies and declarations at the beginning of our interviews about not having any personal experiences to share.* They signed up anyway. They were curious. They wanted to talk. But they made sure to apologize first just in case I heard their stories and walked away feeling as though they had wasted my time with their "unimport-ant" experiences. Like Joy and others, they often had never directly been asked before about themselves, about their own police encounters. However, once questioned, they spent hours talking aloud and listening as they narrated their interactions with officers. *Here*—in the space between as speaker and witness to their own stories—they bumped up against and wrestled with the bound-aries of dominant policing frames that didn't quite fit them and their experiences.

With very clear pictures in their heads about "what" police violence was (*i.e., shootings*), "who" it happened to (*i.e., black men and boys*), and "where" it took place (*i.e., traffic or pedestrian stops*), they struggled with the interpreta-tions and implications of their own stories. *Like ...* [pause] *... they weren't driving in their cars. But ...* [long pause] *... they were just walking down the street with their sister and cousins to the corner store. Wait ...* [even longer pause] *... they were at home with their parents or grandparents or romantic partners. Or hanging out in the school cafeteria, grabbing lunch on a Wednesday with their friends. Or at a college party or shopping at the mall on Saturday evening with close acquaintances. Here*—left in the space between without frames to understand these encounters, they fluctuated between doubt and denial. *Here*, they won-dered what their encounters meant about police violence and themselves. Unsure, some ran immediately and all the way back to what is conventionally known about policing, downplaying their interactions with officers. Unsure, some steadied themselves within the policing and violence frames they knew, making sure I clearly understood how "good" of a girl or woman they were and precisely where and with whom their loyalties lay. Unsure, some stretched out their arms to the unknown, tentatively holding onto what they once knew while staying with their lived experiences and emergent realizations. Cau-tiously peeking over the edges of the unknown in their social worlds, they circled back multiple times in our interviews to incorporate their new aware-ness about their experiences into their expanding understandings of policing. However, no matter if they ran and steadied or stretched and stayed—all of them questioned if what happened to them would be seen as "significant" or "counted" as police violence by others.

Still, some I met were like Abena: *black women who had already talked about what happened, already disclosed, and already reported their encounters.* They knew what lay beyond the edges of what is widely recognized about policing, and, in our interviews, they told their stories once more. *Here*—pushed to the space between, they shared their intimate struggles trying to break through the doubt and denial from police, family, friends, teachers, co-workers, and media that black women and girls' encounters happened and mattered. They called out the ways they were excluded and hated the ways they were blamed. And from *here*, some questioned the utility of black women and girls disclosing violence at all, especially if it could lead to even more of it. Yet, they and others still worked tirelessly to change the punishing consequences that lay on the other sides of disclosures, along with the conditions that shaped there even needing to be disclosure in the first place.

The Secrets of Silence follows the threads weaving together Nema, Joy, Abena, and other black women's stories, encouraging readers to see that silence is not a benign aftereffect or shadow of policing. Instead, silence is a continuation of policing logics in everyday life. And if we listen, or stretch, let go, and expand our understandings of how policing intersectionally reproduces inequality, black women's stories also allow us to see some of the necessary conditions for new worlds: ones with the alternative systems and ways of relating that hooks and other black feminist abolitionists imagine, remember, and dream about—as well as work to make a reality.

Situating the Silence Around Police Violence Against Black Women and Girls

In *America Goddam*, historian Treva B. Lindsey emphasizes that "it's essential when studying violence against Black women and girls to look for the silences, the elisions, and the absences."[37] But what does it mean to look into the silences? To excavate the elisions? To peer into the absences? For feminist and critical race social scientists, it means taking seriously the ways people on the margins make meaning, create knowledge, and resist oppression. Thus, given the "missing-ness" surrounding black women's encounters from so many places, particularly sociology, it was important for me to take an interdisciplinary approach—as our stories on the outer edges of what is conventionally known about policing are unbounded by disciplines.

Everyday Policing: Epistemic Oppression and Policing as an Intersectional Project

When looking into the silences, it's crucial to note that all silences are not the same. There are the silences others impose, then there are the silences people individually and collectively create to navigate violence and find safety in their day-to-day lives. However, black feminist philosopher Kristie Dotson delineates how both silences result from epistemic violence.[38] Simply put, epistemic violence is a refusal to acknowledge, accept, or respond to an individual or social group's experiences, along with a denial of the meaning they make from them. Structurally, epistemic violence encompasses how institutions withhold recognition by framing certain people as illegitimate knowers and pathologically deceptive. Interpersonally, epistemic violence includes the ways individuals uphold these beliefs in their social interactions. Together, Dotson describes how epistemic violence quiets the testimonies of those who do not see certain speakers as legitimate knowers and knowledge producers in our social worlds.

In response, people may strategically hold onto their stories within institutions and with individuals where they feel unsafe. While holding onto their stories, people may come to the realization that certain listeners and those who occupy specific social positions don't have the frames to interpret their narratives or the tools to respond appropriately to their experiences. From there, people don't just hold onto their stories—they stop telling them altogether. They effectively smother their own testimonies. Yet, whether quieted or smothered, Dotson roots these various silences in epistemological ignorance: people's consistent unwillingness or inability to listen to, recognize, and learn from stories that are not their own.[39] Importantly, this unwillingness and inability to listen causes harm and is rooted in domination, producing a distorted knowing about people's experiences.[40] Epistemic oppression, then, is the institutional and intimate exclusion of groups of people and their stories from how we understand, create knowledge, and build our social worlds.[41]

One way I conceptualize everyday policing is by centering moments in black women's stories where people and institutions were unwilling and unable to recognize their encounters of violence and their testimonies. These moments bring "missing-ness" as a social process into view and elucidate one of the most common forms of ignorance discussed in the social sciences—white ignorance. White ignorance systemically ensures people who occupy the social position of "white" maintain legal, institutional, and interpersonal power.[42] This includes the power to determine which people and stories have institutional accounts, or rather which stories matter and which don't. Under white ignorance, knowing is grounded in epistemes that align with and shore up white positions of authority as "knowers" and knowledge producers.[43] From there, knowers actively ignore and violently respond to stories that contradict their perspectives and ability to stay in and garner more power. Thus, as Jennifer C. Mueller states, a white epistemology of racial ignorance encompasses the ways "white people evade and distort the perspectives of people of color and empirical facts of racism."[44] The easiest way to justify these evasions and distortions is by following a belief system that people of color are inherently pathological and thus: "their ways of knowing are flawed. Their methods are inadequate." This allows for our stories and what they reveal about the social world to be disregarded. When this cannot be easily done, we can look to the latest news headline on critical race theory to see how those in power mobilize judicial, institutional, and literal violence in an effort to silence knowledge produced by marginalized groups.

Personally attuned to the "missing-ness," or separateness that emerges from white ignorance and white supremacist violence, sociologist W. E. B. Du Bois famously stated in *The Souls of Black Folk*: "The problem of the Twentieth Century is the problem of the color line."[45] This line demarcates social worlds based on anti-black racism—dictating people's place on one side or the other. Supporting this line, Du Bois says, is a "conspiracy of silence," wherein "it is done quietly; no mistakes are made, or if one occurs, the swift arm of the law and of public opinion swings down for a moment."[46] Most critical sociologists share an understanding of policing, or the "swift arm of the law," as integral to maintaining the color line and the social world as we know it: one where racism determines people's place in society. Consequentially, different stories emerge and circulate on each side of the color line about the purpose of the police. On one side, a common motto is that officers "protect and serve"; however, as Michelle Phelps explains in *The Minneapolis Reckoning*, on the other side, state promises of protection contradict state realities of violence, making this motto feel like a myth for many black people who are often targeted by the police and cannot safely rely on its services.[47] For example, black people are about 2.6 times more likely to be stopped by the police than their white counterparts,[48] and once stopped, face an increased risk of officer searches, arrest, and violence.[49] This violence can quickly turn deadly, with black men being 2.5 times more likely to be killed by the police than white men and black women being 1.4 times more likely to be killed by officers than white women.[50] Moreover, these racial disparities do not end with the police. They extend into every aspect of carceral contact, from fines and fees,[51] court proceedings,[52] sentencing,[53] and carceral confinement, with almost 1 in 10 black adults experiencing imprisonment in their lifetime.[54] As frontline workers for this carceral world, officers do the everyday work of racialization—constructing and ascribing sociopolitical meaning to racial categories by divvying out protection and services to some while surveilling and punishing others.[55]

Consequentially, policing is widely understood as a racial project that uses violence to reproduce people's place within the racial hierarchies that make up the building blocks of our social worlds.[56]

However, violence doesn't work alone. Domination has historically required a veiled "missing-ness" or enforced silence as grounds for reproducing social order. Upon arrival to the Americas, European colonizers engaged in settler-colonialism, wielding violence with the explicit intent of erasing indigenous traditions and communities and taking lands.[57] Throughout slave trade passages, violence was also used to eradicate native African people's histories, identities, and ways of socially relating to one another.[58] In both instances, violence was used to silence—or to suppress the subjectivities, kinship structures, and knowledges of other worlds in order to construct new ones under colonial and racial capitalist regimes. Fearing rebellion and retaliation, slave patrols were organized across the Americas as early as the 1500s to recapture those enslaved who fled the plantations.[59] The first officers, then, were overseers and volunteers who formally and informally enforced people's place.[60] Over time, patrols evolved, transitioning from volunteers and watchmen to formal institutions in the 1800s.[61] In 1838, the first US police department was established in Boston, with many large cities creating their own departments by the mid- and late 1800s.[62] Post-enslavement, white ruling classes created black codes to restrict black people's everyday movements, effectively institutionalizing the continued surveillance of formerly enslaved populations to keep them in their place while the world was remade.[63] Now criminalized for public idleness, black people were targeted by white vigilante mobs, many of whom were members of the police and judicial courts.[64] Thus, as a racial project, policing kept the color line intact as the world shifted from enslavement to Reconstruction, Jim Crow, and now contemporary militarized police institutions.[65] Upholding this color line meant suppressing black life and continuing the formal protection of white people, property, and perspectives.

At the same time, policing has never been an exclusively racial project or one singularly focused on the color line. Black feminist scholars and activists, such as Angela Y. Davis, Andrea Ritchie, Nicole Burrowes, Christen Smith, Mariame Kaba, Sarah Haley, and many others call attention to other lines etching out our social world—and how policing is equally invested in maintaining heteropatriarchal order as it is white supremacy. This order racializes, sexualizes, genders, and ungenders black women at will, making us hypervisible and invisible in ways that suit the building and rebuilding of an intersectional carceral world.[66] In particular, Haley picks up where Davis's influential

Women, Race and Class leaves off and, in the process, brings into view how the often-forgotten gender and sexuality lines become the grounds for carceral expansion during times of social upheaval. First, Davis demonstrates how the prevailing gender social arrangements during enslavement, one where a patriarchal line allowed men to dominate public worlds while relegating women to private ones, didn't apply to black women who labored in fields and domestic spaces.[67] Black women's legibility fluctuated, and stereotypes, such as jezebels, sapphires, and mammies spread stories that worked to legitimate violence as a means to meet the everyday needs of white ruling classes. Then, in *No Mercy Here*, Haley demonstrates how during Jim Crow these distorted stories were a critical resource for public and private carceral expansion.[68] In particular, the policing of black women upheld the continuity in racialized heteropatriarchal and capitalist lines after emancipation *and* as white women entered the paid labor force in large numbers. As the world shifted, black women were targeted, arrested, and pushed into excruciating labor conditions in camps and chain gangs as well as serving paroles in white homes.[69] The distorted stories told about black women allowed for this multiple-domained carceral expansion without much public attention and outcry. Thus, as Roderick Ferguson, Patricia Hill Collins, and others writing on race, gender, and sexuality note, knowledge production and the practice of telling distorted stories are essential to drawing lines that pathologize and work to legitimate violence—a strategy that continues today as post-emancipation laws that prohibit loitering are reanimated, allowing officers to target black lesbian, bisexual, queer, and trans women.[70]

Grounded in these sociopolitical histories that condition legibility, each chapter of *The Secrets of Silence* examines how officers and others reproduce intersecting lines and distinctions in daily life through violence and the suppression and distortion of black women's stories. One historical distinction that persists today is between what Lindsey describes as spectacular and soft killings. Beatings, lynchings, and now shootings are spectacular killings or "fatal incidents when a life is snuffed out; they happen in an instant, a moment."[71] Conversely, "soft killings refer to those that are slow and intentionally imperceptible."[72] Many times, police gender-based and sexual violence, psychological abuse, neglect, and the dwindling health of those left behind falls into this latter designation. Increasingly, however, scholars are focusing on what Rory Kramer and Brianna Remester call the slow violence of policing, or "how contemporary policing practices harm not only the individual stopped but also their peers, families, and communities."[73] This slow violence encompasses policing's impact on intergenerational social relations, failures to provide protection, vicarious trauma, and what Christen Smith points to as the lingering, unquantifiable impact of anti-black state violence.[74] Thus, Korey Tillman argues that we must "broaden the understanding of policing to account for how bodies are restricted, surveilled, prevented, and altered along their paths across time, culture, and geographical context."[75] Yet, as all policing functions to reproduce an anti-black social world, it often forces epistemic distinctions of "most" and "least" vulnerable on the communities policed.[76] This book contributes to this growing body of work on contemporary policing by analyzing the everyday forms of policing that often get minimized and ignored. In doing so, I argue that we must also expand our understanding of policing as an intersectional project that accounts for the regulation of personhood as well as the suppression and distortion of people's stories—as they shape visibility conditions, vulnerabilities, and experiences of harm for black women and girls.

The Silence Matrix: Veils, Hierarchies of Visibility, and The Violence Matrix

Excavating the elisions requires an examination into our deeply held beliefs about vulnerabilities and rights to safety. These beliefs form the bases of our politics, structuring how we bring people and their stories into view. From there, these beliefs condition our practices of protection in everyday life. Indeed, Du Bois describes how it felt to come into consciousness about white politics, or the beliefs and practices constructing the color line, writing: "Then it dawned upon me with a certain suddenness that I was different from the others; or like, mayhap, in heart and life and longing, but shut out from their world by a vast veil."[77] This veil, as José Itzigsohn and Karida L. Brown note, is a "metaphor to describe the work of the color line in the process of self-formation—[which] interrupts interactions, communication, and recognition among people who inhabit social spaces organized around the color line."[78] Able to see through the veil but excluded from social life on the other side, Du Bois developed a double consciousness or "sense of always looking at one's self through the eyes of others, of measuring one's soul by the tape of a world that looks on in amused contempt and pity."[79] Shut out from the broader white world, people become what Audre Lorde calls "watchers," wherein they learn "the language and manners of the oppressor, even sometimes adopting them for some illusion of protection."[80] Thus, whether it is "the swift arm of the law" or "the adoption of language and manners," both sides of a racialized veil develop separate but interrelated politics around people's vulnerabilities, rights to safety, and protection.

The Secrets of Silence offers the silence matrix as a way to observe the dynamic relationship between the police politics of protection on one side of the veil and on the other, black intracommunal politics of protectionism in response to police violence. Specifically, the silence matrix tracks the veiling process—tracing the ebb and flow of black women's fluctuating legibility to see how both their hypervisibility as targets and invisibility as victims create a "missing-ness" in everyday life. In doing so, this book builds on important work by Cathy Cohen, Saida Grundy, and others who center and theorize social life within black spaces. In *Boundaries of Blackness*, Cohen focuses on black people directly impacted by the HIV/AIDS epidemic and subsequent political organizing, detailing how exclusionary politics are adopted and enforced within the context of black people constantly responding to racism, stating:

> African Americans must weigh concerns over the respectability and legitimization of black communities in the eyes of dominant groups against concerns over the well-being of those most vulnerable in our communities, as they struggle against very public, stigmatizing issues.[81]

When weighing these concerns, black communities can engage in secondary marginalization, which involves "reproducing a rhetoric of blame and punishment and directing it at the most vulnerable and stigmatized in their communities."[82] Black intracommunal politics, then, work to manage the public image and behavior of the social group while dealing with broader racial injustices. And these politics have direct implications for black people calling attention to issues of homophobia, poverty, and sexism as to speak about these issues means to risk being seen as someone distracting from racial injustice.

In *Respectable*, Grundy expands upon Cohen's influential work, showing how the veil obscures visibility around interpersonal violence within black communities.[83] Focusing on social life at a historically black college, she finds people compete for resources behind a racialized veil, and one of those resources is legibility. Within this intracommunal competition, a single story about heteromasculine criminalization can take root in black communities and be used to make universalistic claims that hierarchize victims and vulnerabilities.[84] Black men can leverage these dominant framings in the broader world to silence black women and queer men victims of sexual assault. Thus, when people engage in competitions for visibility, they often use what Jennifer Carlson refers to as a politics of vulnerability, which is "a particular kind of political frame for making universalistic claims based on embodied vulnerability. By centering political claims on vulnerability, claims makers can universalize particular standpoints under the politically appealing guise of vulnerability and victimhood."[85] Misrecognition is key to vulnerability politics, to hierarchizing victims and experiences of harm—as it brings into view and elevates certain stories and perspectives while disregarding others. Within black communities, this process often coincides with a politics of respectability, which is a historically black resistance strategy that works to achieve personhood and legibility within the broader world by regulating one's behavior and appearance.[86] However, as Grundy notes, individual and group desires for respectability, along with fear of outside interventions, can constrain a victim's visibility to a binary— of either pathologization or adherence to normative gender roles.

The police also mobilize vulnerability discourses, historically conceptualizing themselves as protectors and guardians.[87] Importantly, this self-promotion is juxtaposed against depictions of black people as racialized, "dangerous" threats.[88] Thus, Collins refers to stereotypes as controlling images precisely because they package together ideologies into stories that are easily passed along—shaping how people bring others into view and subsequent practices for enforcing their interests and realities.[89] These images encapsulate many lines and distorted stories that officers can use to target black people. In this way, Forrest Stuart and Ava Benezra demonstrate how young black men navigate these images and officer surveillance by "getting cover," enlisting black women in heterosexual performances to maneuver around criminalization and narratives about a "deviant" black masculinity.[90] However, black women and girls face distinct controlling images, grounded in misogynoir, that work to justify violence.[91] For example, the jezebel image delegitimizes disclosures of sexual violence by labeling black women and girls as "fast" or "asking for it." In *Hood Feminism*, Mikki Kendall traces how this story traverses the veil:

> For young Black American girls there is no presumption of innocence by people outside our communities, and too many inside our communities have bought into the victim-blaming ideology that respectability will save us, not acknowledging that we are so often targeted regardless of how we behave. The cycle created by racist narratives and perpetuated by the myth of the fast-tailed girl is infinitely harmful and so difficult to break, precisely because of the ugly history of sexual violence against Black women and other women of color.[92]

As such, controlling images create norms we use to evaluate and regulate others. Sanctions go hand-in-hand with these norms, enforcing consequences for violating the ways we expect to socially relate to one another.[93] Ultimately, the distorting stories told about black women undergird the violence matrix, wherein Richie notes "various kinds of abuse in multiple contexts line up to leave black women uniquely vulnerable."[94] As a framework for making visible black women's experiences, this matrix allows us to see how domestic violence leads to police encounters, wherein black women experience even further harm from officers and how an estimated 60–70 percent of black women incarcerated are also victims of domestic violence.[95] It also brings into view the "sexual-abuse-to-prison pipeline," which encapsulates the relationship between sexual violence, controlling images, and schools' punitive responses to black girls in a crisis.[96] This book builds on this understanding of the violence matrix by demonstrating how politics, norms, and sanctions veil, or silence, these harms in everyday life—producing, enforcing, and normalizing white and black heteropatriarchal lines in our social worlds.

A Note on Methods

Storytelling with Interviews and Invading Ethnography

People's lived experiences help us peer into the absences, and, as Cecilia Menjívar argues, they provide a window into the social world in between dominant categories and ways of knowing.[97] To get at experiences in the space between what is legible and what has yet to be named, sociologists rely on standpoint epistemologies. As conceptualized by Sandra Harding, Dorothy Smith, and Patricia Hill Collins, feminist standpoint epistemology emphasizes ways of knowing grounded in lived experiences contextualized by the broader social relations, structures, and histories that produce them.[98] Without accounting for black women's experiences, it is impossible see into the social world at the intersection of anti-black and patriarchal violence, and as Threadcraft states, "visibility, legibility, requires storytelling, narrativization."[99] Indeed, feminist scholars often engage storytelling as a form of political and intellectual activism to speak truth to power and people, to make visible what has been "missing."[100] And as Gloria González-López notes in her study on familial incest, telling people's stories about violence carries political and ethical responsibilities to participants, who vulnerably shared their experiences in hopes that it would change social conditions.[101] Similarly, most of the black women I interviewed shared their stories with me as a praxis of hope that it would somehow change the social conditions for the next black woman or girl. As such, this book explicitly engages in black storytelling traditions that link the (re)telling of people's stories with an ongoing ethical responsibility to care for their narratives.[102]

The stories presented in this book are primarily drawn from interviews with black women who narrated their lived experiences of policing. Our interviews were a part of a larger mixed-methods study on police violence against black women and girls in two urban cities in the southern United States. The larger project comprised three phases, consisting of in-depth and life-history interviews, field observations, and surveys. In the first phase, I spoke with thirty black mothers about the intergenerational talks on policing within their families and communities. While these mothers' narratives are not shared in this book, I mention these interviews because our conversations greatly informed the ensuing methodological decisions. Namely, they lead to a more intentional life-history approach and to centering more diversity among black women. In the second phase, I conducted life-history interviews with a diverse group of thirty-two black women in a predominantly white city in the US South. Their stories are foregrounded in this book. The second and third phases also included field observations of community events on policing, protests, and other social issues as well as local and national surveys. With a focus on black women's stories, I only gesture to the survey in chapter 3 to highlight black women's reactions to participating in them before the interviews. For those interested in reading about the project's phases and survey measures of police violence, more details are provided in the methodological appendices.

In presenting black women's stories, I draw from sociologist Anima Adjepong's invading ethnography, which is a queer of color reflexive practice that pushes scholars to write more transparently about the researcher's presence and embodiment within the text.[103] Invading ethnography makes explicit researchers' impact on interviews and the ways we shape the (re)telling of people's stories. It creates a conversation between readers with the researcher's methodological process and participants. In this case, invading ethnography meant writing into the presentation of stories how numerous black women chose to interview me before answering my interview questions. These moments illustrate how black women wrestled out loud with whether they would share their stories—with me and future readers. They also serve as an additional site from which to observe how black women navigate everyday policing.

Interior Lives Behind a Veil of Dissemblance:
Struggles for Recognition, Emotions, and Multiple Consciousness

Over time, black women learned to guard their stories from others who did not have the lived experiences or tools to understand them—strategically producing silence to physically and psychically protect themselves from literal and epistemic violence. This silence is a part of what historian Darlene Clark Hine describes as a larger culture of dissemblance, wherein black women historically have resisted oppression by giving off the illusion of being open while hiding their inner worlds from others.[104] Dissemblance allows black women to move between social worlds where they face pathologization, violence, and what Paige Sweet refers to as gaslighting—wherein others strategically deploy controlling images and misrecognition to create a surrealness around their lived experiences of violence.[105] Thus, dissemblance allows black women to resist gaslighting and the lines carving out their social worlds.[106] While contextualized by broader social conditions, dissemblance is self-imposed "missing-ness," as Hine states: "The inclination of the larger society to ignore those considered 'marginal' actually enabled subordinate Black women to craft the veil of secrecy and to perfect the art of dissemblance."[107]

It can be challenging, then, to understand the meaning of silence in black women's lives. When is silence suppression? When is it resistance? Or can it be both or something else altogether? Across disciplines, scholars turn to the interior lives of marginalized populations to find answers to these questions. Within the interior life, stories told and untold—and the personal meaning made of them—provide a way to observe how lines are internalized and reproduced or resisted and transformed.[108] At times, some black women sought recognition of their stories, and as political scientist Melissa Harris-Perry argues, the pursuit of recognition and ensuing struggles highlight the power dynamics between individuals and social groups.[109] Using the metaphor of navigating a "crooked room," she describes black women's embodied disorientation maneuvering around misrecognition in their social worlds and their journeys to political consciousness.[110] From the space between, pathways and roadblocks to recognition make visible the intersecting lines drawn in daily life, effectively illuminating the veils through people's attempts to lift and remove them. From *here*, we can trace silencing and how black women develop what sociologist Deborah K. King describes as a multiple consciousness, which, similar to double consciousness, emerges through black women's embodied encounters with and resistance to an intersectional social order.[111]

Consequentially, Harris-Perry argues that struggle for recognition "brings to the fore the emotional experiences of black women as a location for political understanding."[112] Indeed, feminist scholars like bell hooks, Audre Lorde, and Sara Ahmed have turned to emotions, such as fear, shame, pain, resilience, love, rage, joy, and isolation, to show how social orders are reproduced in intimate relations, institutions, and internal lives.[113] Drawing from these scholars, this book takes seriously black women's emotions as an epistemology for understanding the meaning of silence, highlighting their expressions, pauses, hesitations, and back-and-forth conversations with me and themselves.

Black Women and Heterogeneity

When developing this study, I was adamant about including black women like Abena, Joy, and Nema—those with different identities and backgrounds. I knew there was a diversity of experiences among us. I also knew from my own interactions with officers and those of other black women closest to me that most of us feared and had encountered the police, even if we didn't talk openly about what happened during those interactions. Yet, from the very beginning, I received a lot of academic pushback. Sociologists have a long history of reifying "variation" and deploying it in ways that center whiteness, heterosexuality, and masculinity—explicitly and implicitly keeping white heterosexual men as a central reference point.[114] As such, non-black women would confidently tell me: "If you want to know or say anything about black women, you need variation—you need to interview black men and white women." Equally long is the history of social science research as a driver in pathologizing poor black communities in ways that suggest, or at worst, perpetuate, the false belief that violence only happens "over there." So, their advice for my wanting to include black middle-class women? "Their social background means they don't encounter officers or experience violence." Yet, research on the black middle-class shows how they are not buffered from racism and violence, and as Andrea Boyles reminds us in *Race, Place, and Suburban Policing*, officers heavily patrol the suburbs and borders of privileged spaces where the presence of black people disrupts white comfort and intensifies anxieties.[115] Thus, in analyzing the "missing-ness," it was imperative to include black women who were omitted from policing social science research and conversations. Heterogeneity was a critical resource in allowing me to follow the strands linking black women's experiences within, outside, and in between preconceived notions about policing and violence.[116] It allowed me to describe the social world in the space between that connected black women across all of their differences—and also produced distinct conditions under which they and their stories were policed.

Ultimately, the black women I interviewed were mostly from the United States and some were originally from countries in the Caribbean, Central America, or West Africa. They were raised by two parents or one mother or stepparents or grandmother or aunt or older sibling, and almost all of them talked about also being raised by their communities. Some grew up in neighborhoods in the center of bustling urban inner cities, attending public schools, and others grew up in suburban neighborhoods, attending a mix of public, private, and boarding schools. Some still lived in the economic circumstances and communities in which they were born. Some moved far away and to higher tax brackets. Others struggled through "revitalization," displacement, and economic decline. Some had completed college or advanced graduate degrees and worked as doctors, lawyers, and teachers. Some had completed high school or had GEDs and technical degrees and worked as assistants, hairdressers, and on assembly lines. A few were unemployed or between jobs. Regardless of their educational background and job status, most had side hustles to keep a steady income and provide financial support for themselves and their families.

Some of them were activists with grassroots organizations, and a couple of them were police officers themselves. Many of them organized and participated in efforts to help those in their communities, with some putting together protests and community events and others putting together hot plates for their elders down the street. Some of them talked openly about their mental health, their anxieties, depression, post-traumatic stresses, and other disabilities, as well as how they managed and coped and struggled and thrived. Most were cisgender, and a few were transgender, non-binary, or gender fluid. All of them identified as black women. Collectively, they were bisexual and heterosexual and lesbian and queer and partnered and married and single and divorced and remarried and dating and figuring it out. Some had children, some did not, and most discussed othermothering children in their families, churches, neighborhoods, and broader communities.[117] All of them had encountered the police in their lifetime. Many of these encounters were violent. "Missing-ness" connected them across social class, gender identities, sexualities, ages, and geographies.

However, this book does not minimize their differences. The ways these black women were differentially situated at other intersections—in addition to anti-black racism and patriarchy—created unique conditions under which they and their stories were policed. Black women who grew up in or resided in poorer neighborhoods within inner cities had distinct experiences navigating highly surveilled communities and encountering officers in schools, while walking down the street, and other places as they went about their daily lives. Black transgender and gender-fluid women encountered transphobia in their interactions with police no matter the context. Black queer, lesbian, and bisexual women dealt with homophobic violence in public and private places. Black women with disabilities explained how they were punished instead of supported when they called the police during mental health emergencies. Regardless of their identities and backgrounds, black women who lived with police officers in their homes, either as romantic partners, parents, or other family members, shared how they had nowhere to turn and no one to call. Many of them talked about how as black girls, no one would believe them and their stories. And collectively, all of them guided me through and explained shifts in their awareness and understanding of their encounters that are often made "missing."

Outline of Chapters

Each chapter is organized around five sites—or spaces between—where black women encountered and made meaning of violence from officers and others outside of what is conventionally recognized and addressed about policing. Each chapter also centers on four or five black women's stories and asks readers to first listen to these stories without any or much analysis. Some black women are met once. Others show up in multiple chapters, revealing how black women's experiences span many spaces between throughout their lives. Situating their stories within the historical and contemporary conditions of silence, I then trace them through the silence matrix and show how everyday policing accommodates difference while producing indifference—making black women collectively and distinctly vulnerable. Finally, between each chapter, I place black women's voices in conversation with one another to guide readers from one space between to another.

The first chapter, "I Wish I Was Taught to Be Okay in Me," invites readers into the space between the talks about violence from black women's childhood and their vulnerabilities. An intergenerational oral tradition to call out racism and the "missing-ness" in mainstream views about police as public servants, these intracommunal conversations are a space to listen to stories, learn strategies for navigating encounters, and receive affirmation about one's humanity. Thus, black women distinctly recall learning their place through the talks, noticing how they entered and vanished from these discussions. This chapter, then, examines how the talks are a critical site of everyday policing, wherein the silence matrix becomes embodied and legitimated—traveling with black women as they encounter, identify, and work through violence in their lives.

The following three chapters focus on the connections between police, interpersonal, and community violence. The second chapter, "What Happens in Our House" / "You Don't Call the Police on Your Family," centers the space between home and police contact. With intracommunal politics working to make home a safe space from the police, black women had to navigate domestic violence alongside outsiders' pathologization and insiders' deification of black domestic spaces. Their stories about home violence and officers' responses reveal how the lines drawn and redrawn are simultaneously enforced by officers as well as those closest to them. The third chapter, "He's Just Gonna Be Right Back Out There," focuses on the space between conceptualizations of police violence as exclusively police shootings and physical assaults and black women's disclosure of police gender-based and sexual violence. Their stories reveal how officers leverage the cover of multiple veils to target black women and girls, illuminating how sexual coercion is a form of violence made possible by "missing-ness" in our social world. The fourth chapter, "I Was Kind of Scared to Report It," brings into focus the space between black women pushing through silence and the consequences that lie on the other side—namely, officer retaliation and intracommunal backlash. Faced with these punishments, black women made constant, daily evaluations about the risks of speaking and reporting. Accordingly, this chapter analyzes the nuanced ways dissemblance takes on protective features and transforms silence into a radical act of resistance.

The fifth chapter, "When We Gather," centers the space between black women's lived experiences and self-definition. From these journeys, I theorize *gathering* as an alternative process to everyday policing, wherein black women reflected on their lived experiences and reconfigured their relationships with themselves and others. While everyday policing etched out their place in the space between, gathering was how black women practiced abolition feminism in everyday life—linking the sharing of stories and the co-creation of knowledge with the everyday work toward safety and alternative world-making. However, while I show the promises of gathering through its valuation of people and stories, I also show how it could easily give way to everyday policing around differences in identities and backgrounds.

The conclusion wrestles with a question I often asked myself before, during, and after talking with black women: Missing to whom? Black feminist activists and scholars have been and continue to call out the "missing-ness" so that victims will not be "invisible" or forgotten. People frequently post online with #SayHerName to bring awareness to black women's lives and stories. In 2020, we countered the "missing-ness" in protests, writing Breonna Taylor's and Oluwatoyin Salau's names on signs alongside others and chanting them as we marched down the street so they would not be "invisible" or forgotten. Thus, the conclusion asks: Missing to whom? And importantly, what are the lessons learned about policing and world-making when or if we listen to black women's stories?

One final note: since "missing-ness" is built deep into the fabric of our social worlds, readers might find that speaking to the violence that the silence matrix often obscures may make them uncomfortable. That's fine. This book attempts to show how this discomfort and subsequent retrenchment to silence in homes, schools, neighborhoods, activism spaces, and social science research constitutes a distinct vulnerability to violence. However, some readers of this book may be black women with shared experiences of childhood sexual abuse, familial violence, interpersonal violence, stalking, gender-based and sexual violence, retaliatory violence, other forms of harm, or loss of loved ones. These experiences may have gone unnamed and unrecognized. Many of the black women I interviewed anticipated you. The idea of *you* reading their stories and being helped to recognize and legitimate yours gave them courage, and some explicitly cited you as the reason they chose to participate in the study. They wanted you to take care of yourselves as you listen to their stories. They also left messages for you in the space between chapter 5 and the conclusion. *Here*—they challenged the "missing-ness," speaking ahead in time so that you would know that you are *seen, valued,* and *loved.*

Other readers of this book may also know violence and the margins intimately, moving through and between spaces in similar and different ways to these black women. While this book exclusively focuses on the everyday "missing-ness" of black women and girls from understandings of policing in the United States, a centering of their stories in no way meant that they did not see you and that we are the only social group that experiences violence and "missing-ness." Many of the black women I interviewed and met at protests spoke of the connections and distinctions between theirs and others' daily struggles for safety and freedom. Several recognized that within every large social movement fighting against state and other forms of institutional violence were women and gender-nonconforming people fighting against violence on intimate fronts within their own families and communities. They wanted you to know that you too are *seen* and *valued*. And they expressed empathy and solidarity.

Still, other readers may have only read about or studied the margins as a place in our social world described by others whose lives are shaped daily by the master's tools. They saw you, too, and conveyed their wariness.

Last, other readers may have only heard about the margins in passing as they carry on with their lives undisturbed by the "missing-ness," yet undoubtedly benefiting from the margin's existence. Or—there may be readers who are acutely aware of the margins and intentionally target the space between to evade accountability. They saw you, too. They expressed rage and disdain.

Nevertheless, this book takes seriously black women's stories, emotions, and what they wanted shared about their experiences as a political location for understanding everyday policing, even as it may make readers uncomfortable for very different reasons. Borrowing from the words of Alexis, a black woman activist in her late twenties whose story is shared in chapter 5: "You might feel disrupted, and you might feel mad, even. In the long-term, this disruption was positive . . . I'm gonna be uncomfortable anyway, so I might as well say what I'm gonna say."

"nothing is going to happen anyway"

"i mean, i really don't feel like the situation affects [*pause*], well,
let me stop—"

"who's the bad guy? who's the good guy?"

"because i'm like is everything I say [*pause*]
am I going to have to overexplain, you know what i mean?"

"i think it's bullshit!"

"in order for me to protect myself, I feel like I have to have my own back"

"it made me feel like it was more urgent to protect them than myself"

"i wish i was taught to be okay in me"

1

Sadia

"Who are you? What brought you *here*?"

These were the first two questions Sadia asked me as I approached the back corner of the dimly lit, crowded coffee shop. Several books lay open face down, and empty drink cups were messily spread atop her table. I placed my backpack on the floor and took the vacant chair beside her. Without my interview sheet and recorder, we talked. And by talked, I mean I spent the next thirty minutes answering a series of rapid-fire questions about my personal background and journey to the project.

Like many I interviewed before and after her, Sadia wanted to know where I came from, what my police experiences were, why I wanted to know about other black women's stories, and most importantly, how long I had cared. With them, my race and gender were often considered a proxy for someone who might understand their untold and unrecognized experiences of violence. However, this often was not enough. They also wanted to know my story. This *storytelling vetting process*—where black women used my story to decide how I might interpret what I heard—was integral to determining if they would share their stories with me. As someone with experience navigating the space between, I understood the importance of this process. I also understood Sadia less as someone who was closed off or cold and more as someone who had learned invaluable survival strategies over the course of her life. Thus, it was only after sufficiently answering Sadia's questions that she and I moved to an outside patio for more privacy so she could answer mine. Still, we spent an additional twenty minutes of me taking handwritten notes before she eventually gave me permission to record our conversation.

A medium brown-skinned, black African American in her early thirties with dreads, Sadia is fluid in her gender and sexuality. When I asked how she wanted to be identified, Sadia shared that she uses "she" as her pronouns and "woman" as an identifier, explaining why she also politically locates herself as a black woman. Growing up in low-income, predominantly black neighborhoods in a large city on the East Coast shaped Sadia's political commitments then and now as an adult. Despite her professional degree, Sadia worked several jobs to make ends meet, and most of her "free" time was spent engaged in community work.

As we discussed her childhood, I asked Sadia, "Did anybody talk to you about the police at all when you were growing up?"

"Absolutely."

"What were those conversations like?"

"Same conversations I'm having with him," speaking about her nephew whom she was helping to raise. She called these talks "what-to-do-when" conversations, in which she instructed him to make "no subtle movements" and give "short answers." This was also the advice young Sadia and her brother received from their mother and stepfather. While she took the time to pull her nephew aside for these discussions, Sadia described the police talks she had in her family growing up as less a discrete event and more as ongoing "normal conversations." Within these talks, Sadia's mother and stepfather expressed concern for her and her brother's safety, impressing upon them that they were vulnerable to the police.

Growing up on the East Coast, Sadia had vivid memories of 9/11. This event changed the police talk in her family. The nationwide rise in Islamophobia and heightened surveillance of Muslims across racial and ethnic identities worried Sadia's parents.[1] They feared that their family would be targeted by the police because of their names and because they looked "Eastern African." To prepare, Sadia's parents had a series of conversations with both her and her brother. Although these talks happened for them at the same time, Sadia recalled her parents spending "more time" having "more in-depth" talks with her brother, including "multiple conversations about different types of police," like the US Immigration and Customs Enforcement (ICE). They told her brother: "You're tall. You're a tall black man . . . They don't see you as a child," warning him about how police adultify black boys by perceiving them as threatening adults instead of children.[2] That black girls were also targets of adultification did not come up in these conversations.[3] As she reflected on this, Sadia assertively said, "All of those things were the conversations I listened to, but I didn't receive any of that."

"How did it make you feel to get different advice?"

"I was accustomed to it. The boys always got different advice . . . There wasn't really a lot of conversations that were the same for me in regard to my brother."

Rolling her eyes, Sadia tilted her head and smiled knowingly at me, sarcastically explaining how the beginning and end of her talks on policing and violence was that she should "know how to act." Using air quotes to emphasize her point, she assumed I knew exactly what she meant by this. Nodding and smiling back at her, I silently affirmed Sadia's assumption and did not ask her to say more or provide an explanation. *Here,* in the space between, we both knew how black girls were taught to "act" to prevent violence.

Through these conversations, Sadia also learned that some violence could be spoken about. But others? They were to remain hidden. For example, her mother and stepfather talked very openly about her brother's vulnerabilities to police violence and were attuned to how local and national events heightened police surveillance. However, the violence black women and girls experienced were rarely discussed, whether it was at the hands of the police or from people they knew. Thus, the sexual, physical, and psychological abuse wrought by Sadia's stepfather, who often took the lead on familial talks on violence and safety, was something the family didn't dare discuss—not with others, or among themselves. So, when drunken physical and sexual assaults happened to her as a child, Sadia was left alone to figure out how to deal with them. As she got older, she had to leave her home, telling me she spent time "living out of a trash bag" whenever he "kicked me out." Going to her grandmother's house an hour away after experiencing abuse, she emphatically stated: "that was violent."

At her grandmother's home, Sadia still wouldn't talk about what happened. And as a cycle of abuse and leaving home continued over the years with no one directly speaking about it, Sadia *learned* silence. She explained: "It was the experience in black houses where what happens in the house stays in the house. You don't talk to anybody. You don't tell your grandparents about it. You don't do this. You don't do that because it ain't nobody's business what happens in my house."

Sadia didn't dare break these rules. Thus, even though she often turned to her godmother, a "second mother," to discuss "emotional things," she never shared what happened in her parent's house. Keeping the abuse to herself for many years, Sadia "really didn't talk to anybody about that part of my life until later on." Socially isolated from her family, she started cutting herself to cope with sexual abuse.

Over time, from observing which types of violence couldn't be talked about among her immediate and extended family, Sadia said she eventually learned her place. *Here,* she described her family as "old school": "so men had a place, boys had a place, women had a place, girls had a place, and it was different." As she concluded this statement, she was shaking her head, visibly frustrated.

"How do you think about that now?" I asked.

"I think it's bullshit!" Getting angry, she went on to describe how she felt learning her place through silence and violence: "Because—but for a black woman, where would everyone be?! [*We laugh.*] To not acknowledge our experiences or even provide us with skills or tools to be successful in a world that doesn't acknowledge us, puts us behind and makes us care about everybody more than ourselves. I feel like that."

Making meaning of her place in isolation, Sadia explained, "I spent a lot of time making sure I wasn't guilty about not taking care of people and taking care of myself." She linked the pain of learning to "put everyone else's livelihood before your own" with being disposable, explaining, "When you're groomed, if you will, to take care of other people, even in the conversation about how you should protect yourself, it takes away from your importance." She continued, "I wasn't taught about being black and a woman and what that was going to cause for the world if I had the audacity to dream out loud and to be bigger than what society says a black woman should be."

Instead, Sadia was "taught what that was going to be like for a black man." Left alone to figure out how to name, understand, and protect herself from violence, Sadia was adamant about ending this part of our interview with a dream—an imagined talk for herself as a black girl. *Here*, on the outer edges of what is recognized, she intimately wished the talks had told her that "my experiences were gonna be different . . . [and] because I was a woman and because I was a black woman, I had to be mindful of those experiences." Using her imagination to bridge the space between the talks and her vulnerabilities, Sadia decisively concluded: "I wish I was taught to be okay in me."

"I Wish I Was Taught to Be Okay in Me"

THE SPACE BETWEEN THE TALKS AND VULNERABILITIES TO VIOLENCE

No caregiver or parent wants to have the police talk. Yet, in the face of persistent state violence, it's a conversation many have out of necessity—it's a discussion grounded in survival. Thus, the black mothers interviewed in the first phase of this project agonized over *when* not *if* they would have these talks with their children. Balancing their desires to preserve their innocence with their will to protect their lives, these mothers understood, as many black caregivers do: The police talk is a harrowing rite of passage, wherein black youth learn to face the reality that officers are not there to protect them and in fact pose an ever-present threat to their safety and well-being.

The talk effectively explains how policing constructs personhood based on racism.[4] On black youth's side of the color line, keep your hands up, say "yes and no sir," make no sudden movements, and follow the officer's commands are more than directives educating them on what they should do and say when they inevitably encounter the police. They are an interweaving of cultural narratives passed down from generation to generation about what Du Bois refers to as "the swift arm of the law" that upholds the veil demarcating social worlds. In essence, caregivers use these conversations to teach black youth how to see through the "missing-ness" in mainstream narratives that frame officers as protectors and public servants. They alternatively provide counter-frames about police profiling and violence.[5]

Since the emergence of #BlackLivesMatter, this once-secret intracommunal practice to ensure physical and psychic survival has now worked its way into mainstream discourse. News articles, TV shows, and op-eds poignantly describe what it is like for black caregivers to perform this "grim ritual."[6] Even President Biden during his 2023 State of the Union address spoke directly to the talks as socialization practice responsive to systemic racist policing, explaining how on his side of the color line, he and other white Americans don't have to have this conversation:

> I've never had to have the talk with my children—Beau, Hunter, and Ashley—that so many Black and Brown families have had with their children. If a police officer pulls you over, turn on your interior lights. Don't reach for your license. Keep your hands on the steering wheel. Imagine having to worry like that every day in America.[7]

Black families don't have to imagine. Before cell phones, social media, and news reports—black communities relied on oral storytelling practices to teach black youth how to navigate the space between mainstream stories that deny the presence and power of anti-black police violence and black people's lived experiences.

These intimate discussions, then, do more than provide instructions. They function as a guide through any dissonance caused by "missing-ness" in mainstream messages about black people's vulnerabilities. They also affirm black humanity, signaling that despite these risks and realities, black youth deserve to live in a world where they are safe and free from violence. Thus, the talks simultaneously challenge the color line while explaining how officers enforce it. Further, given the focus on safety and personhood, these intracommunal discussions accompany other conversations on vigilante and interpersonal violence.[8] However, even as the talks are a place to learn about vulnerabilities and receive support, only certain people and experiences are recognized, only certain lines are named. At closer glance, very few of the news articles, TV shows, and op-eds highlighted the talks had with black girls about the police and their vulnerabilities. Nevertheless, these childhood conversations are designed to be remembered, and many black women did indeed remember them.

More specifically, they recalled what it was like to find themselves on the margins. *Here*—on the outer edges of what their families and communities would recognize—fears, anxieties, rages, confusions, apathies, and sadness filled the space between the talks they received (*or overheard*) and the realities they faced. *Here*, feeling multiple lines being drawn and redrawn, they noticed the politics of when and where they vanished from these conversations as well as the norms and sanctions around how they reentered. Thus, black women's stories and emotions make visible everyday policing in the talks and how it kept them on the outer edges of their intracommunal social worlds.

For some black women, the impact of continued "missing-ness" was evident in their girlhood. For others, it would be years or decades later before they realized the talks were a space where they learned hard and painful lessons about the margins. In either case, black women's stories demonstrate how everyday policing becomes embodied through the silence matrix, moving with black women as they encounter violence in different contexts throughout their lives. Yet, alongside the silences are black women's resistance. Sometimes, resistance resided in the pauses where contradictions were evaluated and meaning-making filled the space. Other times, resistance lay in the varied ways black women, like Sadia, imagined different conversations where their vulnerabilities were addressed and they were affirmed. Then, there were those whose resistance came directly from private conversations with their mothers, where away from family members they constructed a veil of dissemblance to speak openly about the other lines shaping their lives. Altogether, black women's various ways of resisting, whether through pausing, call-outs, imaginative conversations, or naming lived experiences, elucidates the presence of everyday policing.

Joy

It was early on a Friday afternoon when Joy and I met at a café. An upwardly mobile, light brown-skinned, black, African American, heterosexual, cisgender woman in her early thirties, she has a master's degree and a somewhat flexible schedule working as a counselor. Thus, she was able to leave work a little bit early for our interview. While we stood in line to order our coffee, Joy shared that she found the project's emphasis on black women and policing quite unexpected and unique. Even still, she was hesitant to participate. She didn't know who would show up. She didn't know what it would mean to have a conversation about policing with a stranger. However, she trusted the local organization from whom she heard information about the study and decided to sign up despite her concerns.

Still, her anxieties came up at the beginning of our interview when I asked her, "How do you feel knowing that we're gonna be talking about police or police violence today?" To which she replied, "Oh my gosh. It's weird because last night, I went to go and eat. Right after I left my meeting here, I went to go and eat at—or get food from a restaurant, and there was police in there eating, and I [was] just like nervous, and it comes, it goes. I don't know if it's certain police, and so I was . . . [pause] but then I woke up this morning, and I was like okay, I feel a little better because I'm in a safe environment."

Concerned for her emotional safety during the interview, Joy explicitly made several comments about who she would and wouldn't allow to ask her questions about her experiences. Laughing, she told me, "If you were white, I would not be comfortable talking with you about this, unless you were maybe a down white girl who grew up in a black neighborhood her whole life." Similar to other women I interviewed, Joy consistently talked about the relationship between lived experiences and someone developing the appropriate frames to understand them. For Joy, living in a predominantly black space and having certain experiences were important prerequisites for listening to her story and being able to understand what it was like for her to grow up in Easton. While she might be okay with speaking to "a down white girl" who had specific types of experiences, she had absolutely no interest in speaking to white men about her encounters with the police or any other violence in her life. White men were too socially distant from her. From their place, she doubted their capacity to understand her story. "Because I'm like, is everything I say [pause], am I going to have to overexplain, you know what I mean?" She resolved that these interactions would be "more emotional labor," thus illustrating how many black women I interviewed didn't want to do the emotional work to remember, disclose, explain, and sometimes justify their stories at the same time.

But—Joy was not done giving me the list of people who couldn't interview her. She was also critical of white researchers and anyone, regardless of racial background, from white institutions. From the space between, she hoped that the interviewer was "someone who is, . . . wanting to do it not for curiosity." She paused then added, "'Cause that happens too, with white researchers I find is that they will do things for curiosity purposes and not for the betterment of that particular group. You know what I mean?" Joy was my fortieth interview. By then, I knew both what she meant and that other black women shared her concerns. As I nodded my head, Joy then launched into several questions about the project and my experiences with the police. It was only after she conducted her interview of me that Joy visibly relaxed and giggled while telling me, "I got like three decades worth of stories," and "Let me know if I go on a tangent." For the next two hours, she shared some of her stories with me.

Joy's cheery demeanor changed as she started reflecting on her childhood. Long pauses seemed longer as she oscillated between tearfully looking down at her drink and distantly staring out the back window. It was as if she had been transported back to another place and time, somewhere deep within her memory as she explained that Easton, where she grew up, was a "terrible city" that was "crime-ridden." She grew up constantly hearing "gunshots in the neighborhood." She needed protection as a child but, she explained, "I'm in a city where police officers can't protect me." She felt torn between wanting police protection from neighborhood violence and loyalty to her community: "Oh my gosh. It was hard because I understood in one aspect that Easton was a terrible city . . . but then the other part of me—it was a hard balance because it was like okay, they have to protect, but then it was like, well, they're abusing their power, too. I think I felt this [pause] it was more anxiety-provoking. As a kid, I was always very on edge. I'm in a city where the police officers can't protect me. They're criminals essentially."

Joy's perspective about the police as criminals was partly developed from participating in communal talks in which friends, neighbors, and family members dispensed survival strategies. In her neighborhood, there was a saying she used to hear a lot as a kid: "You'd rather get robbed by a criminal than get pulled over by police." This was because, as Joy explained, police "were harassing people."

For Joy, this lesson hit very close to home as she had several family members who were engaged in illicit activities and were often stopped by officers. From listening in on conversations about the police, she learned that officers were corrupt, confiscating drugs and selling them back to people. She also learned that officers "could kill you and just go plant drugs on you [and] call it a day." Over the years, Joy learned to "say 'yes sir, no sir,'" "be respectful," "don't sass them," "keep her hands on the wheel," and "just answer their questions." Most importantly, "do not move until they tell you to move." This lesson was impressed upon her from the many times she saw what happened to family members during and on the other sides of police encounters. From witnessing, Joy understood very deeply that police "have a certain amount of power, and it's hard."

Despite the police being a constant source of conversation and ire, Joy had only a vague memory of someone telling her that Easton police were "being inappropriate with women during traffic stops and stuff." She gathered these lessons over the years but didn't have anyone to confide in about her fears being a black girl navigating police and neighborhood violence. She couldn't talk with her father. This was because, as she shared, "my father is in prison. My father has been in prison on and off since I was five." There was also no time to talk to her mother—a single parent who worked long hours to ensure the bills were paid. Joy didn't want her fears and anxieties to be another problem for her mother. "I don't want to burden my mom 'cause she's a single parent, and she's being hurt." Imagining a conversation about her experiences of violence, Joy speculated her mother would be agitated and question her: "'Really? You're gonna bring this on me?'" She imagined this reaction because "that's kind of what it felt like my mom's attitude sometimes, and I think it was just a more internalized. This is just our life. This is what it is." Ultimately, Joy understood her family as "very old school" in regard to her place and the broader institutions they had to deal with.

So, Joy found solace and support at school with a black police officer for D.A.R.E.—Drug Abuse Resistance Education—a police school- and community-based drug education program launched in the 1980s as a collaboration between the Los Angeles Police Department (LAPD) and the Los Angeles Unified School District (LAUSD). While these programs were widely praised at the time as an anti-drug program, D.A.R.E. expanded the presence of officers in schools and worked to humanize the police during the War on Drugs.[9] Indeed, Joy smiled fondly as she remembered their "bond," explaining, "I always accepted him as somebody who was one of us 'cause he was black. I'm pretty certain he had a family." His status as someone who was black and had a family was important to her, and, given her relationships with her parents, he became a "father figure." She continued smiling as she recalled how he was "always pulling my ponytails," saying that he was the person in her life whom she could confide in and "wasn't a threat." She appreciated him for giving her this one "positive interaction" with the police, which stopped her from thinking "they're all terrible."

Even still, this one positive relationship didn't ease the constant fear Joy had about her vulnerabilities to police and community violence. "There are criminals essentially. Some of the police officers are criminals. This place is just not safe." Her experiences separated her from others, saying the "many white people who don't grow up in those kinds of environments. They can't always relate to that." Even in her friendships, she felt some distance. "I have white friends, but I don't think that they're ever gonna be able to—I mean, because I can't walk in their shoes, and they can't walk in mine, but I don't think they are even able to empathize. They can, but I don't think they really understand." For Joy, "when you grow up in a city like that where there's no distinction, and the morals are kind of—[*long pause*] it's hard."

Now, as an adult, Joy struggled to shake the anxieties and fears she grew up with, sharing how it took a while "to decipher, even in my personal life" who can be trusted. She reflected on how carrying these pervasive fears and anxieties alone as a child made it difficult to build adult relationships because "I think for me it created this oh my gosh, what's next?" In the view from her place, she questioned: "Who's the bad guy? Who's the good guy? I don't know."

Keisha

Keisha, a medium brown-skinned, black, African American, heterosexual, cisgender woman in her mid-twenties with short, straightened hair, met me for lunch during her work break. As we waited in line to order our food, we made small talk about the local city politics before making our way to a secluded picnic table at the far edge of the park.

"Do you have any questions for me, the project, my experiences with police or anything?"

"No, not really. I think I'll probably have more questions as we talk more."

"Okay. How was the survey for you?"

"I had to think about the last—there was one thing that came up on your most recent experience with a police officer. It was three years ago—I got pulled over . . ." Keisha began to tell me about an encounter with the police and how she "blocked it out." Pulled over for a failure to signal, the officer harassed and verbally berated Keisha on the side of the highway. He asked her what she did for a living, to which Keisha replied that she was a teacher. The officer then yelled at her and questioned her ability to read and follow directions. Not knowing what to do, Keisha was "trying to balance standing up for yourself, but also, I'm trying to make it to work, and I'm trying to make it home." Eventually, the officer let her leave, and she spent the rest of the day "disheveled," crying, and trying to forget the experience.

After sharing this encounter, Keisha moved on to talk about her childhood. For most of her life, she grew up in the same predominantly black middle-class suburb where neighbors looked out for each other. While sitting on their porches, adults in the neighborhood would tell children playing outside, "Oh, I'm watching you," to remind them that someone was there looking out for them. Keisha also recalled learning about the border between her neighborhood and another where she wasn't allowed to go. A single street demarcated her community from where "we knew not to go to the back" as "a lot of shady stuff went on in the back of the neighborhood." As Keisha noted, "Parents just wanted to make sure they were all safe."

Watched by a community and told to stay in her neighborhood, Keisha's parents didn't feel she needed a talk about the police. This was not because the police were absent from the middle-class suburb, but her parents did not deem them as much of a threat "because all the police officers who patrolled our neighborhood were black." Keisha's father also personally knew them and "made it a point to have a relationship with them." So, Keisha explained, the officers in her neighborhood "saw us grow up." However, as she expressed her comfort with the officers in her childhood neighborhood, she was unsure if this comfort was "because they were black" or "because they saw us literally grow up." Whatever the reason, her parents didn't talk to her about the police. Reflecting on this more, Keisha said her father "never told me about it" and her mother "is not somebody who's super open."

Keisha's parents didn't often discuss difficult topics with her. In describing them to me, she told me that they were both "very much, whatever happens, happens. And you just move forward." Keisha did, however, have a talk about sexual violence. In this conversation, she "got the talk about sexuality, and boys will be boys." Specifically, she learned that it's "your job" to protect yourself and that she needed to "dress a certain way" and "be aware of my body." Her parents were "so down my throat" about these messages, she explained, because they didn't want Keisha to get pregnant.

Keisha's parents also imparted the rule that violence, in general, "had to be, whatever's in the house stays in the house. That whole thing." Keisha hated this rule—both then and when we met. "That don't really work for me," she said before going on to explain that she was "somebody who needs to talk about it if it happens." This included Keisha's concerns about police violence. For example, when an officer fatally shot twelve-year-old Tamir Rice in Cleveland, Ohio, Keisha grew very concerned for her brother's safety. So, she took it upon herself to have the police talk with him so he was "aware of these things." She wanted him to know "that I see him" and that "if something like that ever happens—not necessarily to the extent of a Tamir Rice, but if you ever feel uneasy about a situation, I'm here to come talk to." This conversation with her brother was important because she was "a little bit more understanding" and "he'd probably come talk to me before he went to go talk to my parents." Keisha didn't recall if her parents had the police talk with her brother. However, there were differences in how she and her sibling were treated regarding safety. For example, she rode the bus. But her father drove her brother to school. To Keisha, her father's extra effort for her brother could have been to ensure he was safe. "I don't know if that's the reason why they did it, but, when I was growing up, I rode the bus."

Although Keisha didn't get a police talk as a kid, she did have a conversation with her father after receiving a ticket during her frightening encounter with the officer that she recounted earlier in our interview. "His whole thing is you say nothing, you just take it and go, but I have a smart mouth. I hate feeling like—[pause] this is my parents' whole thing with me. I just hate feeling disrespected, and I feel like respect is a two-way street. Even, sometimes, the way my parents talked to me growing up, I was always the one that was just like, 'I feel like there's a better way to say this. You can get your point across without berating me and belittling me.'"

In comparing how she felt with her parents and her interaction with the officer, Keisha explained that she learned to "self-correct a lot." She even tried to talk with her parents about why she didn't feel like she could talk to them about this police encounter or other experiences of violence in her life. "I feel like they had each other, and then, when my brother was born, they tried to protect him. I don't know if it was just cause it's my personality. They always felt like I was independent, but I always felt like I couldn't go to them for things, so I felt like I had to be independent."

To protect herself, Keisha began to "detach from certain situations" and carry her experiences on her own. Even though she now had people she could turn to for support, when violence and other difficult things happened, she said she doesn't "feel the weight of it until I feel the weight of it." Keisha felt alone in protecting herself because in the view from her place: "In order for me to protect myself, I feel like I have to have my own back."

Abena

Abena and I had communicated about the project via text several times. But a recommendation from another study participant whom she trusted helped me secure an interview with her. Although she said, "Um . . . I feel fine talking to you," she was still very hesitant at the beginning of the interview over the phone late in the evening, sounding distant.

A dark brown-skinned, black, African, heterosexual, cisgender woman in her early thirties, Abena has a high school degree and worked as a receptionist. She grew up in a black community that had since changed. "White people have come over, and they have raised taxes like tremendously [and] it pushes the black people out." There was sadness in her voice as she described the impact that gentrification and displacement have had on the community's relationships, as she no longer recognized many of her neighbors.

Growing up surrounded by family and close friends was important to Abena. She received the police talk but said these were more of a communal conversation in her neighborhood where she and the other black kids in her community had discussions about police and other violence more broadly. Within these talks, they learned to expect harsh treatment from the officers who patrolled their neighborhood. "They would just say . . . just be careful on how you act outside. Because you know, you can act someway at home, you can play fight and all that kind of stuff and you'd be okay, but if you go out to school and stuff like that . . . then of course they are going to handle you a little differently than we do at home."

These warnings were given to everyone regardless of gender. Police, Abena learned, see them all as "just black people [*pause*] 'cause [*laughs*] it didn't matter, it was just black people that were fighting [*pause*], it didn't matter if it was a girl or boy, so it didn't matter." Her perspective was reinforced by her observations of officers at school. "And I went to a predominantly black school [*pause*] and to be honest . . . We all had white police officers. We didn't even have black police officers. And, of course, if kids got into fights, they would handle them very, very, very, very roughly and these were kids." These police assaults were a common occurrence at Abena's school.[10] She explained that officers did not care what age the kids were, remembering police assaulting "elementary, middle school, and high school kids." Indeed, she had vivid memories of watching "grown men" assault "little boys" or "really handle them really rough." Frequently witnessing these encounters was traumatizing for Abena and bolstered the messages she learned about the police from her neighbors. It also reminded her that she had to be very careful at school. Unlike at home, where she could "play fight" and "be okay," at school, it might be met with police violence.

Abena also learned another lesson during her community talks—you do not call the police. "We really didn't call the police like that [*pause*], we really didn't." She anxiously explained, "I would never, if I had ever had to call police [*pause*] it would be very [*pause*], it would be very detrimental. I wouldn't just find myself calling the police for anything because it's just so scary. It's so scary. So, I just don't want to do it. I wouldn't want to do that at all. It's just [*pause*] if it's like a life-or-death situation, and I see someone, I don't even know, then [*pause*] I just would not want to call the police at all." Abena went on to share stories about how she and her friends worked to protect each other at school when there was "fighting and stuff." They would say to each other, "No, we're not going to call the police; you going to have to calm down . . ." The consequences of calling the police were reinforced by watching how officers responded to different crises in her neighborhood. When residents saw officers abusing someone, "It's like, well, that's just how they are. It was like basically you live in a so-called white man's land, so you just basically have to abide by the white man's rules." Abena eventually concluded: "You just had to deal with it" on your own.

As we continued talking about her childhood, Abena disclosed that she was sexually assaulted by an adult in a position of authority at her school. Speaking to how schools are sites of sexual violence and social control,[11] she was afraid to involve the police or another authority figure. So, she kept the incident to herself for a while, struggling with what it would mean to tell someone and reach out for help. Eventually, she spoke with a friend who supported her in disclosing the sexual assault to adults at school. However, as more people found out what happened, Abena learned that people blame black girls for these types of experiences.

If someone was doing something to you, that you did not feel comfortable, [*pause*] yeah you may have said something, and they would be like, "Oh! Just stay out of their way!" Basically, [*pause*] it wasn't like "Oh, sweetheart, let's see what we can do about this, you know." It was basically, "Just stay out of their way [*pause*] and maybe they will just leave you alone." It's like, I'm telling you what this person is doing, you know. And it's kind of like if you react in a negative way. [*long pause*] It's like, what's wrong with *you*, why are *you* acting like this. [*pause*] It's like, did you not see this person and I've been telling you what's going on! [*pause*] . . . They only see you pop off! As soon as you've made it to your limit [*pause*] and like, I can't take this anymore. [*pause*] I done told, I've said something, I've written it down, I've told the principal, whoever, counselors, and it's nothing going to happen.

Abena painfully described what it is like for her reaction to sexual abuse to be seen as a problem instead of the violence she experienced and the person at school who inflicted it. And during our interview, she shared how it felt to grow up watching this person continue to work with children. She also shared her other experiences, repeatedly telling me after each disclosure that there was no point in black women and girls speaking about violence because "nothing is going to happen anyway." From the space between: "They only see your reaction; they don't see what causes the reaction."

Kristen

Initially planning to do our interview in person, Kristen had to travel at the last minute for a family situation. So, we ended up speaking over the phone late one evening. She is a medium brown-skinned, bisexual, cisgender, black, African American woman in her early twenties. Coming from a middle-class family, she was "curious" about where our conversation would go. As a kid, Kristen lived "in the suburbs in a predominantly white place" right outside a large metropolitan city. As one of the few black students at a predominantly white school, Kristen's parents made sure to have "many, many conversations" with their children about the police and navigating white spaces.

Kristen proudly remembered how her parents were her biggest advocates at her school. For instance, when teachers singled out Kristen for being "loud and aggressive" and forced her to go to alternative school, her mother confronted the school's administration, telling them that "the language you are using to describe my daughter is because she is black." Both parents were "really affirming" for Kristen. She went on to explain that they often "affirmed for me that I definitely wasn't crazy" when she experienced racism. Emphasizing her gratitude, she recalled how "some of my other black friends who lived in this super-white place didn't have that." Worse, some parents would "sort of gaslight them," questioning their children if what they were experiencing was indeed racism or something else.

Kristen had numerous talks with her parents, where they helped her "identify something as racism." If she was confused, she felt comfortable going to either one of them and stating, "'Oh, hey, this happened to me, and I don't know if it's racist or not.'" From there, they would have familial conversations to figure out if something was racist or "racially tinged" and work together to address it. Through these conversations, Kristen's parents ultimately helped her develop what she called a "race consciousness." ·

When talking about the police, Kristen spoke very openly about the messages she received from her parents. Importantly, she remembered she got her "negative feelings" about the police from her father. "My dad hates the police," she told me, and he was "extremely confrontational" with them. Her father explicitly said, "Fuck the pigs, fuck the cops," a lot when she was growing up. Moreover, she learned specific rules from her father. "You don't trust the police, like you don't call the police on your family, don't call the police when something is going down [*pause*] like you only call the police in the absolute last resort, like somebody needs to be dying for you to call the police." Kristen made sure to stress each point over the phone as she recited her father's list of "don'ts."

Kristen's race consciousness about the police extended to how she evaluated her relationships with white people. Her parents told her not to trust her white friends to defend her if she is with them and they encounter officers. "[My parents] often talked about the ways in which white people weaponize the police." They cautioned her to expect white people to "throw your black ass under the bus," and that "the police will be gunning for you if y'all get caught up in something." In such a situation, Kristen was advised to "just be quiet, don't say nothing, don't do nothing . . . just comply, comply, comply," as compliance is "better than being killed."

However, her parents also insisted that Kristen not let police "use their power" over her, saying, "If they violate your rights, let them know. You know your rights, and they can't do that to you. And they can't take advantage of you." Kristen recognized that these messages were "contradictory," and from her perspective, they "show how complicated it is to be black and navigate around the police." She was unsure there can even be "right advice" for dealing with the police, given they had so much power.

When I asked Kristen if she and her brothers received the same advice growing up, she hesitated to answer. Carefully considering the question, she finally said, "Yes and no." Kristen eventually went on to explain that she and her brothers all received the same contradictory advice to "know your rights and, you know, try to be respectful," but also to demand respect from the police: "Don't let them talk to you any kind of way." But, as the "only girl," her parents also insisted that she learn to control her temper. "So out of us, I'm the one with the mouth, the one who will cuss you out and ask questions later." She paused, then added, "I'm also the one, [*pause*] well, [*pause*] we all have tempers, mine is just a little shorter. So, there was definitely kind of a [*pause*] special conversation that was had with me."

Kristen audibly worked through being singled out for "a special conversation" about her temper potentially causing a problem with the police, growing unsure about this messaging in our interview. She expressed how at the time, she considered this side discussion to be "less related to gender and more related to my disposition, like as a person." But "looking back at it now," she might "identify those things as sexism," explaining, "I didn't then. I just read it like [*pause*] I didn't see it as I'm being treated differently because I'm a girl. I just thought, I'm being treated differently because I'm Kristen. And so now, [*pause*] thinking about it now that I'm older, [*pause*] I wonder how much those two things can be separated from one another, [*pause*] like if that's even possible."

Kristen had reasons to wonder as her parents disagreed about whether black women and girls were even vulnerable to police violence. In these heated disputes, her father emphasized his and her brothers' heightened risks to violence over hers and her mother's, repeatedly saying "especially as a black man in America." As she recalled this statement, Kristen deepened her voice over the phone to imitate her father. Every time he made this point, her mother would intervene with, "Fuck that! [It's] as a black person!" As Kristen recalled, her mother passionately explained:

No, history has shown us many, many times that the police don't give a damn if you are a man or a woman. Like, they will enact the same type of violence upon you. It is not about gender; it is about blackness. And specifically, when it comes to gender, [*pause*] there are different gendered forms of violence [*pause*] that women face that men do not [*pause*] or that are unique to women.

Kristen repeatedly paused as she attempted to delineate and name the different forms of violence and their relationship to "blackness" and/or "gender." While she didn't elaborate further on what her mother meant by this, after conducting so many interviews with black women who struggled to name certain experiences, I assumed she was referring to sexual violence.

I asked Kristen how these conversations made her feel at the time, and she paused again, this time for much longer. Eventually, she responded, speaking in a lowered voice: "Like, my brothers were more in danger than me. Like, my brothers had a closer proximity to police violence than I did. It made me feel like it was more urgent to protect them than myself." Kristen admitted that "even now, like being conscious of gendered violence against black women, I still evoke my brothers often when thinking about, or talking about police brutality." She worried, "What would happen to my brother if he is walking down the street or if he was driving in his car?" After taking another long pause, Kristen summed up her memories of these conversations, proclaiming they "made me think that violence happens more to black men from the police than to women." While Kristen said she now sees black women's "unique" vulnerability to police violence, her shift in perspective "hasn't changed" her actions as she continued to worry more about her brothers than herself. She struggled to shake the belief that, when violence happened, she's "the one with the mouth."

The Conditions of Silence:
Black Families Surviving State and Epistemic Violence

The talks are a space to share stories and co-create knowledge about the police and other types of violence that may be "missing" from mainstream narratives. Thus, black women searched these conversations for language to help name their vulnerabilities and lived experiences, and more, they looked for instructions on how to access protection. Instead of receiving guidance and support, many found themselves in the space between. *Here*, they felt the drawing and redrawing of lines in intracommunal conversations that veiled them and their stories, and ultimately, many black women that I interviewed came to see the talk's elisions as demonstrating their value and worth within their families and communities. Yet, to understand the current iterations of the talks black women receive, we must situate them within the sociopolitical histories of state and epistemic violence that necessitate these conversations in the first place.

———

Under chattel slavery, the white ruling class used violence to break down the social relations and languages that held previous social worlds together and instill white capitalist heteropatriarchal order. This order systemically held black people captive and extorted their labor while also drawing lines allowing white men to dominate public spaces and relegating white women to domestic ones. As slaves, black women were forced to work alongside black men in fields and denied the conditional protection afforded to white women. Thus, black women's experiences under slavery and after call attention to the incoherence and contradictions of race and gender lines.[12] Their stories also illuminate how beliefs about protection became relationally intertwined with one's place. Consequentially, historian Kali Gross shows that we can trace black women's hypervisibility as targets and invisibility as victims across regimes in relation to protection, wherein the exclusionary politics of protection means "black women were not entitled to the law's protection, though they could not escape its punishment."[13]

Oftentimes, overseers used gratuitous violence indiscriminately against black people regardless of gender. Black women, men, and gender-nonconforming people were all subject to this violence. Black women were raped for resisting enslavement as well as sexually exploited for their reproductive labor, but this in no way precluded the reality that gender-nonconforming people and black men were not also victims of sexual assault and exploitation under this regime.[14] At the same time, black women and gender-nonconforming people were also whipped and lynched, experiencing lethal plantation violence in similar ways to black men.[15] However, as violence was used intentionally to break down social worlds and inscribe a new dominant order, specific acts of harm were linked to, and sometimes disproportionately inflicted upon, certain enslaved people.[16] Thus, violence was wielded both indiscriminately in its practices and in ways that reinforced white elite heteropatriarchal taxonomies and frames. In this way, Collins states:

> while violence certainly seems central to maintaining separate oppressions—those of race, gender, social class, nationality/citizenship status, sexual orientation, and age—violence may be equally important in structuring intersections among these social hierarchies.[17]

Importantly, stories told about violence using the dominant order's languages and logics in no way meant—both then and now—that various and numerous acts of violence did not happen beyond or at the intersections of these categories. Refusing to acknowledge, name, and contend with that reality was then and still is the purpose of epistemic violence—with the explicit intent to separate, dominate, and reproduce a white capitalist heteropatriarchal social world.

Today, the naming of violence is still tied to this language through controlling images, which shapes our ideas about who is a threat and who is entitled to protection. Stories told reinforce racialized, gendered, and sexualized no-tions about "innocence," "deviancy," "dangerousness," and "criminality"—expanding and restricting recognition and dictating our perceptions of real-ity.[18] As such, stories grounded in pathologies are critical to the expansion of policing throughout US history. And from slave patrols during chattel slavery, organized lynch mobs during Jim Crow, and the political wars on poverty, crime, and drugs that ushered in the eras of militarized police and mass incarceration—each shift in carceral regime strategically deployed controlling images about criminality and vulnerability to maintain white elite heteropa-triarchal dominance. Indeed, scholars have written extensively about the con-trolling images of black men as "rapists" and "predators" and how framing white women and children as their intended targets is used to maintain social control, from lynching to the funneling of resources into the carceral state.[19] These images—and in particular, their relationship to one another—are used to tell stories that generate fear among white populations. Capitalizing on this fear, white vigilante mobs and the police have historically used the guise of providing protection from "the other" to justify the existence and expansion of policing and the carceral state.

However, controlling images about black women that change and contra-dict each other have also been used for carceral expansion, consistently align-ing around the white slave-owning and elite class's aim to normalize the use of violence to build and rebuild their public and private worlds. Thus, as mam-mies, black women were a-gendered and asexual, an image that framed them as safe to be in white homes for the purposes of exploiting their domestic labor. This story pushed black women out of view and made them into invisible caretakers who could appear when needed to nurture the well-being of white families.[20] More, this story was particularly critical to domesticating the car-ceral sphere after emancipation, wherein black women on parole were forced to provide domestic labor for white women working outside the home.[21] Yet black women were also conversely gendered and sexualized as jezebels, which made them hypervisible and described them as difficult or unsafe to be around because of their presumed excessive sexual appetites.[22] Now, in these same domestic spaces, black women were considered dangerous to white family stability as controlling images concealed their vulnerability to sexual violence and held them ultimately responsible for any sexual violence inflicted upon them. Further, alongside both of these images, black women were gendered as aggressively "man-like."[23] This story made black women visible through physical labor and their ability to perform manual labor on plantations with black men. And given an increase in demand for cheaply-paid manual labor after the abolishment of slavery, black women were targeted by the police and forced to labor alongside black men in prison labor camps and chain gangs.[24] However, the sapphire image meant that any and all of black women's resistance to violence was seen through the lens of them being illegitimately and disproportionately angry or violent. This story framed black women as manipulative "loud mouths" who instigated violence in the first place.[25] Throughout regimes, black women were subjected to various acts of lethal, physical, and sexual violence, and this violence occurred in public, private, and in-between spaces.[26] However, controlling images worked to rationalize and normalize violence against black women, effectively serving as a way to epistemologically hide these harms and keep them from being named, known, and addressed. As a form of epistemic violence, they did this by preventing the naming of violence against black women and girls altogether, and when named, restricting the frames to those that blamed them for it. Thus, controlling images, and the narratives they carry, simultaneously creates vulnerabilities to violence and silences black women's testimonies.[27]

Within black spaces, a politics of respectability developed over time to allow for a semblance of control in a social world pervasively shaped by distorting narratives. Respectability, as Evelyn Brooks Higginbotham notes, "equated public behavior with individual self-respect," and thus, encompassed black people's psychic work toward self- and collective respect within a social order that persistently refused to recognize their personhood or right to safety.[28] As a form of resistance, respectability involved socially distancing oneself from stereotypes, and at the same time, worked to demonstrate worthiness of protection by moving toward ideal images grounded in the dominant order.[29] The family is a key institution for examining this process, and hooks invites us to see these relations as a critical space for coming into consciousness about inequality:

> Family is a significant site of socialization and politicization precisely because it is there that most of us learn our ideas about race, gender, and class. If we ignore family and act as though we can look to other structures for education for critical consciousness, we ignore the significance of early identity and value formation.[30]

Importantly, hooks points to the constrained agency within black families to resist and adopt ideology. And as a longstanding oral tradition, the talks on violence are situated in this constrained space—wherein historical and ongoing state and interpersonal violence make these conversations necessary, and families have autonomy over the content of these discussions. The talks, then, reveal what is recognized at the intracommunal level about violence and the police. And given that conversations about violence reflect the dynamic adoption, resistance, and transformation of social order in everyday life, what is untold or distorted is just as important as what is shared.[31]

For example, in *Growing Up Jim Crow*, Jennifer Ritterhouse describes how parents, neighbors, and extended kin taught black children racial etiquette, or

> a set of rules, a script, and part of a process, the power-relations process by which a viable relationship between dominant white and subordinate black—and therefore "race" itself—was negotiated on a day-to-day basis.[32]

These talks emphasized performing acceptance of white politics, norms, and rules without internalizing them. A key part of resisting internalization were caregivers vocalizing that while these performances and strategies were important for safety, white politics don't get to define black children's personhood, sense of worth, and value within their own community. However, gender and class lines shaped these socialization practices, etching out when and where norms and rules were critiqued and resisted or adopted and internalized. Thus, while black families across social classes relied on avoidance and respectability to navigate violence, black middle-class families more heavily relied on respectability. Black middle-class families also used respectability to socially distance themselves from black working-class families through stories that pathologized their homes, children, and socialization practices. Gender distinctions were also adopted, with stories that exclusively linked physical and lethal violence to black boys and sexual violence to black girls.

As black caregivers seek to protect black children from modern police, the oral tradition of teaching black children how to navigate state violence persists. So, too, do the class and gender distinctions. Today, respectability is a familial strategy for black boys and girls alike; however, black boys are more likely to receive messages about policing as a systemic social issue grounded in racial injustice.[33] These talks emphasize the power of policing, explicitly naming how black boys have minimum control over the outcomes of encounters and, therefore, should not internalize the ways officers see them.[34] Yet for black girls, not only is their risk of lethal violence minimized and ignored, social class shapes whether caregivers frame police sexual violence as a systemic social problem or as an individual issue for which black girls are personally responsible. Further, black working-class families are more likely to consider police sexual violence as a systemic social problem and impart strategies for navigating encounters alone and at night.[35] Conversely, black middle-class families are more likely to see police sexual violence as an individual issue for black girls who don't behave as "ladies," therein, teaching adherence to respectability norms and black heteropatriarchal familial power as pathways to safety.[36]

Understanding these histories, I engage hooks's emphasis on family as a significant site for observing socialization into political consciousness about violence and the lines that etch out our social worlds. Indeed, hooks traces her own journey as a theorist back to her girlhood, where she grappled early on with gender politics within the context of her family and what it meant to speak about violence from the space between:

> I remember trying to explain at a very young age to Mama why I thought it was highly inappropriate for Daddy, this man who hardly spoke to me, to have the right to discipline me, to punish me physically with whippings. Her response was to suggest I was losing my mind and in need of more frequent punishment.
>
> Imagine, if you will, this young black couple struggling first and foremost to realize the patriarchal norm (that is, of the woman staying home, taking care of the household and children while the man worked) even though such an arrangement meant that economically, they would always be living with less. Try to imagine what it must have been like for them, each of them working hard all day, struggling to maintain a family of seven children, then having to cope with one bright-eyed child relentlessly questioning, daring to challenge male authority, rebelling against the very patriarchal norm they were trying so hard to institutionalize.
>
> It must have seemed to them that some monster had appeared in their midst in the shape and body of a child—a demonic little figure who threatened to subvert and undermine all that they were seeking to build. No wonder then that their response was to repress, contain, punish. No wonder that Mama would say to me, and then, exasperated, frustrated, "I don't know where I got you from, but I sure wish I could give you back."
>
> Imagine then, if you will, my childhood pain. I did not feel truly connected to these strange people, to these familial folks who could not only fail to grasp my worldview, but who just simply did not want to hear it. As a child, I didn't know where I had come from. And when I was not desperately seeking to

belong to this family, community that never seemed to accept or want me, I was desperately trying to discover the place of my belonging.[37]

Speaking from the space between, hooks describes the process of learning her place and her intimate journey to find the place of her belonging. In doing so, she analyzes the relationship between the dominant social order outside her family and the dominant social order within it. Similarly, I triangulate how Sadia, Joy, Keisha, Abena, and Kristen describe their gender socialization within the talks with their awareness of their vulnerability to violence, personhood, and sense of worth.

The Silence Matrix: Politics of Protection and Protectionism

While a popular motto of the police is to "protect and serve," perceptions of police legitimacy are largely shaped by race, gender, sexuality, and class. Black, LGBTQ+, and working-class people are less likely to trust the police and more likely to believe that officers treat them unfairly compared to their white, heterosexual, cisgender, and middle- and upper-class counterparts.[38] Thus, the talks challenge white, elite, heterosexual, and cisgender views of police as public servants and protectors. As such, these conversations speak directly to the police politics of protection. Attuned to the "missing-ness" in mainstream messaging, black communities and families teach black youth that officers will see them as a racial threat to public safety. To demonstrate this reality, the talks frequently include discussions of adults' prior police encounters, the lived experiences of others, recent and ongoing accounts of police violence in the news, and historical anti-black state violence. As such, the talks teach them to see the color line and socialize them into Du Boisian double consciousness, wherein black youth learn "this sense of always looking at one's self through the eyes of others."[39] For example, Kristen learned a "race consciousness," whereby her experiences of racism were named and affirmed as real by her family. This vocalization of racism dispelled any dissonance around her experiences and fortified her resistance to racial gaslighting. Indeed, she recalled, "Some of my other black friends who lived in this super-white place didn't have that." Further, these discussions grounded her understanding of policing in structural power; she concluded that "with officers having so much power," there couldn't be "right advice" about the police.

Whether black women received or overheard the talks, these conversations were a significant and intimate site of critical consciousness development around police and other types of violence. They carried the lessons from these conversations with them, distinctly recalling adults' strong emotional reactions to police politics. When she was growing up, Kristen's father said "fuck the pigs, fuck the cops." Sadia's family was terrified of increased police surveillance after 9/11. Community members anxiously warned Abena that they were targets of the police—something she came to understand through watching officers assault her peers at school. Black women across all their differences collectively learned that the police have too much power, or as Joy said, "They're abusing their power too."

Learning to see the color line and its enforcement through violence, black women came to view policing as a method of maintaining a white social order. For example, Kristen's parents taught her that "white people weaponize the police" and to be extra cautious around officers when she was with her white friends. Abena learned that "it was like basically you live in a so-called white man's land, so you just basically have to abide by the white man's rules." Joy stated that being able to maintain views of police as protectors and public servants—and not having to see officers as a threat to their safety—was indicative of white elite racialization as "many white people who don't grow up in those kinds of environments" were not forced to develop frames to understand the types of experiences she had growing up. Indeed, research shows that white families try to avoid conversations about racism and the police after high-profile police killings.[40] Thus, the talks effectively dispel the mainstream myth of "protect and serve" grounded in white racial ignorance that distorts and avoids how policing functions in black communities.

While black women learned about their exclusion from the politics of police protection based on racism, caregivers socialized them into the intracommunal politics of protectionism. However, black women confronted their continued "missing-ness" in their families and communities as they learned that protection from the police only extended to certain people, vulnerabilities, and oppressions. For example, black women primarily learned about black men and boys' systemic risk to lethal and physical police violence outside the home. *Here*, in the space between, they felt the talks reproducing a gendered double consciousness—or way of looking at policing that emphasized spectacular, masculinized forms of violence (*i.e., lethal violence*), locations (*i.e., public places outside the home*), and victims (*i.e., black men and boys*).[41] This masculinization was very common among the black women interviewed, as the talks themselves are often defined as racial socialization for black boys.[42]

Black women understood, both in their childhood and as adults, that the talks were grounded in the historical experiences of black men and boys under anti-black regimes and the present-day reality of their risk of being killed by the police.[43] Thus, black women with boy siblings, cousins, neighbors, and classmates joined their families and communities in being responsive to these risks.[44] They recalled several of these "normal conversations" and their personal versions of Kristen's anxieties around: "What would happen to my brother if he is walking down the street or if he was driving in his car?" Taught to see, recognize, and understand the vulnerability of black men and boys to encounters outside the home, they learned and passed along strategies to avoid being killed and physically assaulted. Thus, Sadia had conversations with her nephew about "making no subtle movements." Keisha talked with her younger brother after the fatal shooting of Tamir Rice. Abena and her peers worked to "calm down" everyone when fights broke out at school.

Collectively, the talks—received and overheard—dispelled any dissonance about racism and police violence against black men and boys. They do this by explicitly locating the problem with anti-black policing, affirming their humanity, and confirming that black men and boys' fears and rage were valid, real, and important. As such, these conversations cultivated empathy for the black men and boys in their lives while also forging solidarity between family and community members. When black boys were given individual strategies to navigate hostile and potentially deadly interactions with officers, it was understood that they have minimal or no control over the police in these encounters.

But—this main talk did not expand to hold space for other people's stories. While the talks challenged the "missing-ness" grounded in racism, these conversations mirrored and even facilitated the "missing-ness" of others. Thus, black women found that the content within and boundaries surrounding the talks became highly contested sites of gender and sexuality politics, illuminating the presence of other lines dictating what would be made visible and what would continue to be rendered "missing." As a consequence, there were little to no systemic connections made between policing and how black women, gender-nonconforming people, and LGBTQ+ people are also victims of deadly police violence,[45] how there is a risk of police sexual violence against all black people, including black men and boys,[46] and how the home is a context in which police violence and other acts of violence occur.[47] In the place where black women were supposedly taught how to see through the "missing-ness" and name vulnerabilities, they instead continued to encounter epistemic oppression within their intracommunal worlds, learning exclusionary counter-frames that made it difficult for them to speak about their experiences of violence.

And *here*—outside of mainstream *and* intracommunal recognition—black women were left alone without counter-frames to name their vulnerabilities. *Here*, many worried what the unchallenged "missing-ness" signaled about them and inferred meaning about their place and worth within their families and communities as well as broader society. Finding themselves in the space between, black women felt isolated and solely responsible for protecting themselves, as Keisha said: "In order for me to protect myself, I feel like I have to have my own back." Learning about her place through violence and silence, Sadia, as previously noted, said, "Men had a place, boys had a place, women had a place, girls had a place, and it was different." This was also because a structural understanding of policing grounded in racism and power, or that there cannot be "right advice with officers having so much power," shifted when we look at where and how black women and girls entered these conversations—if they entered at all.

The Silence Matrix: Norms and Sanctions

It is important to note that when calling out these conversations as intimate sites of erasure, none of the black women in my study advocated against the intracommunal protection and care that black men and boys received. However, many passionately discussed how the talks failed to lift the veils around the other lines shaping their lives and include them in intracommunal recognition and support. Finding themselves on the margins of these vital conversations, black women noticed how they were located in the talks through gendered norms—particularly racial loyalty and gendered respectability.

Respectability norms pressure black girls to be "good girls" and "ladies" to protect themselves from everyday violence. This pressure suggests that black girls are, ultimately, responsible for the violence that they experience. In *Between Good and Ghetto*, Jones describes how black girls must contend with respectability politics when strategizing how to protect themselves, wherein "gender violations are likely to open them up to a series of public and private sanctions."[48] The Combahee River Collective also explains how difficult it can be for black girls to move through dissonance around their lived experiences without the ability to name what continues to be veiled:

> As children we realized that we were different from boys and that we were treated differently. For example, we were told in the same breath to be quiet both for the sake of being "ladylike" and to make us less objectionable in the eyes of white people. As we grew older we became aware of the threat of physical and sexual abuse by men. However, we had no way of conceptualizing what was so apparent to us, what we knew was really happening. Black feminists often talk about feelings of craziness before becoming conscious of concepts of sexual politics, patriarchal rule, and most importantly, feminism, the political analysis and practice that we women use to struggle against oppression.[49]

While it was difficult to put a name to the violence, the Collective still felt what was happening to them. From the space between, black women I interviewed also felt how conceptualizations of violence elided their lived experiences. These feelings alerted them to how structural understandings of power shifted to individual blame when they reentered the talks through gendered language grounded in respectability norms.

As such, black women noticed how they were taught to take on individual responsibility for violence through lessons about controlling their behavior, bodies, and appearances. Keisha learned that "boys will be boys," and thus, she needed to "dress a certain way" and "be aware of your body." Sadia remarked upon the differences between her and her brother's talks, where she learned she should intuitively "know how to act" to prevent violence. Kristen was pulled aside for a "special conversation" as the "only girl," where she learned to individualize her experiences and see her behavior or "temper" as a problem. While she recognized that all her siblings had tempers, from Kristen's perspective, the talk was "less related to gender and more related to my disposition, like as a person." Thus, the talks reproduced a gendered veil, bringing black women and girls into view through pathologies as well as explaining the violence against them as an individual issue—rather than a community or political one—that they were solely responsible for inciting and protecting themselves from.

Alongside respectability, black women learned what Richie calls the trap of loyalty, wherein they were pressured to put the safety of the family, especially men and boys, above their own well-being.[50] This gendered norm is partially grounded in a genuine fear of the consequences for involving officers in a crisis. As such, black women were warned not to call the police for help or assistance, as Kristen summed up: "Like you don't call the police on your family." Abena wouldn't call them unless it was a "life-or-death situation," even then, she was unsure. To adhere to these rules, black women learned silence and that they should reproduce their own "missing-ness" in a crisis. This internal reproduction of a gendered veil was a critical part of protectionism politics designed to prevent police interference in black communities.

Yet, this silence was more than just about not involving officers in a crisis. It included seeing anyone who was not a member of the nuclear family as an outsider to issues of familial violence. Protectionism silence around the police, then, was also a gendered "missing-ness" used to legitimate silence around experiences of violence within the home. *Here,* talking to anyone—even extended kin, neighbors, and friends—was constructed as a betrayal and seen as disloyalty to the black heteropatriarchal nuclear family structure. Thus, Keisha learned that "whatever's in the house stays in the house." Sadia learned not to speak about her experiences of sexual violence in the home, stressing that: "It was the experience in black houses where what happens in the house stays in the house. You don't talk to anybody." Cut off from support within their families and communities, Sadia explained how reentering the conversation through these norms signaled her place and worth: "When you're groomed, if you will, to take care of other people, even in the conversation about how you should protect yourself, it takes away from your importance."

Sanctions enforced politics and norms. Within the talks, sanctions took the form of blame and ostracization. For example, Abena described how respectability was used to blame her for a school authority figure sexually abusing her as a child to divert attention away from him: "It's kind of like if you react in a negative way [*long pause*], it's like, what's wrong with *you*, why are *you* acting like this [*pause*]. It's like, did you not see this person and I've been telling you what's going on!" Speaking directly to a gendered veil, Abena explained how bringing black women and girls' experiences of violence into view through the gendered language of respectability created a lack of empathy for their encounters on the other side of it. As such, she theorized how legibility on the other side of racialized and gendered veils meant "they only see your reaction; they don't see what causes the reaction."

Norms were also sanctioned through the pathologization of black women's "mouths," which were explicitly framed as a source of deviance and of inviting punishment. Drawing on the legacies of the past, black girls often experience gendered racism in institutions through the framings of their mouths as loud, confrontational, and aggressive.[51] Conversely, silence is associated with being ladylike and knowing one's place. Within the talks, these messages were linked to black women and girls' vulnerabilities to violence. Kristen was seen as "loud" in school, and while her parents challenged this messaging as racist in a predominantly white space, she also learned that in her family, she was "the one with the mouth" at home and could incite violence by speaking. Keisha was also taught that she had a "smart mouth." Throughout my interviews, blaming black women's and girls' "mouths" exacerbated feelings of shame and the internalization of the silence matrix.

Everyday Policing and the Reproduction of Intersectional Inequalities

Situated behind multiple veils, black women had to work their way through messages that completely or partially excluded them, leveraged them for the protection of others, and individually blamed them for violence. As such, many felt this process of "missing-ness" as intersectional lines carved out and normalized their place on the margins. Thus, we can witness the historical and ongoing relationship between literal and epistemic violence in the talks through frames distinguishing intersectional vulnerabilities to spectacular, slow, and soft violence.

Drawing and Redrawing Lines of Exclusion: "Missing-ness," Knowledge Production, and Protection

As attempts to keep black youth safe from police violence, the talks functioned as a form of epistemic and literal protectionism. Adults and peers epistemo-logically drew from black people's historical and present-day lived experiences to call out the "missing-ness" in mainstream views, naming how perceptions of officers as public servants are alternatively grounded in white ignorance and experiences. Caregivers believed that internalizing white ignorance around policing would be dangerous to black youth and those around them. Further, black women also learned to see white people's ability to weaponize police and deny the consequences as a function of whiteness and power.[52] Thus, black women left these conversations with the ability to recognize the color line and see police violence as a systemic social problem. Black women from working-class childhood backgrounds had these conversations within their nuclear

families, extended kin, and communal networks. Alternatively, these talks
were mostly restricted to the nuclear family among black women with middle-
class childhood backgrounds. Finally, contrary to research that focuses on
black mothers' socialization, including my own work, when present, fathers
and stepfathers lead the talks on violence.

Buttressing black women's psychic resilience to racism and policing, the
talks helped them develop a race consciousness as a form of resistance.
At the same time, black women distinctly recalled still being confused about
their vulnerabilities and experiences. In naming this confusion, they speak
to how after calling attention to the ways policing enforces a racialized veil—
the talks reproduced "missing-ness" around their gendered vulnerabilities.
Here, their emotions alerted them to vulnerabilities and experiences associated with other lines. *Here*, they confronted how while the talks directly
named policing as a function of white supremacy, it often failed to incorporate heteropatriarchy as co-occurring lines shaping police practices and social order. Thus, it excluded those who were not cisgender heterosexual black
men and boys. This exclusion encompassed both a denial of black women
and girls' equitable participation in the intracommunal story-based knowledge production process around violence and a denial of protectionism. In
the absence of these stories, some concluded that black women and girls
were not targets of police violence. The combined public and intracommunal
"missing-ness" triggered a misrecognition of the social problem. This misrecognition then became the grounds to legitimate the continued everyday
policing of black women and girls' stories—which, if shared and listened to,
would challenge their "missing-ness" from the talks in the first place. As such,
"missing-ness" constituted a circular logic, which veiled and excluded other
experiences while centering and elevating black heteropatriarchal viewpoints
and experiences. Similar to white ignorance, which evades and distorts racism, heteropatriarchal ignorance evaded and distorted heteropatriarchal
oppression.

Drawing and Redrawing Lines Through Coerced Inclusion: Bringing Others Into View Through Pathology or Support

After being excluded, two pathways to intracommunal legibility emerged:
pathologizing narratives or coerced support through normative roles. Both of
these pathways maintained the dominance of black heteropatriarchal perspectives and social arrangements. While pathologies justified and led back to

more exclusion, inclusion was based on support for black heteropatriarchal politics of protectionism. *Here*, on the outer edges, black women reappeared in the talks through gendered norms and sanctions that restrictively supported black men and boys and the black heteropatriarchal family structure. Non-pathologized legibility came through their loyalty to protecting black men and the black family above anything else, including their own safety. To challenge these politics and norms, as Cohen similarly notes, meant to incur the risk of being brought into view through pathology and seen as someone engaging in alternate politics that distracted from racial injustice. Again, this viewpoint is grounded in heteropatriarchal ignorance and dominance, which misrecognized the "missing-ness" of black women's stories to mean that there is no social problem. To resist this absence, then, meant to be labeled "the problem" by trying to bring attention to other lines that others did not recognize or consider as important. *Here*, black women learned that speaking about violence and the other lines was synonymous with betraying their families and communities. Thus, speaking led back to pathology and exclusion. In my interviews with black women, all of them learned and confronted this socialization into black heteropatriarchal politics and how it was used to withhold recognition, assert dominance, and enforce others people's interests and realities.

Loyalty was best conveyed through black women adopting silence, or making themselves "missing" behind other veils. For many, this came with the internalization of narratives that viewed gendered and sexualized differences outside of heteronormative roles as well as experiences of heteropatriarchal violence through pathology. Thus, black women across all their differences highlighted how the talks about sexual violence ascribed blame to them. Black lesbian, bisexual, and queer women also spoke about how they either did not receive any messages about black LGBTQ+ people's vulnerabilities and experiences, or mostly heard narratives where they became visible through pathology. Finally, black women who had middle-class childhoods were those most likely to be explicitly taught to see their "mouths" as a source of deviance and precursor to violence. Sometimes, their mothers conveyed these messages, but most learned to see their "mouths" as inciting violence from the men in their lives. Consequently, many black women came to see themselves as deviant for speaking about violence. Having learned through the talks to prioritize other people's safety over their own, they were left with limited to no options for community-sanctioned support around domestic violence—a point discussed more in-depth in the following three chapters.

Normalization of Intersectional Inequalities: Dissonance, Isolation, and Apathy

When policing was grounded in structural understandings of the color line—the problem was considered systemic and led to collective protectionism politics. However, heteropatriarchal lines were unnamed or framed as individual issues, thus black women were left individually responsible for finding protection from violence, especially gender-based and sexual violence, whether from the police or people they knew. As such, black women described "missingness" through feelings of isolation in direct relation to other people's ignorance and apathy. However, resistance to everyday policing took many forms. Some called out how policing as an everyday social logic was taken up by those closest to them in our interviews. Joy cited numerous contradictions and similarities between police and communal violence. Kristen witnessed her mother push back and eventually pull her aside to have private talks where she learned to name and identify violence and other lines (*this part of her story is discussed more in chapter 5*). Abena grounded herself in her lived experiences—eventually coming to name and theorize how black women and girls were brought into view through respectability. Keisha worked to value and protect herself from harm despite the messages she received. And Sadia stated what she learned was "bullshit," and instead imagined new conversations where she was affirmed and "taught to be okay in me."

"i wish i was taught to be okay in me"

"who are you? what brought you here?"

                              "are you here to help me or are you here to hurt me?"

"who's the bad guy? who's the good guy? i don't know"

          "the conversation can go many ways . . ."

                              "because i'm like, is everything i say [*pause*]

          am i going to have to overexplain, you know what i mean?"

          "i think i'll probably have more questions as we talk more . . ."

"cause, like, talking about it for me is what makes it even more, like,
yeah, no, *this* is violent"

          "nothing is going to happen anyway"

                              "what happens in our house"
                              "you don't call the police on your family"

2

Kristen

As discussed in the previous chapter, Kristen had "many, many conversations" with her family about racism and police violence. During these talks, her parents spoke about various social issues and affirmed her experiences with racism outside the home. Kristen was grateful for how they advocated for her at her predominantly white and middle-class suburban school when teachers discriminated against her. Throughout these experiences, she was extremely proud that her mother and father helped her develop a "race consciousness," or ability to see, navigate, and resist racism.

When it came to interacting with the police, Kristen learned to know her rights, be cautious when she was with her white friends, and comply with officers' commands to avoid being killed. These conversations were mostly directed at her brothers, so she recalled listening in on their talks about the police. With all the high-profile cases of police brutality against black men and boys, Kristen understood why. However, her mother tried to include her and the risks of police violence faced by black women and girls during these conversations. But she was shut down by Kristen's father, who emphasized the threat to black men and boys in ways that minimized her vulnerability as a black girl. As the only daughter, Kristen was also singled out for conversations about her disposition and told to watch her temper with officers. Given the risks of police violence to family members, Kristen still vehemently agreed with her father's warning to never talk to the police. And throughout our interview, she spoke very openly about these and other lessons about violence that she learned in her family.

However, Kristen noticeably grew anxious when she spoke about experiences within her home. *Here*, in the space between home and police contact, she lowered her voice and chose each and every word very carefully. Cautiously, she said, "I know for me, there was [*pause*] I know that my dad, [*pause*] my dad always has this thing. [*pause*] Like he has this thing about the sexualization of bodies." To help me understand what she meant by this, Kristen gave an example that occurred often outside the home. "Like, he is that person that who is like, 'Uh uh, that little girl should not be walking around in a bathing suit with her tummy out, these folks could be looking at her [pause] and you know that girl with those short pants [pause] people are going to be thinking she's fast.'" Saying this aloud made Kristen very uncomfortable, and it was clear through her pausing and lowered voice that she was hesitant to speak more about it. But she did. Except this time her example was how the monitoring of little girls' bodies and clothing shaped experiences *within* her home. "So, for me, things like shorts, or little spaghetti straps or things like that, he was always weird about it [pause] like 'Go put on some more clothes, or don't be walking around your brothers like that' and those sorts of things. [But] like my brothers could be shirtless, but I couldn't be pants-less, and for damn sure, like being shirtless was completely out of the [pause] like wearing a sports bra, just a sports bra [pause] that would be completely totally out of the question."

Noting the gendered differences in dress codes, Kristen didn't have a place to talk about these and other experiences within her childhood home. So, she was hesitant when she said: "I think my dad was a pretty violent person. And we don't really [pause] there really wasn't the space to talk about that. My dad was—is a violent person."

"What do you mean?"

"He [pause] my dad was never like the sort of [pause] so we never like [long pause]. No. Actually, I'm going to be honest. We kind of got the shit beat out of us pretty often."

Kristen struggled at first to name these experiences—working through whether, and if so, how, she wanted to speak about them during our interview. Deciding to share her story and "be honest," she described how her father would make them "take off their pants" and undress before he "beat their asses." Kristen was shocked to hear her voice, to hear herself name and say these experiences out loud. "Even saying that out loud makes me realize, damn, [pause] like that [pause] I don't think that was okay. I don't think it's okay [pause] to make somebody take off their clothes and also how terrifying that use to be."

This violence, Kristen explained, was her "dad's response to things often . . . like 'you piss me off, you do something I don't want you to do, you going to get your ass beat.'" She told me that she was "really specifically using *beat* because like [pause] my dad use to for real like beat our asses." As she spoke on these beatings, she reflected: "Like damn, [pause] I don't really think you're supposed to hit your kids *that* hard or like *that* many times, or with some of the things we were like hit with." In her home, violence was not only used to enforce the dress code. It was also used to solve "disagreements." For example, if she or her siblings had conflicts or a different opinion than her father, he would "like square up and go . . . like we finna fight. Or like, I'm going to beat your ass, or steal off on you, or punch you." In these moments, Kristen clarified that while they all were beaten, her brothers were the ones her father was the most likely to "steal off on" or "punch."

However, it wasn't just physical assaults. Kristen's father would "scream; it's not even yell . . . scream." She detailed, "My dad was also [pause] on top of just being physically violent [pause] now that I'm thinking about it [pause] my dad was also extremely verbally violent [pause] he wouldn't necessarily use harsh attacks, like he wouldn't attack your person by calling you anything fat or anything like that, but he would definitely cuss you out, like, 'What the fuck?! You stupid motherfucker!'" Further, Kristen stated, "Dad is homophobic [pause] he uses the 'f word' or used it often [pause] and other extremely pejorative things that I'm not even going to say." Kristen was ashamed of the things her father said. Reflecting more on this during our interview, she went on to share that she was "actually quite embarrassed to even think about these things now" and refused to talk more about the details of her father's homophobia.

"Why are you embarrassed?"

"Because, I mean he's said some really AWFUL things, [pause] just awful. Things that are embarrassing, [pause] like, oh my gosh."

Kristen quickly followed up this admission with how her father's views of LGBTQ+ people have since changed. While she didn't want to tell this part of her story, she wanted to assure me that he no longer held these homophobic views. Yet, the messages she received from him still lingered and were hard for her to shake. So, she shared, "[I] never talked to my parents about my sexuality," or what her life is like for her as a bisexual black woman.

When Kristen's father got violent, she also didn't ever think about calling the police or even talking to other family members about the abuse. She speculated that if she did, she would be met with, "Well, you got whupped because you are supposed to get whupped, and you are a kid, and these are adults, and this is the natural order of things." For her, this violence was "kind of normalized" as a form of discipline. She learned from it that "there's really nothing to talk about [pause] you got a whupping, and there is nothing else to talk about."

Later, as a teenager and now as an adult, Kristen eventually had conversations with a few of her black friends about their experience of whuppings or beatings. From these talks, she came to realize even more how "for us, it's sort of normal" to see this violence as discipline. "I've had this conversation many times with like, black folks, like with my black friends. And they're like, yeah, girl, you know my daddy done picked up the shoe on me, or like, let me tell you about my momma and her switch, or like, my grandma and her extension cord [pause] or stuff like that." Kristen stated, "Now that I'm older, I sort of problematize those things . . . I don't think it's okay to pick up a shoe and hit somebody with it."

Despite problematizing the abuse from her childhood, Kristen understood "how effective violence can be." But she concluded it was "not always sustainable for, like, control" and that she was currently "trying to unlearn that violence is not always the most logical response to, like, a disagreement with another person." Part of this unlearning is thinking through the "different relationships" she had now with her parents. Discussing her mother, she shared, "So, I've talked to her about how Dad ran the house off of fear [pause] so you don't do something, you do something out of fear that you would be hit [pause] it was fear and intimidation." Whereas her mother "is the opposite." Privately, she and her mother "talked about how Dad ruled off of fear and Mom was more respect." She further explained:

> My mom, we have a very amazing relationship. Our relationship is excellent. And I told her I think it has a lot to do with the fact that you didn't resort to violence every time there was a problem. You didn't think that the solution to every problem was I'm going to beat your ass. Instead you talked about it, you tried to understand, like, why did you do this stupid thing that you've done, child, like, let's talk about it, and I'm going to try to understand it, like, how do you feel [pause]. It was an attempt to understand a thought process and have a child understand, like, this is why this is wrong, and this is why you shouldn't do it, and this is what you should do instead.

Kristen concluded, "I really have a deeper appreciation for that now" and the ways talking and working to understand one another "sustained" their relationship. Conversely, Kristen and her father "have a difficult relationship." This is because, as she explained, "I'm not afraid of him anymore [laughs]. When they had disagreements now as an adult, Kristen said she let him know: "Dad! I'm not scared of you anymore!" [laughs] "No! I said no! I'm not going to do it, and there is no amount of screaming and yelling and cussing me out that you can do." She demanded that he "respect me now" and told him that he "can't just talk to me any kind of way anymore cause I'm not a kid!"

Kristen disclosed these experiences of familial violence toward the beginning of our conversation. As we kept talking, she returned to them and shared other incidents. *Here*, in the space between during our interview, she audibly worked through new insights she had about her story from talking more openly about her father's abuse—incorporating her childhood experiences into her adult understandings of violence. From the space between, she shared: "And this is why it's really interesting to sit here and talk about things and *really* talk it out. 'Cause, like, talking about it for me is what makes it even more, like, yeah, no, *this* is violent."

"What Happens in Our House" / "You Don't Call the Police on Your Family"

THE SPACE BETWEEN HOME AND POLICE CONTACT

"What happens in our house" is a saying I frequently heard while listening to black women share their experiences of intimate partner and familial violence. In telling their stories, some like Kristen lowered their voice to ensure no one overheard them. Others, like Gina, whose story is to come in this chapter, talked loudly as they described domestic violence and officers' responses. Yet, no matter how black women chose to share their stories, they all spoke to how officers and others engaged in everyday policing around the home. Many times, black women used the saying "What happens in our house" as shorthand to quickly convey the politics around why they kept their stories to themselves for so long or as long as they did. They sometimes spoke it as a call, knowing I would know the response. Nodding, my body would stiffen as I replied, "stays in the house." *Here,* in these intimate moments of call-and-response during our interviews, there was a deep and shared understanding among us: We do not speak to others about the harms that happen between us in our homes.

According to the National Coalition Against Domestic Violence, 45 percent of black women have experienced intimate partner violence in their lifetime.[1] These encounters have a lifelong impact as victims of domestic violence are more likely to suffer from depression, anxieties, post-traumatic stress disorder (PTSD), and other types of mental health disabilities.[2] Less is known about the experiences and outcomes of familial abuses against black women from different backgrounds. However, in *Battle Cries*, Hillary Potter provides a glimpse into these social worlds, showing how childhood violence, like the kind Kristen experienced, form a critical pathway to intimate partner violence in adulthood for black working- and middle-class women.[3] Yet, this violence is often made "missing" because to tell the stories would make us look critically at our private lives.

Thus, black women's stories of domestic violence illuminate everyday policing in our private social worlds, and a shared awareness of the saying "What happens in our house, stays in our house" connected the black women in this study across backgrounds, identities, and times in their lives. Spoken as a principle and a warning, Sadia, a gender-fluid black woman with a working-class background, explained in the previous chapter why she remained silent for years about her stepfather's sexual abuse:

> It was the experience in black houses where what happens in the house stays in the house. You don't talk to anybody. You don't tell your grandparents about it. You don't do this. You don't do that because it ain't nobody's business what happens in my house.

We also see that Sadia and others get angry and push back against this "missingness." For example, Keisha, a cisgender black woman with a middle-class background, also learned that it "had to be: 'whatever's in the house stays in the house.'" However, she quickly followed up with: "That don't really work for me." When we met, Keisha was adamant about her need to speak openly about her experiences within her home just as much, if not more, than her encounters outside of it.

At the same time that black women learned that domestic violence should "stay in the house," they also learned that "making it home" should protect them and others from the police. Or, as Abena said in the previous chapter, "Of course they are going to handle you a little differently than we do at home," to demarcate that she should expect violence from officers and safety from those around her. Thus, black women were taught to idealize the home, to see it as a safe place from racism and violence even as the reality that emerged in my interviews was that it was one of the most frequently shared points of police contact due to officers responding to domestic violence.

Teyanna

"So, my first question for you is do you have any questions for me before we get started?"

"No, I'm an open book. You got me."

"I wanted to ask you, how did you feel taking the survey? What was the survey like for you?"

"It made me reflect a lot. And then I thought about how much I really don't, [*pause*] or rather how afraid I actually am of the police. That's what I got from the whole thing, though."

"Did it bring up anything specific for you?"

Teyanna is a dark brown-skinned, black, African American, bisexual, cis-gender woman in her early thirties whom I met in the summer of 2020 at an anti–police violence protest. Although we initially met in person, we decided to conduct our interview over the phone due to the ongoing COVID pandemic. When I asked her about whether the survey brought up anything for her, she began to tell me about officers' responses to the domestic abuse in her home throughout her childhood.

When it came to talks, Teyanna didn't remember any childhood conversations about the police. Instead, she mostly learned about officers through the D.A.R.E. program at her school. Unlike Joy, the program did not humanize the police for Teyanna. "I was always scared to go near them because they carried weapons. I remember that. I wasn't scared of them as people, but scared of their weapons, and I associated them with the weapons in that sense." Thinking more about if the police talk happened in her family, she speculated, "Maybe my mom and my dad had it with my brothers." If they did, she "wasn't there for it" but she further shared, "I just would imagine that they would, because in my father's head not that he loved me and my sister less, but in his head, he knew how hard it was to be a black man 'out there.'" Teyanna continued, "I don't think he thought the same for us. I would like to think maybe 'cause—[*pause*] I don't know . . ." Trailing off, she struggled to make sense of what the absence implied about how her father felt about her and her sister. Eventually, trying to explain exactly what she meant, Teyanna said her father assumed "we would never really do anything to get in trouble."

I asked her how this assumption made her feel. "I don't know. [*pause*] They [read brothers] were spoiled from day one. From day one, my mom was like— my mom had my sister and I handled like we were . . . [*pause*] I guess she just always expected that we had [*pause*] like we would know what to do in these kinds of situations 'cause we were raised understanding that we were black women and we already had two strikes against us, so be careful." The expectation to "be careful," as well as the assumption that she would automatically know how to navigate situations that went unnamed, shaped how Teyanna perceived herself then as a child and now as an adult. "In that respect, I feel like I did have something that my brothers maybe didn't quite understand." This "something" she's referring to was a feeling of independence, as she explained how she didn't feel comfortable calling the police or relying on others. For Teyanna, she would "rather figure it out for myself, to be honest."

Yet, calling the police was a frequent occurrence in her childhood home. At the beginning of our interview, she described how her "father was an alcoholic" and "combative." When he would become abusive, "cops would have to be called to the house." She remembered how the police "were always really nice" to her but also how she "watched what they did to him." "A good one," or positive encounter, was when officers were "being helpful" and removed her father without hurting him. Recalling one of these incidents, she said, "Maybe I was maybe like eight, and I was trying to protect my mom, and things got crazy, and we had to call the cops. I remember them letting me sit in the back of the car with them, and then when the paramedics came, they made sure I got in there. They made sure to take care of me and then asked the paramedics if I could have a teddy bear. That was positive." She kept the toy for years, saying: "It was a positive experience in a traumatic situation."

Other times, however, Teyanna and her siblings saw officers physically assault her father, and she oscillated in the meaning-making of these encounters as she worked to make sense of what she witnessed. On the one hand, she said her father was "combative" and "not compliant" and that officers treated him "rough" but "maybe not abusive," so "it wasn't as traumatic." Yet, on the other hand, there were times when officers were really violent with her father. "But a few parts of it did stick out in my head how they treated him," and they could be "*really* rough with him." Teyanna "never really watched anybody put their hands on another person like that up until that point." Observing her father in these "rough" encounters with the police was "traumatic" for Teyanna.

Altogether, she shared how the domestic violence, along with officers' inconsistent responses, continued to impact her, saying, "A lot of that goes into actually who I am now because of those experiences." She explained more when discussing how she coped with what she witnessed, nervously disclosing to me, "I do have—I do have mental illness. I suffer from depression, with PTSD. And we're not sure yet, that BPD (bipolar disorder) on Friday." When we met, she was waiting for her official diagnosis. While Teyanna continued to seek mental health support around her experiences of violence, she and her siblings were also working to reconcile with their father. For them, this included her father apologizing to all of them for drinking and the domestic violence he inflicted throughout their childhood. When reflecting on her father's journey to giving this apology, she explained it was "a long way for him" to recognize the impact this violence had on Teyanna and her siblings. In reflecting on her experience receiving it, his apology "did stir feelings," but ultimately, it felt "cathartic." She elaborated, "It helped me let a lot of things go . . . You're lucky if you get that, though. In that respect, I'm blessed." Although the apology significantly helped her, Teyanna stressed that she continued to deal with the long-term implications of what she experienced and witnessed in her home. From her place: "It's just always there, like that kind of trauma never lets up."

Danielle

A dark brown-skinned, black, African, bisexual, cisgender woman in her mid-twenties, with shoulder-length black hair, Danielle and I met at a café one early afternoon and sat on the outdoor deck for privacy. About her childhood, she said, "We grew up poor. But we transitioned to another tax bracket before I even realized that we were poor. Then, we moved." Although she had some childhood memories of her first neighborhood, she mainly recalled growing up in a middle-class, suburban community with her mother staying home to care for Danielle and her sister.

"I know so much of those talks are happening now, but no. We never had that talk." Though Danielle did not identify a specific conversation, she did learn from her parents over time how to respond to the police. She was told to "be nice to them," be "stupid kind," and, "they're helpful, but also try to stay away at the same time." Recognizing that these were "very conflicting messages," she didn't question it because, as a kid, she said: "this is what my parents told me to do. That's what I'm gonna do." Further, she emphasized that in her culture, "you never question your parents."

When we transitioned to talking about her experiences with the police, Danielle shared that her "first interaction was when I was in high school." Initially hesitant to talk about it, she said she had "a family situation." After pausing for a while, she disclosed, "Me and my dad were getting into it [*pause*], and it got to the point where it was physical." Describing her father as "a strong human being," Danielle was terrified and "didn't know how to handle" the situation. She eventually broke free, ran to her room, and barricaded herself there and called the police. While she was waiting for the police to arrive, her father tried "to knock my door down." She was afraid of what would happen to her if he got in, and he stopped only after she yelled at him that she had called for help. When the police arrived, Danielle was in shock from the assault and still barricaded inside her room. So, the officer, who Danielle describes as "white or Latino," first spoke with her father. Then, when coming to talk with Danielle, the police had little patience for her not immediately exiting her room. She described how they quickly grew frustrated with her, saying: "They were coming at me, [pause] saying because I'm of age I can go to jail." Upset, she yelled through the door, "This is not why I called you guys!" So, they left.

I asked Danielle how the police response made her feel, and she angrily replied, "Oh, awful. It made me feel awful. [pause] If I'm calling you because I feel unsafe, but you're saying I can go to jail because I was trying to defend myself. It doesn't say much." However, Danielle didn't get a chance to further explain her feelings about this incident as we were interrupted by a white woman, the only person sitting at the other end of the patio.

"Sorry. I overheard that. I had the same situation. Did they take you to jail?"

"No, they didn't," Danielle said stiffly.

"They took me to jail." Without asking, she went on to tell us her story of familial violence and officers' responses.[4]

Danielle and I were shocked and visibly agitated as we waited for her to stop talking. After the woman finished detailing her own encounter, the tone of our conversation shifted since we were made aware that someone was listening to us. I asked Danielle if she would like to go somewhere else, but she wanted to remain where we were as we talked casually about other things.

A few minutes later, the woman left. After we were completely alone on the patio and our conversation could be private, Danielle went back to telling her story. Her experience with the police left "an awful taste in my mouth" and caused her to "never call them" again for help with other assaults from her father.

"Did you talk to anybody about it?"

"No. My family, we grew up that you don't talk to anybody outside of your family. I would just talk to my mom and sister about it."

When she and her sister were alone, they talked about how "messed up" the abuse was with their father. However, while her mother would acknowledge that "what he did was wrong," she would also try to get Danielle to understand that she was "trying to make the marriage work." She would rhetorically ask Danielle, "What can you do about it?" Imitating the indignance in her mother's voice, she shared how this response from her "felt shitty." But "at the same time, it's a culture thing," Danielle explained, "Essentially, men can't do any wrong. The way my father grew up—we'd always make these excuses for him. He was an only child, a son, all this stuff. He wasn't raised to truly consider anybody else."

Danielle's experiences of abuse in her childhood home, coupled with the police response, her mother's reactions, and warnings against reaching out to others for help, isolated her. Unable to talk about what happened, she explained, impacted her ability to build relationships because "I wasn't able to ever effectively communicate." Left alone to move through this trauma, Danielle had "mental breakdowns." The cycle—comprised of each domestic incident and silence—"brought me into a depression." Over time, she became conscious of how unprotected she was—both by police and her family. In the space between, she poignantly shared: "I wasn't guaranteed any safety."

Gina

Sitting in a park close to her job, Gina had just gotten off of work. A light brown-skinned, black, Latinx, bisexual, cisgender woman in her early thirties with curly brown hair, she was candid throughout our conversation. We went back and forth between sitting at a picnic table and walking a nearby trail during our interview, first talking about her volunteer work in her community and a recent relationship that had just ended. Shifting to talk about her childhood, Gina noted that she grew up middle-class in a military family, so she and her brother did not receive a police talk as children. Gina reasoned that they "never [had] any of those kinds of talks and stuff" because of "cultural differences" or possibly because she "grew up in a biracial family, so it [police talks] was never a thing." She recalled how she only "knew to never talk to police" from her black friends, whom she would hear having talks with their parents. Yet, living on a military base prompted her parents to stress that Gina and her brother were supposed "to listen to the MPs, military police." And it wasn't until years later, when Gina and her brother were adults, that her parents had a substantial talk with them about the police.

Her parents were motivated to have this talk after Gina's brother was pulled over and after the death of Sandra Bland in jail after she was arrested during an aggressive traffic stop. Gina shared, "We first had our real 'police talk' maybe two years ago." During these conversations, her father, who is Mexican and

Spanish, did not see police violence as "a race thing." From his perspective, the problem was that people needed to "just listen" to officers when they gave them commands. In response, Gina's mother, who is black, would get "really heated," arguing that she was "raising a black boy at the end of the day and he has to know different things." As she noted, her parents had this talk for "more so [my] brother." Even though she was present, Gina listened more than participated, and in the process, she learned to "put your hand on the steering wheel, give them the information they need, [and to say] 'Yes, sir. No, sir.'" When the conversation did focus on Gina, it was less about the risk she faced as a black woman and more to warn her to behave. Her mother said, "I know your mouth, too." Therefore, Gina "needs to sometimes don't even talk back," with her mother urging her to just "get out of there and then you can do what you need to do after." Gina learned that she ultimately needed to "just know when to talk sometimes."

When we transitioned to her encounters with the police, Gina disclosed that most of them happened around "domestic disputes." She detailed one situation in which her friend and her friend's boyfriend "were getting into it" when her friend called her instead of the police. Upon arriving at her friend's home to break up the fight, her friend's boyfriend was the one to call officers. Once the officer, who was black, arrived, he scolded them, telling them, "Y'all need to stop. You lucky I came up here and some of my other police officers didn't because it would've been a totally different situation. Somebody would've got hurt, or somebody would have been for real going to jail." The officer then let them know he was giving them all "a pass" because he sympathized with the situation and "know these things happen with domestic disputes." Reiterating that they all "need to just cut it out," he did not take them to jail.

Gina was initially very relieved. But these feelings changed when the officer pulled her aside and immediately "tried to flirt with me after." He asked her, "What do you like to do on the weekends? What's your number?" Taken aback, Gina was at a loss for words. When we met, she still was. "I was like . . . [long pause]." Unable to finish her sentence, she eventually told me that she felt "frustrated," saying, "Because I'm like, what if we were in a situation like I don't know you and you tried to sexually push up on me to say, 'Well, I'm gonna take you to jail if you don't.' So, it's always kind of like those things of feeling uncomfortable."

Gina went on to tell me about another domestic violence incident. This one spilled over from her home to her college campus and involved an ex-boyfriend that she had just broken up with. "I was trying to break up with this guy, and

I had cut things off with him, and he came up to the school and basically trying to say, 'You can't leave me.'" Her ex "grabbed my backpack and swung me down to the ground." She gestured her body to emphasize how hard he had to throw her and pointed out, "I'm not the smallest girl, either." Trying to defend herself, she went into "fight or flight, like, no, I'm not going down like this." Yelling at him to "get off" of her—the two of them started fighting.

Others on campus witnessed this assault but did not intervene or offer help. "People were in the hallways literally watching this entire domestic dispute of a man put his hands on a woman, and teachers are looking out the door, and not anything happening." Eventually, the police were called, and she explained how the white officers arrived and "grabbed me up like I was the aggressor." By that time, her ex had "kind of stopped" attacking her, so the cops were dismissive and told her, "'I don't know why y'all are acting like this.'" They also singled Gina out as a student at the college and scolded her: "You go here and all of this" and reprimanded her by saying that she should not be behaving like that on campus. She was incredulous at how the officers treated her, and yelled, "Are you serious?! Wait a minute. Y'all are supposed to be protecting me, the student. I go here. He doesn't." She tried "to talk about the situation" with the police but was quickly made aware that "they were not trying to hear it."

Witnesses finally started speaking up and supported Gina's story, telling the police, "No, he tried to fight her." It didn't matter. Both she and her ex-boyfriend "got written a simple assault ticket" because, she explained, "there were marks on me and there were marks on him" from defending herself. Further, the officers chastised Gina about the public location of the assault and told her "'Okay, well, you need to figure out what you're gonna do with this situation because the president of the university, he doesn't want these disturbances and stuff.'" She pushed back against the officers for blaming her for the "disturbance," and asked, "Can we address how he came up to the school to fight me?" Gina's pleas made no difference. In the end, the officers' responses to her and her friend's domestic violence situations left her with "no faith" in the police. In the view from her place, she questioned: "Are you here to help me or, are you here to hurt me?"

Veronica

Veronica is a black, Latinx, non-binary, transgender woman in her mid-twenties with an expansive sexuality. She and I connected through a mutual contact in my field site, and since we were in the first couple of months of the

COVID pandemic, we decided to interview over the phone instead of in person. We also spent the first twenty minutes talking about COVID and the lockdowns before easing into talking about her childhood.

Veronica described what it was like growing up in an immigrant working-class family and neighborhood. While she did not recall a specific conversation about the police with her parents, she did remember how "family, friends, neighbors, and peers [that] nobody really had a positive mindset of police." This caused some confusion for a young Veronica as "society teaches you about police are gonna be outstanding, super members of society. They're out here to protect you. They're keeping the streets clean, [pause] they describe them as superheroes." These conflicting messages made Veronica always feel "weird being in a community of people who hated and did not trust the police." However, she went on to say, "I realize that I just hadn't developed those experiences yet with the police to understand that perspective." Her views, however, eventually "changed over time," stating, "the more world experience or life experience I developed." This included going back and forth between living at home and in a shelter with her mother because of the domestic violence from her father, as well as her experiences with intimate partner violence.

While being in what she described as "an abusive relationship," Veronica had repeated contact with officers. In one instance, her partner at the time went to her apartment, sharing: "they broke the door down, and I had to fight him outside." Once outside, the neighbors called the police. Knowing that cops were coming, her partner "had just left" when they arrived at her home. She described the assault in detail to the police: "I showed them my bumps and my bruises, scars, and scratches and stuff I had just gotten." But the white and black officers, she said, "told me they couldn't do anything about it cause I was trans."

As Veronica detailed, "They didn't see it as domestic. The officers didn't see it as domestic abuse because I was a biological male to them," and told her that the violence "doesn't count." For the police, "This is just the same as two guys fighting in a bar, right?" Angrily, Veronica pointed to her door and rhetorically questioned the officers, "Why is my whole door kicked in?! What?! This doesn't count as a break-in or something?! Like nothing." She worried that her boyfriend would return and hurt her. When she told the officers this, they said, "Oh, well, if he comes back, you call the police again." Disappointed and left to defend herself, she heatedly pointed out, "They didn't even give me a case number."

Her boyfriend's physical and psychological abuse continued and escalated. He enlisted strangers to target Veronica. He "actually had put my address on Craigslist," so "there were people jiggling my doorknob at night." He stalked her and repeatedly came back to her house. She told me, "He had fought me and was telling me all the kinds of things that crazy lovers tell you, only then— he left again." Each time, Veronica was left alone to defend herself: "I was scared for my life." And every time her partner came back to her home, she called the police. But each time the police responded to the attacks on her, she frustratingly said, "They didn't do anything."

On one occasion, officers gave her a number to a counselor. Following another assault, Veronica called the counselor instead of the police. The counselor was "very, very nice and made me feel like that she cared." After talking with her for some time, Veronica disclosed to her one of the reasons she believed her boyfriend kept attacking and stalking her and that she was unsure then if she should tell the police. She was also unsure if she wanted to tell me. "The only way that they were gonna do anything about it that I knew is I had to reveal a crime that he was committing that had nothing to do with me, honestly." I could hear Veronica working through whether she wanted to share this part of the story. She eventually said, "I guess I'll let you know."

Without prompting, she revealed, "The reason why he's beating me up is because I know he has child porn." She explained this was "why he started getting really physically violent is because I had found out that he was downloading child pornography." She didn't tell the police because "they were just so awful," and she was trying to protect him. Taking on the responsibility for trying to get him to stop on her own, she kept "telling him that this is really bad. This is not good; he needs to stop. This is dangerous," and "instead of him stopping, he turned it around to me because I knew."

After sharing this with me, Veronica clarified her desire to protect him from the police. "I didn't tell the police the first time because I didn't—I thought that . . . [pause] I don't know. I don't know what I was thinking. I should have told them the truth." Between wanting to protect him, being attacked by him, and being left to defend herself numerous times, Veronica eventually felt she had no choice but to share this information with officers in hopes that they would take the case more seriously. For her, she said, it was "the only way that I could get him out of my life." This is because after another assault that left her scared for her life, Veronica explained, "they're about to leave me again with no case number."

Once the two white police officers learned about the child pornography, "that's when they started to get involved" and "finally were like, 'Whoa, okay. Now, we can do something about the child pornography, but we can't do anything about him beating you up.'" While still disregarding her abuse, the police engaged Veronica's help in investigating her boyfriend. Even then, they continued to be "so awful the entire time" and "bully me into the station to talk about what happened in order to find the computer and stuff." After they got what they needed, the officers drove her home, and in the car, joked to Veronica, "Oh, I bet you won't date guys like him anymore." Veronica distinctly remembered how this felt, being in the car, listening to them insult her, and thinking to herself, "This is so dumb. You guys are so stupid." She sarcastically responded to the officers, telling me her response to them—"I didn't know that he was watching child porn when I met him."

"All of these things" made it "just such a nasty, sour experience," thinking it was, as she described, "the perfect time for police to get involved and to find someone threatening me with violence." Instead, they "never did anything. They only did something whenever I reported the other time." Throughout this experience, "it ended up becoming very victim-blaming. The detectives in the car were blaming me for having a bad relationship."

When I asked Veronica how she coped with all of this, she pointed to the initial counselor and the free counseling she received from a local women's shelter. The counselors "seemed to care," stating, "She made me feel well enough to share what I was really scared about my ex . . ." They "helped me recognize that what happened was really weird and really long." They helped her feel "safe enough to share that information with the police that came to the apartment." So, she pursued counseling after the initial incidents with her ex. "I did a lot of anxiety counseling, did a lot of self-validation counseling, just so much work." Reflecting more on this experience, Veronica stated, "The only people I felt that were helpful were empathetic women." She continued:

> It made me feel like I wasn't in the wrong and what was happening to me was wrong. It helped with feeling secure in my experience. It helped with developing my life beyond that experience. It helped me learn how I got in the situation and how to prevent getting in these situations and what to look out for because I wasn't prepared for life to be an abusive relationship.

From counseling, she learned "how to find support and how to utilize support and not to be ashamed of asking for help and not to be ashamed of anything." While the counselors helped Veronica, in her words, "develop my life beyond that experience," the "whole experience, again, made me just really untrusting of cops." Moving forward, she did her best to have no contact with the police, even if she needed help. This was because she didn't "want to be told that the one you're dealing with doesn't count as assault." From the space between, "Well, I don't want to be victim-blamed again."

The Conditions of Silence: Black Women Navigating Home Pathologies, Domestic Violence, and Carceral Feminism

With vulnerabilities to officers tied to "out there," black women learned to stay silent about their experiences of violence in the home to protect their families and communities. On their side of a racialized veil, making intracommunal violence "missing" signaled their loyalty as speaking to the police and outsiders was framed as betraying their families. Thus, silence fortified their intracommunal world from outsiders. However, it also left black women and girls' experiences of violence from insiders unnamed and unaddressed. *Here,* "what happens in the house" historically has been, and continues to be, critical to understanding the everyday policing of black women and girls.

————

There is a long and complex history of social scientists gazing into black homes. This history becomes even more complicated and, at times, damaging when investigating inequality and violence. The Moynihan Report is one of the most infamous examples. After declaring respective wars on poverty and crime in the mid 1960s, President Lyndon B. Johnson commissioned Assistant Secretary of Labor Daniel Patrick Moynihan to investigate social unrest and precarity within black communities. This led to *The Negro Family: The Case for National Action*, a report that effectively indicted black single mothers and "broken homes" for poverty and crime.[5] Less discussed is how the report heralded sociologist E. Franklin Frazier's assessment that black middle-class families have made significant progress because they are "more patriarchal and protective of [their] children than the general run of such families."[6] Thus, the report not only pathologized poor, black single mothers, it also deified black, middle-class, heteronormative families. In each case, heteropatriarchal authority—state or familial—was seen as a pathway out of poverty, crime, and violence. Importantly, both pathologization and deification dehumanized black families and centered white, middle-class nuclear structures as an idealized norm. In this way, scholars like Dorothy Roberts, Brittany Battle, and Janet Garcia-Hallet bring our attention to how family regulation and carceral institutions are similarly animated by these familial pathologies and idealizations. In particular, they illustrate how the state targeting of black families is steeped in the devaluation of black life and the investment in protecting white, heteronormative, nuclear family structures and norms.[7] For example, in *Invisible Mothers*, Garcia-Hallet demonstrates how pathologizing black mothers' reliance on othermothers and extended kin allows the state to justify its continued surveillance and criminalization of formally incarcerated black mothers.[8] As such, family regulation institutions frequently collaborate with the police to track, surveil, and punish black families.

Importantly, the 1960s onward saw an unprecedented rise in monetary support to federal and local police.[9] Similar to the past, stories about deviancy proliferated the media and were used to shift the resources and militarization of police departments. This directly led to a surge in officers' presence in black neighborhoods across the country and to what many refer to as the overpolicing/underpolicing paradox, where communities of color are highly surveilled and criminalized but are neglected when they need help and services.[10] Prior to the war on drugs, policing in the United States was primarily the function of local and state law enforcement. This new era in US policing, however, ushered in the rise of the prison industrial complex, which also involved the systemized integration of family regulation institutions. With each war on poverty, crime, and drugs in the 1960s and '70s funneling in more resources, police deepened their collaboration with other social service institutions, increasing their capacity to surveil and criminalize black homes. In the 1990s, broken windows policing, in which officers target what they see as social disorder—wherein white, wealthier communities are framed as "order" and black, poor communities are seen as "disorder"—exacerbated these practices.[11] Thus, Susila Gurusami and Rahim Kurwa describe how broken windows policing logics were used to target black homes—domestic spaces the broader carceral world saw as "broken."[12] Grounded in the pathologization of black kinship and life, they discuss how homebreaking emerged as a practice of police surveillance and raiding of black domestic spaces, which further constructed a pipeline from black homes to jails and prisons.

It is no surprise, then, that the home becomes an important site of resistance for black families. To protect these spaces from outside gazes—and all the pathologizing, surveillance, and violence that come with it—home gets intra-communally constructed as a type of safe space, a reprieve from police and others who would devalue black life and social relations.[13] Thus, home silence is a protectionist reinforcement of a racialized veil—an act of literal and epistemic resistance to white supremacy and state violence. Yet, in the process of distancing and shielding the home from white gazes and carceral institutions, home becomes a moral and political site, wherein black families worked to create idealistic families grounded in heteronormative and patriarchal ideals.[14] Thus, home is where a healthy hostility to the police can be coupled with moralizing demands of how to behave in hopes of protecting family members from the brutality of the state. Yet these demands can come at a cost. Alongside a strategic silence emerges a coercive silence that renders black women "missing" from notions of home safety. *Here*, black women experience what Richie calls gendered entrapment, wherein they have to maneuver around social stigma and criminalization in the broader social world and pressures to conform to black heteronormative familial ideals within their intracommunal ones—all while navigating domestic violence.[15] In describing social life in this place, she writes: "In the private sphere of [black women's] lives they were deeply misunderstood by people closest to them, betrayed by their loyalty to their families and communities, and abused and degraded in their most intimate relationships."[16] Thus, black women experience what psychologist Jennifer Gómez refers to as cultural betrayal around domestic violence, coming to the realization they can be harmed by those closest to them, and yet, still expected to remain silent to protect their abusers from outsiders.[17] This culturally distinct form of gaslighting accompanies intracommunal sanctions for speaking to outsiders, exacerbating the mental health consequences already associated with domestic violence.[18]

Importantly, domestic violence encompasses different types of intimate relationships, including romantic or sexual partners, parents, extended kin, and any others who have consistent access and close proximity to the household.[19] Among these relationships, domestic violence spans humiliation, emotional and psychological abuse, verbal harassment, physical assaults, stalking, and sexual violence, as well as threats, intimidation, and manipulation.[20] Nearly half of all black women experience domestic abuse in the context of intimate partner relationships at some point in their lives.[21] And nearly a third of all black women killed each year are murdered by romantic partners or someone within their kinship network.[22] Today, this violence is widely considered a serious issue. However, it was not until the 1970s that anti-violence feminist activism made significant strides in transitioning these forms of violence from ones that were "missing" to a systemic social problem that warrants public recognition and resources. As a result, the 1970s and '80s saw an increase in public awareness, shelters, crisis centers, and support groups. However, black women confronted barriers to receiving support, including limited access to safety nets and culturally competent services that understood the simultaneous broader and intracommunal conditions they faced.[23]

In the 1980s and '90s, carceral feminist responses to domestic violence took root, bringing about deeper collaboration with the police as a way to publicly legitimize the fight against domestic violence and provide protection for victims.[24] For example, the Violence Against Women Act (VAWA) in the mid-1990s federally recognized domestic abuse as a crime and further increased collaboration between the police and community groups providing social services. Over time, the adoption of mandatory arrest policies forced many state and local police officers to arrest someone or both parties during domestic violence disputes.[25] Black women and girls face a range of officer responses to domestic abuse, spanning neglect, potential arrest, and other types of police violence. In terms of officer neglect, Andrea Ritchie writes how "denial of protection is also a form of police violence, and increases vulnerability to other forms of violence by signaling to abusers and bystanders that violence against women of color is acceptable."[26] While mandatory arrest laws were intended to protect victims, they allowed officers to arrest black women who defended themselves. And alongside the risk of neglect and arrest, officers can leverage these vulnerable moments to sexually harass and coerce black women and girls. Thus, the silence examined in this chapter is contextualized by the interplay between the broader social and intracommunal worlds and, in particular, the history of home pathologization, intracommunal protectionism, and carceral feminist pushes to involve the police in domestic violence. In analyzing Kristen, Teyanna, Danielle, Gina, and Veronica's stories, I ground my analysis in the lessons black women learned about the home and their lived experiences with officers and others.

The Silence Matrix: Politics of Protection and Protectionism

Black women confronted the politics of protection in the space between home and police contact, or, as Veronica learned throughout her life, that officers were far from the "superheroes" and "super members of society" that mainstream messages depict them as. She theorized feminist standpoint theory as she reflected on her story, or how knowledge is situated and based on social position and experiences:[27] "I realize that I just hadn't developed those experiences yet with the police to understand that perspective" of her community who "hated and did not trust the police." Grounded in legacies of homebreaking, black women received messages like the one Kristen's father gave her: "You don't call the police on your family." Yet, in the space between, they were given little to no guidance on who they should call when they encountered intracommunal violence. *Here*, black women felt what Amber Joy Powell and Michelle Phelps call dual frustration around their gendered, racial vulnerability, wherein they needed protection from domestic violence but feared reaching out to officers and incurring the risk of police violence.[28] *Here*, they were left with interpersonal or "family situation[s]," as Danielle said, that they "didn't know how to handle" on their own.

With minimal to nonexistent support, some black women, like Kristen, called no one and told no one. They adhered to protectionism politics that prioritized the safety of the black family structure and the black men who were abusive in their lives. However, some eventually engaged in what Monica Bell defines as situational trust, where they constantly evaluated their distrust of the police against their evolving risk of harm and made strategic decisions to reach out to the police for protection.[29] These evaluations occurred during moments when they or someone close to them were being physically attacked. Therefore, some stepped outside of protectionism politics—making the strategic decision to call the police despite warnings against it. Thus, with no other options, Danielle protected herself by running to her room, locking the door, and calling the police.

Officers' inconsistent responses, in many cases, exacerbated black women's dual frustration. For example, Teyanna constantly evaluated her and her family members' need for protection from her father against their entire families' risk of police violence. Employing situational trust, she called the police and sometimes had positive experiences. Other times, she witnessed the police physically assault her father. She ultimately concluded that she was afraid of the police and would "rather figure it out" on her own and find alternatives in the future. In other cases, black women confronted their exclusion from police protection. In another example, an officer quickly grew frustrated with Danielle for not leaving her room, so he spoke to her father. With only his account, the officer threatened to take Danielle to jail, further illuminating the exclusionary politics of protection whereby black women and girls are subjected to state punishments but cannot access state protections.

For many black women who repeatedly called the police, the cycle of domestic violence coincided with a cycle of police neglect. *Here*, being assaulted by her boyfriend continually puts Veronica in contact with officers; and the police neglect makes her vulnerable to more abuse. While Veronica did not want to call the police, she feared for her life—so she kept calling. To officers, however, Veronica was a "nonideal victim," as they used pathologies about her race, gender identity, and class to bring her and her testimony into view.[30] This obstructed recognition. As she noted, "The officers didn't see it as domestic abuse because I was a biological male to them." Alternatively, it is only after she mentioned an "ideal victim"—in this case, children subjected to child pornography—that the police mobilized into action.

The Silence Matrix: Norms and Sanctions

Persistently brought into view through controlling images, officers saw black women as deviant and culpable in their abuse. These stories undergirded police neglect, harassment, and the criminalization of black women. And in many ways, these responses served as a sanction to their resistance to abuse. For example, similar to the black women in Potter's study on domestic violence within black relationships, Gina, Veronica, and Danielle, came to understand over time how they would not be protected because officers would not see them as victims. Black women also struggled to see themselves as victims of domestic violence, and Potter states, "The inability to view themselves as victims aided in the women's inclination to respond to their batterers' violent acts with corresponding force."[31] From the space between, she notes how fighting back is a dynamic form of resistance as black women reclaim their agency and engage in self-defense.[32] Thus, Veronica said, "I had to fight him outside," Danielle barricaded herself in her room, and Gina went into "fight or flight, like, no, I'm not going down like this." Seeing black women's resistance through the lens of pathology, officers threatened to arrest Danielle, with her sharing: "If I'm calling you because I feel unsafe, but you're saying I can go to jail because I was trying to defend myself. It doesn't say much." When Gina's boyfriend stalked her and assaulted her at school, police "grabbed me up like I was the aggressor." She was also charged with assault. Further, the police sanctioned the spillover of violence from private spaces into public ones, as, she recounts, officers were apathetic to the abuse and more concerned with the incident occurring on campus, telling her she "need[ed] to figure out what you're gonna do with this situation because the president of the university, he doesn't want these disturbances and stuff." Last, officers sanctioned Veronica for reaching out for help, engaging in trans-exclusionary politics that do not consider trans women to be "real" women.[33]

Within their intracommunal social worlds, black women and girls primarily came into view through respectability and racial loyalty. These legibility pathways lead back to gendered entrapment, wherein conformance to ideals of "good girls" and "ladies" and submission to the black heteropatriarchal family structure were seen as legitimate strategies to ensure safety. Thus, Jones writes:

> Good girls do not turn wild in the streets; instead, they spend the majority of their time in controlled settings: family, school, home or church. Good girls are appropriately deferential to the men in their lives. Good girls are not sexually promiscuous, nor are they anything other than heterosexual. Good girls grow up to be ladies and once they have achieved this special-status position they become committed to putting the needs of their family first.[34]

Importantly, silence is a critical part to being a "good girl," and speaking about violence dissents to the intracommunal politics of protectionism. Thus, Kristen was singled out as the "only girl" and taught to see her disposition as a problem, internalizing that she was "the one with the mouth." As an adult, Gina's mother told her she "knows your mouth, too," and to avoid violence, she "need to sometimes don't even talk back."

While intimate partner violence went unaddressed, familial violence between parent/adult kin and child relationships was seen as normal. Thus, Kristen struggled in our interview to name the violence in her parental relationship, believing that her experiences in the home would not garner empathy from those around her. Thus, she states others in her intracommunal social world would say: "Well, you got whupped because you are supposed to get whupped." In Spare the Kids, historian Stacey Patton sheds light on how this type of corporal punishment became normalized over time due to white supremacy. "During Jim Crow, whupping was used as a survival tactic to teach black children proper racial etiquette so they would not risk being beaten or lynched by whites."[35]

These punishments are still used today, and more, can be seen as a legitimate method for socializing black youth into protectionism politics. Thus, corporal punishment is not often intracommunally seen as abuse, and instead, framed as a benefit for black children despite the harmful impact on their physical, psychological, and emotional health.[36] Further, these forms of punishment can be specifically used against black girls to reinforce ideals about black nuclear heteropatriarchal families and gendered respectability, or more specifically, to curb their sexuality during adolescence, wherein, Patton states, "a young woman's chastity is somehow a reflection of her family's values."[37] Given that adhering to "good girl" norms is considered a pathway to safety, Kristen's father worried about outsiders seeing her as "fast" and asking for sexual violence based on her attire. In the process of socializing her away from these images, he sexualized her body as a form of protectionism, surveilling and controlling her gender and sexuality in the home through violence, homophobic slurs, and restricting her attire. Even as she explained how violence was used to enforce familial order, she knew others would frame the abuse as "You are a kid, and these are adults, and this is the natural order of things" between parents/adult kin and children. This was also reinforced through hearing friends' stories as she got older about how close family members also used a "shoe," "switch," or "extension cord" to assault them. These stories, along with her own experiences, further signaled to Kristen that this abuse in the parent/adult kin and child relationship was "sort of normal."

For many, exclusion from police protection was mirrored in intracommunal exclusions from protectionism. While Danielle understood that she could not "talk to anybody outside of your family," she sought safety and comfort from within her nuclear family. Her little sister empathized with her, but her mother's adherence to protectionism politics meant that she prioritized the marriage. For her, "trying to make the marriage work" meant ignoring domestic violence because "what can you do about it?" These multiple exclusions meant not only did black women's experiences go "missing," but wanting to address violence could be seen as breaking up the family. As such, they were sanctioned for reaching out for help. Feeling violence and the silence matrix carving out their place, numerous black women felt their distinct vulnerability to heteropatriarchal violence on both sides of the color line and lamented: "I wasn't guaranteed any safety."

Here, without real options for protection, black women became vulnerable to police sexual coercion. Thus, when Gina's friend calls her to intervene in a "domestic dispute," at first, the officer empathized with how he "know these things happen with domestic disputes." Then, he told them they were "lucky" he responded to the call instead of another officer. With someone else, they could have gotten "hurt," or they could "for real [be] going to jail." Naming their exclusion from police protection and describing his power to arrest and assault them, the officer then used his discretionary power to give them all a "pass." However, he immediately followed this up by sexually harassing Gina

and asking her for her personal information. Unprotected in the space between, she felt "frustrated" and "uncomfortable." She recognized the potential
consequences of saying "no," and explained that he could "take me to jail if I
don't." In this way, Gina's story showed how officers can leverage the lack of
protection in the space between to target black women and girls in exchange
for leniency within the broader carceral system—a process further explored
in the next chapter on police gender-based and sexual violence.

Everyday Policing and The Reproduction
of Intersectional Inequalities

Between outsiders' pathologizing and insiders' deifications of the black
family—black women felt the space between the conflicting stories told about
home and the realities they navigated in their everyday lives. For them, home
was as a paradoxical space: one where they learned racial solidarity and labored
alongside their families and communities to maintain safety from the police,
and one where they experienced and witnessed violence from officers and
others. Learning silence as protectionism, most black women I interviewed
were hesitant to speak about this part of their stories, and their ambivalence
was reflected in their narratives shared in this chapter. While home silence was
a response to historical and ongoing oppression, from listening to black
women's stories, it was clear that this silence was not meant to protect them—
so, it didn't. Further, there was a sense that our unwillingness and inability to
speak about domestic violence, in all its forms, was a critical link in the
"missing-ness" of black women and girls' stories from conversations on policing: How could they speak about what happened with the police if they
couldn't speak about why officers were called in the first place?

Drawing and Redrawing Lines of Exclusion:
Police Neglect and Familial Lack of Support

Broader carceral and intracommunal worlds align around minimizing and disregarding heteropatriarchal violence—reinforcing white and black heteropatriarchal lines in everyday life. Across all their differences, black women learned
that you do not call the police on your family. When we met, most black
women still agreed with these rules and worked to uphold a racialized veil
between them and the police. However, they learned through their experiences
that this also meant upholding heteropatriarchal veils around interpersonal

violence. This silence cut them off from accessing support from extended family and community members. Importantly, they were not given alternatives for seeking protection. Thus, when confronted with domestic violence, some called the police anyway. From there, officer responses often reinforced the need to uphold a racialized veil, and the absence of community-sanctioned alternatives to the police meant that black women were left in a cycle of abuse with little to no options for safety. Consequentially, black women found that their exclusion from protection on one side of the color line influenced their vulnerability to violence on the other. Left in the space between, feeling multiple lines of exclusion being drawn and redrawn, black women described the pain of coming into consciousness about not being guaranteed safety from officers or those closest to them.

Drawing and Redrawing Lines Through Coerced Inclusion: Pathology and Protecting Heteropatriarchy

While Teyanna's story showed how officers can use incidents of domestic violence to inflict violence upon black men, most of the black women I interviewed described how officers showed leniency toward abusers and sympathized with domestic abuse. Thus, Gina recalled the officer empathized with domestic violence as a normal part of heterosexual relationships and that he said he knew "these things happen with domestic disputes" before sexually harassing her. Additionally, when Danielle's father physically assaulted her, the officer did not provide protection and primarily relied on her father's account. Alongside this exclusion, she also navigated her mother's decision to protect her marriage over her safety and recognized that her father "wasn't raised to truly consider anybody else." From her place, Danielle intimately witnessed the promotion of hegemonic black heteropatriarchal structures and ideals as an effort to resist pathology, which ultimately entraps black women in violent relationships. Altogether, the politics of protection and protectionism aligned through empathy for heteropatriarchal violence and protecting these structures, viewpoints, and relations.

Normalization of Intersectional Inequalities: Rationalizing Violence and "Missing-ness"

Victims' legibility around heteropatriarchal violence was tied to pathology and rationalizations of violence in everyday life. Thus, for Kristen, familial violence was rationalized as normal and a legitimate method for instilling norms and enforcing heteropatriarchal structures, wherein her father would say "extremely pejorative things" about LGBTQ+ people that she did not want to disclose in our interview. In Veronica's story, officers also used pathologizing narratives, bringing her experiences into view through transphobic frames, telling her "they couldn't do anything about it cause I was trans." Under the many lines drawn through police politics, officers explicitly told her that the abuse "doesn't count" as intimate partner violence. Black women struggled to make sense of the dissonance of messages about what it meant to "make it home" in order to find safety and warnings that stressed "what happens in the house" should "stay in the house." They recognized how officers and others shared practices of violence and silence. Thus, from their place, black women and girls' strategic attempts to call upon officers for protection should not be taken lightly. Very cautiously did they engage in situational trust, often weighing the pros and cons of external and intracommunal risks during ongoing abuse. And the stress of making these decisions and their potential consequences for themselves and others caused immense anxieties.

Given these conditions, resistance took many forms. First, black women choosing to tell their stories that were supposed to "stay in the house" is a form of resistance that defied the idealization of black homes and heteropatriarchal lines that veil their experiences. Thus, Kristen recognized that by speaking with me she was lifting veils she had learned and internalized throughout her life, and she questioned throughout our interview whether she was going to "be honest" about her experiences. Although Kristen did not reach out to the police or others for help, as she got older, she and her mother eventually had one-on-one conversations about violence away from her father (*these conversations with her mother are discussed more in chapter 5*). From home, Teyanna, Danielle, and Veronica's decisions to call the police were also acts of self-protection and resistance. For Teyanna, this resistance can be understood through how, despite her fear of officers, she and others called them for help. However, given officers' inconsistent responses, she questioned the utility of the police. Similarly, Danielle resisted by calling the police even though she was told to stay away from them. And throughout Veronica's cycle of domestic abuse and police neglect, she engaged in self-defense, persistently advocating for her case to be taken seriously and calling out officers' victim-blaming tactics. Last, while Gina did not call the police, she did fight back on behalf of herself and her friend. Despite messages and practices that devalued black women and girls and left them unprotected, these black women's seeking help during a crisis demonstrates that they still believed they were entitled to safety.

"what happens in our house"

"you don't call the police on your family"

                                        "i wasn't guaranteed any safety"

"'cause like talking about it for me is what makes it even more like,
yeah, no, *this* is violent"

        "it's just always there, like that kind of trauma never lets up"

"some people think, it's really tiny things that don't matter, but it shapes you"

"well, i don't want to be victim-blamed again"

        "are you here to help me or are you here to hurt me?"

                                "he's just gonna be right back out there"

3

Gina

Gina was first introduced in the previous chapter. Growing up middle-class and on a military base, she and her brother didn't get the police talk from her parents, with the exception of being told to listen to the military police. However, the death of Sandra Bland, as well as her brother getting pulled over by the cops, prompted her parents to finally have a substantial police talk. In this conversation, Gina's parents argued about whether race plays a role in policing. For her father, who is Latinx,[1] race did not, but for her mother, who is black, it did. Despite her mother emphasizing racism, it was Gina's brother who was viewed as particularly vulnerable to police abuse, given that he is a black man. Conversely, it was Gina's behavior of "having a mouth on her" that her mother noted as something that needed to be controlled to avoid police violence.

During our interview, Gina explained that domestic disputes have put her in contact with the police, including when she tried to protect a friend from being attacked by her boyfriend. In that case, Gina was sexually harassed by the responding police officer. She also disclosed another experience in which an officer sexually assaulted her at a local bar. Out one night with friends, Gina "got into a little dispute [*pause*] with this guy and had been drinking a little bit." To break up the fight, the bouncer called the police. The responding black officer took advantage of restraining Gina to grope her: "And while he was grabbing me, he was grabbing all up against my body, too. I'm like, 'Get off me!' I had, of course, a little dress on cause I'm going out . . . he just grabbed, and then we fell to the ground." On the floor, the officer continued groping Gina, putting "his hand all on my ass" and "touching all over me." She yelled for the officer to get off her. But he kept "literally groping" her in front of everyone.

When he let her go, he began "acting like it wasn't a thing." He accused her of being too "drunk" and making it out to be like "I don't know what I'm talking about." Moreover, Gina described him as saying he was doing her a favor by not arresting her. She explained to me that while she was "tipsy," she was "coherent enough to know what's going on" and that she was being assaulted. Unsure of what to do, Gina left the bar.

A few weeks later, Gina saw the officer again. She tried to ignore him, but he approached her, asking, "Weren't you out here a couple weeks ago showing your ass and stuff?" Angry at how he described the assault, Gina confronted him, replying, "Yeah, but wasn't you also grabbing my ass?" This time, the officer was not alone. He was with his partner, who appeared confused by the verbal exchange. The officer who groped Gina tried to downplay the accusation in front of his partner and said to him, "You know we get all kinds of people out here." Turning back to Gina, he said, "But we don't need to have no problems. But I'll make sure I check out for you next time if there's something and make sure I'll look out for you and all." Gina disclosed the assault to a friend, who exclaimed, "Hell no, you report his ass!" But Gina felt uncomfortable reporting and wanted to move past it. "I didn't say anything 'cause I was just like, whatever. Sometimes you just let men be men kind of thing, that situation, but . . ." She paused and never finished her sentence.

When I asked Gina how she coped with officers harassing and assaulting her, she responded, "I didn't. I think it was just one of those things you just don't even think about it in the moment, and so you just keep it pushing." She concluded, "Boys will be boys," and said she had "no faith in police." The department, "they ain't going do nothing about him anyway. They just be like, okay, one person said something." Reflecting on why she and other black women don't report police gender-based and sexual violence to departments, she said, "I think that's a lot of times what happens is we just want it to be over, we don't want no problems, and so we don't allow reports to be made or extra work to make [a] statement 'cause a lot of times we just trying to get on to what we got to get on to next."

Despite claiming she wanted to just move on, Gina sometimes wished she had reported the assault. She wondered if it could have helped the next black woman he did this to because it "would have been one of those situations to where I did bring it up to say at least because then that establishes a pattern if it is." Ultimately, in the view from her place, reporting still didn't make sense because "he's just gonna be right back out there."

"He's Just Gonna Be Right Back Out There"

THE SPACE BETWEEN VIOLENCE DEFINITIONS AND DISCLOSURE OF POLICE GENDER-BASED AND SEXUAL VIOLENCE

The most common question I received in academic spaces about black women's stories was: "How are you defining violence?" At first, the question admittedly made me feel apprehensive and defensive. Making my way through lessons that I, too, had picked up as a black girl and stumbling through newly learned conceptual tools, I attempted to describe the specific details of what exactly made something *violent*. Then, while interviewing black women and analyzing their police encounters, the question made me feel angry and defeated. I struggled to convey all I was hearing when they intimately shared their police interactions with me. Finally, one day after finishing another presentation of the stories in this chapter, someone inevitably asked me "the question" again. Feeling my apprehensiveness and anger coalesce into a rage, I came to recognize the doubt and gatekeeping behind the question as the same threads weaving together black women's challenges in disclosing their police encounters.

More directly, no one asked for my definition of police violence after hearing me discuss black women's stories that were similar to those frequently covered in the news and virulently circulated on social media. In those moments, others readily recognized the potential tragic and deadly consequences of police encounters. Instead, the question was repeatedly levied at interactions that lay outside of police shootings and officers' threats of lethal force. The question also revealed skepticism around harassment, catcalling, and various forms of sexual assault as acts that fell short of rape as an unspoken threshold for sexual violence. On the outer edges of what is widely recognized about policing, others hesitated to call the harms that officers inflicted on black women and girls *violence*.

After receiving this question innumerable times over the years, I eventually understood through the query's pattern—or timing and tone—that when most people asked for my definition of violence, what they often meant was:

"Is this *really* violence?" Importantly, Collins writes, "Viewing the very defini-tion of violence as lying outside hierarchical power relations of race and gen-der ignores how the power to define what counts as violence is constitutive of these same power relations."[2] Thus, the definitions of violence we use to bring harm into view are socially constructed, and more, feminist scholars often critique the ways dominant definitions do not account for gender-based and sexual violence.[3] Today, widely accepted police violence definitions are primar-ily drawn from news media outlets and sourced databases, research institutions, officer convictions, and police department administrative data.[4] However, black women have historically been denied access to positions of power within these spaces and excluded from how they produce definitions of police vio-lence.[5] And as shown in the previous chapters, black women and girls' exclu-sion from knowledge production processes around violence also extends to their intracommunal worlds where they confront barriers to sharing their stories. Yet, black women and girls must contend daily with how these differ-ent spaces conceptualize violence as their definitions expand and restrict how others see and respond to their experiences. And thus, definitions of violence create and obstruct pathways to disclosure.[6] Therefore, the query "How are you defining violence?" led to the conditions analyzed and the questions ad-dressed within this chapter: How do black women experience and understand harm from officers that lie outside of common definitions of police violence? How do they decide to disclose these encounters?

While I found in my interviews that black women from different social backgrounds did, indeed, experience police violence in ways that fit common conceptions of officer use of force (*e.g., chokeholds, physical assaults, threats of lethal force with a gun, tasing, and vicarious exposure to police fatalities and vio-lence*), this chapter is not about proving these encounters happen in their lives. Many activists and scholars have already shown that they do. Instead, this chapter focuses on the encounters black women knew were downplayed as significant acts of police violence, ones that are often made "missing" in our social worlds. Thus, I focus on police gender-based and sexual violence outside of rape. I do so not to reify these experiences as forms of harm that are exclu-sive to black women and girls but to emphasize how these interactions speak directly to how violence and the silence matrix carve out our social worlds every day and people's place on the margins. From their place, black women consistently identified police gender-based and sexual violence as encounters that deeply affected them, interactions that they rarely, if ever, reported or dis-closed, and as harm they felt others would minimize and not take seriously.

Ashley

"I don't feel nervous. I can say I'm excited, I guess."

Like some other black women I interviewed, Ashley was interested in talking with me after taking the pre-interview survey. Similar to others, it was the first time Ashley felt that her encounter would be recognized as a meaningful form of police violence. So, she told me she was excited to finally discuss an interaction she saw represented on the survey and had kept to herself since she was a kid.

Ashley, a dark brown-skinned, black, African and African American, heterosexual, cisgender woman in her early thirties, has a high school degree and works several jobs. After one of her work shifts, she met me for the interview at a local park. Quickly noticing a nearby farmer's market and festival running that evening, she and I decided to walk around and chat about her day since she had just gotten off work. Eventually, we found a secluded picnic table far enough away from the music to allow us to hear each other and gave us some privacy. While I reviewed the interview protocol, Ashley intently watched a soccer game nearby. I asked how she felt knowing that we were going to discuss police violence. At this, she turned back to me, smiled, and refocused her attention on our conversation.

Ashley grew up "in a really small town." There, she "knew about all the police officers and how they were generally." Yet no one talked directly with her about the police because, as she put it, police violence was not a "thing" back then in the way "it's important now." She detailed, "We didn't have to, and I don't regret or are upset at my Momma for not telling me anything like this because you don't know the future." Instead, Ashley learned how to interact with officers by attentively watching those around her. From her observations, along with the tragic death of a family member by an officer—of which she "heard different stories" about what happened—she understood that when "I walk past them, you know, I don't say anything to them. I try not to even look at them."

Although she tried to stay away from police as much as possible, keeping her distance proved difficult due to officers responding to domestic violence in her childhood home. When first mentioning this, she said, "One time, I called the cops myself because we have a really evil stepfather. [*pause*] I don't wanna talk about it . . . blah . . . blah . . . blah." Her voice trailed off as she waived her hand to dismiss the story. We moved on to other questions about her childhood. Yet, it quickly became apparent that it was difficult for Ashley to talk about her interactions with police as a kid without talking about her stepfather. When I asked Ashley if she had to call the police as a child, she disclosed that "something happened in the family where he actually put his hands on my sister."

As we continued to talk, Ashley changed her mind about telling this part of her story. She tried to intervene on her sister's behalf. But her mother held her down "so I wouldn't go over and help her." With her mother restraining her, Ashley watched her stepfather physically assault her sister. She shared that "it was so bad" that she kept trying to wrestle herself away from her mother so she could get help. Eventually getting loose, Ashely "ran to the neighbors and called the cops." Once the police arrived, she explained to the officer what happened and told me that she was "really hysterical" while speaking to him "because I literally saw this grown man beat on my sister."

However, the responding officer had little patience for Ashley being emotional and repeatedly told her to "shut up" and that he was "trying to help me, but I won't stop talking!" This response shocked Ashley and deeply "hurt" her. She felt she would have been treated differently if she were white, comparing the officer's response to "videos with some really hysterical white people" [*laughing*] and how the police "have not told them that." Moreover, with her sister's refusal to speak with the officer about what happened, he told Ashley that he met her stepdad and that "he seemed fine and okay. [And] it didn't seem like he did anything." With that, the officer left.

After Ashley shared this story, I wrongfully concluded that this domestic violence incident and ensuing police interaction were what she expressed interest in being "excited" to finally talk about. However, when I asked to confirm, she explained that she had talked about her stepfather's abuse with "so many people" and that her entire family "knows all about him." Instead, the encounter she was "excited" to finally have a chance to speak about occurred earlier in her life, "when I was nine or ten years old." She said that up until now, this experience was "just something I just kept to myself."

This encounter involved an officer catcalling her as a child. For Ashley, this experience, she said, was "the first time I felt sexualized by someone." She had very detailed memories of that day, remembering where she was, what she was wearing, who she was with, and how she felt during and after the incident. Ashley said she, her sister, and a cousin were walking to a local corner store in their neighborhood. She smiled fondly, recalling how much fun they had being "cute," playing "dress up," and wearing "these spaghetti-strap dresses" and "fake little nails."

Ashley's smile quickly disappeared as she abruptly stopped in the middle of telling this story. Worried about my impression of how she was dressed, she anxiously explained, "But I'm nine" and "was not developed whatsoever." She made it a point to let me know that she and her family members "weren't looking 'fast' or anything like that." She grew increasingly nervous while making these statements. I nodded and agreed with her, telling Ashley they were all "just kids." At this, Ashley laughed and noticeably relaxed, settling back into the bench as she continued with the remainder of her story.

While "walking down [the street]" with her sister and cousin, "this cop literally slow[s] down" and drives "in front of us a bit." Pulling slightly ahead of them, the officer "full stops" and waited "until we came into view." Then, when they passed his patrol car, the officer rolled down his window and cat-called. During this encounter, Ashley distinctly recalled how he stared at their bodies, "literally look[ing] me up and down." She tells me that she could not tell his exact race, but "I know he was not black," and she details how she "still remember[s] his face. He had sunglasses on." Getting angrier as she remembered how she felt during the encounter, she elevated her voice while imitating his gaze at her body and rhetorically asked, "Who does that?! Who stops just to, you know, and then look me up and down?!" Further describing how she felt, Ashley said, "I never felt so disgusted in my life. [*pause*] I felt really gross. [*pause*] It's something that sticks with me to this day. [*pause*] I still remember his face. [*pause*] He knew whatever, how he was looking at me, was not okay." From this encounter, Ashley said she "learn[ed] that people look at me differently." And most importantly, she further explained, "I never want[ed] someone to look at me like that again."

Consequentially, this encounter impacted Ashley's relationships with her body and sister. She said, "I didn't want to be crawling around my older sister anymore" and decided "I never wanted to be like my sister ever again." She told her sister: "Don't put fake nails on me anymore. Don't put no more lipstick on me." Reflecting more on their relationship, she said, "To that day, I wanted to be the exact opposite of her." Her sister "always wondered why" their relationship changed. For Ashley, "to know it was a cop . . . that first sparked, these are not good people." In the view from her place: "Some people think it's really tiny things that don't matter, but it shapes you."

Veronica

First introduced in the previous chapter, Veronica grew up in an immigrant working-poor family. She noticed early on the differences between how mainstream society depicted the police as protectors and the negative views of the police among her family and community. Initially struggling to make sense of these divergent views, Veronica's critique and fear of the cops developed over the course of her life. This included when the police discounted the stalking and abuse she experienced from her ex-boyfriend and how this treatment was grounded to their transphobic dismissal that she could be the target of intimate partner violence from a man.

Another experience that impacted Veronica's perception of the police was an officer harassing her when she was a high school student. She pointed out, "One of the questions that they asked in the survey was, were you belittled by a police officer?" Having answered yes to this question, Veronica detailed during our interview how a white officer bullying her at school was "my first experience with being belittled." These interactions had been on her mind since taking the pre-interview survey, and she had been "visibly remember[ing] that 'cause it was in a big group of kids, and [a] bunch of my peers."

Before sharing her story, Veronica stressed how she was "well-behaved," "kept my head down in school," and "minded my own business." She juxtaposed these comments about her character with how the officer and others at her high school saw her as "flaming" and targeted her as "that gay kid." She elaborated, "My name was 'that gay kid,' and then my deadname.[7] Every single time I was addressed, it was 'that gay kid, [deadname].' It wasn't even just students. It was by teachers. It was by everyone. Coaches, including one of the ones was a police officer or he was an SRO [school resource officer]." The officer, who often initiated the bullying, she said, "thought I was choosing to act gay for attention or something" and decided to "make fun" of her by "'click[ing] it on' and swish[ing] his hips whenever I was walking by." She called out how the officer's harassment "validate[d] it" to peers, and that since he did it, "why wouldn't the kids do it?" Over time, the harassment transitioned to assaults; peers would throw books at her and repeatedly physically attacked her at school. The officer would watch these attacks. "The cop didn't do—[pause] no one did anything throughout my entire grade school career."

When I asked Veronica if she had talked to anyone about these incidents or reported the officer, she replied, "No. I didn't report the bullying because it was normal, honestly. He wasn't the only one who did it." Constantly being bullied based on her race, gender identity, and sexuality, Veronica said, "I ended up developing feelings of complete isolation and othered—I was very othered." The bullying caused Veronica to become "very depressed" because "it felt like no one cared about whether or not I was being bullied or not. I just really kept to my own . . . and blamed myself for a long time." She continued,

"I was just realizing that I wasn't supported by anyone in the community. That includes police, who are supposed to be protective of the community. If I wasn't still being bullied and being assaulted, having faith in that, and having death-directing stuff—the police, even that person, didn't do anything to handle it. Yeah. I just felt really bad all the time."

The bullying and lack of protection impacted Veronica's educational performance. She "just stopped going to classes" to protect herself because, she said, "I just didn't want to be around other people 'cause I never felt supported." She shared, "I ended up missing one-third of my entire high school experience because of bullying," which meant that "I missed so many days of school that my mom had to go to court several times." Consequentially, completing high school "was a miracle," and she only "graduated because I did all online classes."

From officers harassing her at school and other police encounters, Veronica became "very aware of how I could be perceived by police" and "definitely recognized that police officers had some racial biases . . . [and] a gender bias or a LGBT bias." She began to "just notice that they never were there when I thought they should be . . . [and] whenever I asked for them to be there, it always turned out to be something that I would get lashed out for because I was different." Specifically, Veronica recognized that she was targeted because "I was black. I was poor. I was queer." And in the space between, she came to understand, "I wasn't guaranteed any safety."

Robin

Robin is a thirty-five-year-old, light brown-skinned, black, biracial or multiracial, heterosexual, cisgender woman with a master's degree and two jobs. We met at a local bar early one morning before she headed to work and sat on an outside patio deck. Although she and I had spoken several times before we scheduled this interview, she admitted that she was "kind of anxious" about talking about the police and her experiences. Indeed, she was reticent at moments throughout our conversation, giving short answers and pausing for long stretches of time.

During our interview, Robin did not make any specific references to her childhood social class background. However, she did share that she learned about the police from two places—her mother and television. From her mother, she learned that officers "abuse their power" and that she "just doesn't go to places where there is a lot of police." With her mother, she "would watch like, the police show *Cops*, we would watch like, *America's Most Wanted*. So, we would see like, stuff on TV." From her mother and the police shows they watched, Robin learned to stay away from officers and to only interact with them when she needed help.

Transitioning to talk about her police encounters, Robin grew apprehensive as she recalled multiple incidents in which officers exacerbated a situation. One encounter involved a domestic dispute between her and her partner that also included "a psychiatric emergency." Fearing for their safety, Robin's fiancé called the police to report that she was having a mental health crisis. Instead of providing help, the two white officers arrested Robin for assault. She believed the response was partly due to racism. "If they had really listened to what was going on, they would have brought me to a psychiatric hospital, not jail . . . they didn't call a mental health officer, and I think partly because my fiancé is white and I'm black."

After being arrested, the situation worsened, and Robin spent eleven days in jail with little psychiatric treatment or mental health support. Her repeated requests to speak with a psychiatrist were refused. Further, she was given the wrong medication, to which she had an allergic reaction. For Robin, this was the most horrific thing she's ever been through. She laughed derisively as she stated, "I know that the jails have, like, so many people that have, like, mental health issues. It's just like, it doesn't help you get better, [*laughs and pauses*] it just makes everything worse."

In addition to this encounter, Robin was mocked and neglected by an officer after a sexual assault at a local mall. She shared that while shopping with two guy friends, one of the acquaintances followed her into the bathroom and raped her. "[He] followed me into the restroom; I knew him, we were acquaintances, [*pause*] we were there together with another man, but I didn't think he would come into my stall and try to, you know, do something."

While recalling more details about this sexual assault, Robin began to speak in a monotone voice. We stopped the interview and checked in about how she was doing. She was adamant that she wanted to continue telling her story and went on to share with me what happened after the assault.

Robin immediately reported the rape to a black police officer at the mall. In response, he "pretty much just laughed." She elaborated, "He didn't pay me any attention; he just, like, laughed at me and you know . . . [*pause*] I mean, I told him what happened. I was like, hey, this guy just took advantage of me. He just—[*pause*] he just—[*pause*] he just didn't do anything, he was just, like, 'Oh, you're being stupid,' or whatever." The officer's response made Robin "feel like, [*pause*] horrible" and left her to deal with the assault on her own. Eventually, she went and found her other friend and told him what happened. This friend supported her, "helped me get away" from their acquaintance and made her "just feel safer." I asked Robin if she made another attempt to report her assault or the officer for his response. She replied that "after I talked to that one police officer, I never tried again."

Explaining how she coped with this experience—both the assault and the officer's response—she said, "I mean . . . [*pause*] I don't know. [*pause*] I think we went to, we went to a, um . . . [*long pause*] I mean, I tried to overdose, actually. So, I ended up, I wound up [at] the hospital for a little bit . . . [*pause*] like medication . . . [*pause*] and . . ." Robin did not finish her sentence. Shortly after, we decided to wrap up our interview early without going through the remaining questions. She eventually said, "I mean I went to a police officer, and I expected there to be, like, concerns, or take a report, or something, but he didn't do anything."

Nema

Nema, an eighteen-year-old, dark brown-skinned, black, African, heterosexual, cisgender woman in her first semester of college, was first introduced in the beginning of this book. She and I met at a local coffee shop to conduct our interview. Sitting on the outside patio for more privacy, I explained the purpose of the study and asked Nema if she had any questions before we started. Cradling her backpack and hugging it closely to her chest, she leaned her body forward over the table and answered, "No, ma'am." She went on to tell me about what she was learning in her mass incarceration class. This made her more "reflective" about "police interactions with minorities in inner cities and things like that." Alternatively, being from a white, middle-class suburb, she believed she did not have much to contribute and quickly tried to temper any expectations for the interview about herself and her story. To Nema, "certain aspects of police brutality and interaction[s]" only impacted particular black people and people of color. During our interview, it became apparent who Nema felt "the situation affects," as she spent most of our time together referring to her brother's interactions with officers and her guy friend's fatal encounter with the police that happened in her suburban neighborhood.

Nema initially did not remember having any police talks while growing up. For her, despite the incidents that happened around her, the police were "not something we talked about" because "it wasn't really like a thing," considering police violence to be a more recent social problem. As we kept talking, Nema remembered her mother's concern about her interacting with the police once her older brother had "legal issues" and got "involved with the law." Her brother's interactions with the police prompted a police talk for both him and Nema. She remembered her mother warning her brother about his "white friends" in their suburban neighborhood and that he "should be careful." Nema explained, "She always tried to make him understand that those friends have money, and they can get out [of trouble with the police]. You may be stuck in that situation for a variety of reasons, the skin color, the fact that you don't have money like they do, things like that."

Nema's mother also pulled her aside and told her to "be wary" because her brother was "doing this and all that, so just be careful." Nema also recalled a memory of watching from the backseat of the car as her mother got "pulled over one time." In this encounter, she taught Nema "how you should act in situations" like this. She described how her mother's behavior changed and suddenly became "submissive," "put[ting] her hands out," and saying, "Yes, sir" and "No, sir." When the interaction was over, Nema's mother turned to her and said, "Whenever that ever happens, just put your hands out there and be careful. Don't reach for anything unless they ask you." I asked Nema how it felt to see her mother doing these things, and she got angry as she responded, "That bothered me because my mom's a headstrong, independent woman."

As we wrapped up our conversation and started packing our things, Nema began to casually tell me about one more experience she remembered. This time, the police encounter was hers. About a year before, when she was a high school senior at her private boarding school, Nema had a "really bad experience" online with students that prompted police involvement. Called to the principal's office, she was confronted by three officers. One black officer, noticing her discomfort, pulled her aside and offered to help, telling Nema, "You know, we're black in this world. [. . .] I'm gonna help you out as much as I can. Just try and go along with it, and they'll put it away." Afraid of getting in more trouble, Nema was grateful for the officer's support when he said he would "help me out as much as [he] can" and initially viewed this as a positive experience with the police.

The officer then started showing up unexpectedly at Nema's dorm. Arriving at night when she was alone and dressed for bed, he would talk with her for long periods of time about his work stresses on the force, personal life, and relationships, and even what it was like for him to be a father to a teenage girl whom he compared to Nema. Feeling uneasy and living far away from home,

Nema sometimes called her mother to listen in over the phone during some of his "visits." Growing increasingly concerned, Nema eventually checked in with the principal at her boarding school and was shocked to learn that her case had been closed for quite some time. Yet, when she expressed her anxieties to the officer about him visiting her alone at night, he warned Nema that he could still punish her by giving her a ticket.

Initially quite talkative and leaning in with inquisitiveness, by the end of sharing her story, Nema's demeanor drastically shifted. Watching her closely, I observed how the reality of her situation grew in her consciousness and made itself visibly known in her body while sharing her story. She began to show signs of nervousness, occasionally looking over her shoulder and physically turning away from me and the table. It appeared that Nema was realizing— quite possibly for the first time—that she was being groomed and stalked by a police officer and was potentially at risk for other forms of violence. She grappled for a frame, a way to name and make sense of this encounter. Not able to finish her sentence, in the view from her place, she said in a faint voice: "Well, he said he had a daughter, too, [pause] so [pause] I like to think that . . ."

The Conditions of Silence: Defining and Disclosing
Police Gender-Based and Sexual Violence

In the space between definitions and disclosure, black women's accounts demonstrate how everyday policing constitutes a distinct vulnerability to violence. Rarely are black women's stories the bases of how police violence is conceptualized and addressed by legal institutions, media, and communal conversations. Ensuing definitions of violence, then, reveal where black women and girls are left institutionally and communally unrecognized and unprotected. Many black women I interviewed came to understand this, to recognize that they had to navigate their interactions with officers alongside how institutions and others defined violence in ways that made their encounters "missing." Thus, at the root of the question "How are you defining violence?" is the historical and ongoing struggle of who gets to tell the stories of harm in our social worlds.

———

Like other violence, gender-based and sexual violence is about power. To establish and maintain heteropatriarchal social worlds, the state has historically wielded this power through the act of violence and by controlling who has access and legitimacy to tell the story. During US enslavement, masters believed that they were solely authorized to construct the narrative—subsequently arguing that they were entitled to inflict sexual violence against black women and girls based on their legal claims to them as property.[8] At the same time, black women could not make legal claims to their own bodies and their testimonies about sexual violence were devalued by the courts.[9] By disregarding black women's personhood and testimonies, the state effectively legalized sexual violence and criminalized black women's ability to tell their stories and resist. And in a social world without fear of state punishment for inflicting these harms, enslavers and overseers used the threat and act of sexual violence to keep black women physically and psychically in their place.

During Jim Crow, black women and girls continued to be subjected to routine sexual violence from state actors, with experiences spanning rape and lynchings to various types of sexual assault and everyday sexual harassment. Many of these harms were silenced as black women and girls feared reporting their encounters due to white men's power to influence the courts as well as the reality that their attackers could also be members of the courts and police departments.[10] Historian LaShawn Harris details how this collusion from multiple actors and the denial of legal protection meant that officers and others in black women's communities could inflict gender-based and sexual violence with impunity.[11] Thus, gender-based and sexual violence by the police, both then and now, is predicated on what Bell defines as legal estrangement, or black women's "marginal and ambivalent relationship with society, the law, and predominant social norms that emanate from institutional and legal failure."[12] As such, these harms are conditioned upon how we legally and socially construct police violence in our social worlds without including the full spectrum of black women and girls' lived experiences.

In *America Goddam*, Lindsey describes the historical and present-day gendered lines in how we conceptualize police violence, wherein spectacular killings dominate how researchers, policymakers, and others bring police violence and victims into view.[13] While there is no mandatory reporting of any type of police violence by police departments in the U.S., police killings persistently receive more media attention and have primarily been tracked by citizen groups, local organizations, independent researchers, and news outlets. In particular, the *Washington Post*, Fatal Encounters, and Campaign Zero's Mapping Police Violence track incidents of officer-involved fatalities covered in local and national media to create open-source databases.[14] Prior to 2020,

The Bureau of Justice Statistics' (BJS) Police-Public Contact survey didn't account for police sexual violence and conceptualized officer use of force through a wide array of physical and verbal harassment.[15] Finally, police departments across the United States keep their own administrative data on officer misconduct, typically documenting violations against department policies.[16] Importantly, research using these sources persistently find racial disparities in lethal force and physical assaults, often attributing them to officers bringing people of color into view through perceptions of threat and danger.[17]

At the same time, Lindsey draws our attention to police soft killings—or everyday, "intentionally imperceptible," ways that policing reproduces an anti-black social world.[18] These harms, such as black women's experiences of police gender-based and sexual violence, work to reproduce this world in our daily lives. However, media, research, and conversations on policing seldom incorporate these harms into definitions of police violence. Given these absences, black feminist activists and researchers arduously work to define and account for a continuum of these harms. INCITE!, a network of radical feminists of color working on various issues of violence, defines police gender-based and sexual violence as acts of sexualization, harassment, sexual assault, rape, coercion, and other sexualized harms.[19] In "Shrouded in Silence," Ritchie comprehensively outlines the barriers to reporting these types of encounters, specifically defining police gender-based and sexual violence as "any act taking advantage of police authority and power to engage in sexually harassing, degrading, discriminatory, violative or violent acts."[20] The report further argues that the exclusion of these acts from widely accepted police violence definitions and policies impacts how officers target those on the margins. In social worlds that leave these harms undefined, officers are uniquely positioned to know which forms of violence don't have policies to address them, are not taken seriously by departments, and remain untracked by oversight groups. They can subsequently leverage the gaps in policies and reporting mechanisms to inflict gender-based and sexual violence with no accountability. Here, Brooklynn Hitchens and colleagues describe how young women are subjected to punitive chauvinism, "wherein male police officers use coercive power to hassle, threaten, and manipulate young women who lack the power to protect themselves."[21] In light of these power dynamics and conditions, many activists and scholars working on police gender-based and sexual violence make no distinction between on- and off-duty officers as the police can draw on their authority at any time.[22] Thus, officers' infliction of these harms deviates from how sociologists traditionally perceive police violence as a result of racialized threats or danger. Police gender-based and sexual violence alternatively brings into view officers' strategic decision-making to use the lines carving out our social worlds to target the spaces between, particularly over long periods of time.

An example is the case of former Oklahoma police officer Daniel Holtzclaw, who carefully selected his victims to evade accountability—as he understood how difficult and dangerous it would be for black women and girls to report the encounters and that very few people would believe them over a police officer. Using police databases to research many of his victims beforehand, Holtzclaw targeted black women with criminal records in low-income neighborhoods.[23] Over an extended period of time, he committed numerous acts of sexual assault and terrorization.[24] During the trial, his defense strategically brought black women and girls into view by depicting them as deviant, attacking their credibility and character based on their race, gender, and criminal records. Holtzclaw was eventually prosecuted, and criminologist Phillip Stinson and colleagues use publicized police convictions like his to create a database of officer sexual crimes—finding that officers systemically target girls under eighteen years old.[25] However, legal estrangement and the minimization of police gender-based and sexual violence creates difficult and dangerous pathways to disclosing, reporting, and seeking convictions. The risks of stigmatization, police-court collusion, and police retaliation stop many black women victims from disclosing the gender-based and sexual violence inflicted upon them, resulting in much of this harm never making it into media-sourced, department, and crime databases (these pathways and barriers, along with how black women made sense of them, are discussed more in depth in the next chapter).

Policing, as an institution and social process, is built on this violence and marginalization. More specifically, policing uses various acts of violence as a way to build and maintain white heteropatriarchal social worlds. In Before the Badge, Samantha Simon explains how police departments occupationally ensure they remain white, male institutions, stating: "For many decades, the police only considered white men to be appropriate candidates for the job, maintaining this demographic composition by implementing exclusionary hiring practices and creating a hostile environment for anyone who was not white, a man, heterosexual, and masculine."[26] Over the past sixty years, however, the racial composition of police departments has shifted slightly as people of color now occupy the position of officer. This, in large part, is due to federal policies making workplace discrimination illegal and campaigns to diversify the police during times of social unrest.[27] At times, diversification is promoted as a means to build trust between police and the communities "they serve." While policing is still a majority-white male occupation today, almost one in three police officers in local police departments in the United States are now officers of color.[28] Yet, as Simon cautions, police departments are still racialized, gendered organizations that socialize all officers into their roles—a critical part of which is protecting the dominant order. Thus, the diversifying of police departments has, at best, been shown to have mixed results—with some studies showing no influence on officer-homicides, others demonstrating an increase in police violence against black populations, and still other research finding a reduction in discretionary stops and violence.[29] What remains largely missing in these mixed results is the impact of police diversification on gender-based and sexual violence against civilians. To my knowledge, however, there are no sociological studies on the race of the police officer and its impact on police gender-based and sexual violence.

Over the past decade, the #BlackLivesMatter, #SayHerName, and #MeToo social movements have worked to share the stories of those impacted by different types of violence.[30] Black women and girls' experiences of police gender-based and sexual violence sits at the intersections of these movements. Their stories illuminate how police gender-based and sexual violence—of all types—is central to reproducing intersectional domination in daily life. Thus, this chapter works within this historical and contemporary understanding of police gender-based and sexual violence as a method of putting black women and girls, like Gina, Ashley, Veronica, Robin, and Nema, and their testimonies in their place.

The Silence Matrix:
Politics of Protection and Protectionism

Black women disclosed a range of police gender-based and sexual violence, including sexualization, gender-based and sexuality bullying, sexual harassment, neglect, sexual assault, and police stalking and coercion. These harms are often made "missing" in our definitions of police violence, and victims of these types of violence more broadly are made visible through narratives that blame them for encounters. Given these conditions for visibility, many black women shared that our interviews were the only, or one of few times, they had ever discussed their encounters. Several pointed to the survey as the first time they had seen a measure or categorization of their police encounters included in an understanding of police violence. Thus, Ashley was "excited" to finally talk about her experience of police sexualization after seeing it on the survey. Similarly, Veronica brought up the pre-interview survey as an opening to talk about her encounters, noting, "One of the questions that they asked in the survey was, when were you belittled by a police officer?" Answering yes, she went on to disclose her experiences of police gender-based and sexuality bullying at school. For many that I interviewed, the survey signaled that the study recognized a variety of gender-based and sexual violence, which ultimately created a non-pathologized pathway for lifting veils and sharing their stories.

Police sexualization involves officers making black women and girls visible through hypersexualized controlling images that frame them as promiscuous, "fast," and deviant. Corresponding acts of harm include officers flirting, staring them down, directing unwanted sexual attention at them, and solicitation for sexual acts.[31] In sharing her story, Ashley disclosed that an officer sexualizing her—in this case, stopping his car to look up and down her body "when I was nine or ten years old"—had been "just something I just kept to myself" for a long time. Sexualization often coincides with adultification, wherein black girls are viewed as adults devoid of childhood vulnerability and undeserving of protection.[32] These beliefs frame sexualization as a "minor" form of harm; however, sexualization is linked to depressive symptoms and has lasting consequences for black girls' perceptions of their bodies and self-esteem.[33] For Ashley, this encounter indeed left a lasting impression on her self-image as the officer sexualizing her made her feel "really gross" and acutely aware of her body. As she summed it up, she "never felt so disgusted in my life."

Sexualization also signals exclusion from protection and vulnerability to other acts of sexual violence. Indeed, Ashley learned about her exclusion from police protection from this encounter, saying that "he knew . . . how he was looking at me was not okay." His position of authority underscored her vulnerability: "to know it was a cop . . . that first sparked, these are not good people." She now recognized that people looked at her differently and resolved that "I never want someone to look at me like that again." In writing about the sexualization of black girls, Monique Morris states that "no matter their size or age, they were vulnerable to a particular type of sexualization that rendered Black girls as objects of desire, even without their permission."[34] Ultimately, sexualization is facilitated by the racial, gendered, and sexualized dehumanization of black girls and beliefs that hold them individually responsible for managing white and black heteropatriarchal gazes. Thus, Ashley concluded her story by juxtaposing the broader perceptions of police sexualization as a minor form of harm against the reality on the way it drew lines on her body and impacted her self-image, emphatically stating: "Some people think it's really tiny things that don't matter, but it shapes you."

Police gender-based and sexuality bullying involves officers making black LGBTQ+ and gender-nonconforming people visible through racialized transphobic and homophobic pathologies. This pathologization is grounded in images and narratives framing them as inherently deviant for not complying to heteronormativity and a strict gender binary.[35] Subsequent acts of harm include officers using harassment, derogatory names, and assaults to put them in their place.[36] In sharing her story, Veronica detailed how a school resource officer bullied her based on her gender identity and sexuality. Seeing her through pathologizing frames, the officer persistently called Veronica "that gay kid," used her deadname, and "'clicked it on' and switched his hips whenever I was walking by."

These were also public attacks on Veronica in front of her peers, and Brandon Robinson describes how officers targeting LGBTQ+ and gender-nonconforming youth in public places sends a message to others in their social worlds.[37] This message says: Since officers will not protect them, they will also not punish those who target them either. This simultaneous lack of protection and signaling constitutes a distinct vulnerability for LGBTQ+ and gender-nonconforming youth in public and private contexts. Indeed, Veronica recognized the implications of the officer's public bullying, stating how he "validat[ed] it." Teachers and other kids at school joined in the harassment, which eventually escalated to assaults and "death-directing stuff." Excluded from the politics of police protection and protectionism among police, teachers, and students, Veronica said: "It felt like no one cared about whether or not I was being bullied or not." She further explained: "I wasn't supported by anyone in the community. That includes police who are supposed to be protective of the community." In schools, LGBTQ+ and gender-nonconforming youth are more likely to experience bullying than their heterosexual and cisgender counterparts.[38] This harassment directly works to make genders and sexualities outside of heterosexuality and the gender binary "missing" from our social worlds. And ultimately, this pervasive bullying eventually caused Veronica to leave school, sharing that she did not report the officer "because it was normal, honestly."

Police sexual harassment and assault involves officers making black women and girls visible through hypersexualized and criminalized frames. Similar to sexualization, police sexual harassment and assault is grounded in controlling images about black women as deviant, sexually promiscuous, aggressive,

undeserving of protection, and not believable.[39] These forms of police violence include a range of acts, from flirting, making comments on one's physical
appearance, and asking for phone numbers or personal information to body
searches, sexualized touching, and forcible penetration.[40] In sharing her story,
Gina details multiple experiences of police sexual harassment and assault. In
the previous chapter, we learned of an officer sexually harassing her during a
friend's domestic dispute with her boyfriend. The officer first names his power
to arrest and assault them, and after giving them a pass, he proceeds to flirta-
tiously ask Gina for her personal information. Feeling frustrated, Gina named
her exclusion from protection and how the officer wielded power in the encounter to sexually coerce her, stating, "I'm like, what if we were in a situation
like I don't know you and you tried to sexually push up on me to say, 'Well, I'm
gonna take you to jail if you don't.'"

In another encounter, an officer used his power to sexually assault Gina at
a local bar, restraining her and groping her body while other people watched.
She later confronted him about the assault in front of his fellow officer. Police
sexual violence, like Gina's encounter, is structurally enabled through officers'
access and lack of accountability.[41] Importantly, officers can leverage their
institutional power to gaslight black women, using stereotypes and their discretionary power to manipulate and distort interactions.[42] Thus, the officer
attempted to cast doubt on Gina's ability to remember the details of the encounter before explicitly offering protection in exchange for her silence, as she
remembered him saying: "But we don't need to have no problems, so I'll make
sure I check out for you next time if there's something and make sure I look
out for you and all." *Here,* protection was really for the officer, not for her. Gina
recognized her exclusion from protection and was aware of the broader discourses around gender-based and sexual violence that "boys will be boys." In
the end, she had "no faith" in the police department taking her report seriously.
She recognized that she would not be believed; therefore, she made the strategic decision not to report the officer because it would be difficult to hold him
accountable, "They ain't going to do nothing about him anyway."

Police neglect involves officers making black women visible through controlling images that dehumanize, criminalize, and see them as superhuman and
not capable of feeling pain. The act of refusing to provide protection to black
women or help in a crisis is based on these narratives and signals that abuse
against them will go unsanctioned.[43] In sharing her story, Robin disclosed
multiple experiences of police neglect, one during a mental health crisis and
another following a sexual assault. In the first encounter, Robin had a

psychiatric emergency during a domestic dispute with her fiancé. Mobilizing the police politics of protection, the responding officers prioritized making sure her fiancé was safe and denied their pleas for mental health support. Importantly, neglect not only leaves black women and girls vulnerable to more abuse, but it also encompasses carceral punishments for seeking help.[44] This poses a distinct vulnerability for those with disabilities, which are criminalized and punished.[45] Thus, the officers arrested Robin for the dispute, wherein she spent almost two weeks in jail without adequate mental health treatment. In reflecting on this experience, Robin shared, "I know that the jails have, like, so many people that have, like, mental health issues. It's just like, it doesn't help you get better [*laughs and pauses*]; it just makes everything worse." She explicitly called out police politics of protection, particularly her exclusion and her fiancé's inclusion, stating that if the police had just "really listened to what was going on, they would have brought me to a psychiatric hospital, not jail . . . they didn't call a mental health officer, and I think partly because my fiancé is white and I'm black."

Robin's exclusion from protection also shaped her experience of sexual assault. After reporting to an officer that she was raped by an acquaintance, she explained he "didn't pay me any attention," "didn't do anything," and "pretty much just laughed at me." The officer's response to her disclosure compounded her initial trauma, making her feel "stupid" for being sexually assaulted. These moments delegitimize black women as victims of sexual assault and discourage future reporting.[46] Thus, in recognizing her exclusion from police protection, Robin made the strategic decision to not report her sexual assault again or the officer. "After I talked to that one police officer, I never tried again." A guy friend ended up providing support and getting her home.

Police stalking and coercion also involve officers making black women and girls visible through pathologies that sexualize, criminalize, and dehumanize them. Whereas black women victims are often ignored or treated as invisible, they receive unwanted attention through police stalking and coercion. Officers follow them, ask for sexual favors, and use their power to inflict various acts of sexual violence.[47] This violent attention involves officers weaponizing "missingness" from definitions and discourses as well as legal estrangement to target black women and girls, sometimes offering protection or leniency in exchange for silence.[48] In Nema's encounter, an officer recognized her isolation and how she was distinctly vulnerable. He then exploited her exclusion from the politics of protection and racial loyalty to target her. First, he positioned himself as someone Nema could trust because of how racism systemically excludes black people from police protection, telling her: "You know, we're black in this world. [. . .] I'm gonna help you out as much as I can. Just try and go along with it, and they'll put it away." He followed up by offering her protection, or a pathway to safety based on racial solidarity. This pathway made sense to Nema, and she recognized her vulnerability to punishment in relation to her white peers at her boarding school. Thus, she readily accepted the officer's help.

Importantly, police sexual coercion involves officers grooming black girls and using their power to punish and exploit them over long periods of time.[49] Using exclusionary politics and racial loyalty to ingratiate himself and facilitate trust, the officer groomed and stalked her. He visited her at night when she was alone in her dorm. Unsure at first of how to interpret his visits and unable to name what was happening, Nema fluctuated between being grateful and calling her mother to listen in. She eventually learned that her case had been closed for quite some time and subsequently confronted the officer. In response, the once seemingly helpful officer warned Nema that he had the power to punish her and get her in more trouble whenever he wanted. Without a framework to name her experience and a pathway to safety, Nema came into a deeper awareness of what had happened by talking about it during our interview. While she did not explicitly state whether she experienced additional forms of sexual violence from the officer, her words trailed off in her attempts to name her encounters in the space between.

The Silence Matrix: Norms and Sanctions

Discourses on gender-based and sexual violence delegitimize black women and girls' encounters by framing them as deviant and sexually promiscuous. Black women were similarly framed in intracommunal conversations, as gender-based and sexual violence was made visible to those around them through norms that pathologize and blame victims. Even when others acknowledged black women experiencing gender-based and sexual violence, it was usually explained by the respectability of their behavior, appearance, and ability to conform to heteronormative ideals. This, in turn, encouraged conformity and silence as pathways to protection. Further, the systemized linking of individual characteristics to their risk of gender-based and sexual violence impacted black women's encounters, if, and when they disclosed them, and how they chose to protect themselves and their stories. Fearing blame, black women shared their stories with those they trusted and many stated that they did not disclose these incidents for years—if they ever did. Most who experienced gender-based and sexual violence expressed fear that others would use gendered norms as a basis to blame them. This blame was also weaponized by officers. For example, Gina shared how the officer directly leveraged respectability and rape discourses that discredit black victims of gender-based and sexual violence.[50] In his attempts to gaslight and shame Gina for the sexual assault, the officer asked her, "Weren't you out here a couple weeks ago showing your ass and stuff?" He also insinuated that her drinking delegitimized any report she would potentially make.

The fear of this type of blame was also evident during our interviews. Gina paused while sharing her story to quickly explain why she was wearing a "little dress" and to let me know that even though she was "tipsy" at the time, she still knew she was being sexually assaulted. Veronica also let me know that despite bullying at school, she was "well-behaved" and a good student who "kept my head down in school" and "minded my own business." Ashely was aware of how people see black girls as "fast." So, she, too, abruptly paused while sharing her story to let me know she was nine, not "looking fast," and was not "developed whatsoever." In lifting the veils and disclosing, black women worked to protect themselves and the interpretation of their stories.

Finally, Ashley showed how discrediting norms and sanctions can be internalized and imposed upon others as a means of self-protection. Not only did the officer's sexualization impact her view of her body, it shaped her relationship with her sister. Associating the incident with how she and her sister played dress-up, Ashley decided that she "never wanted to be like my sister ever again." She refused to let her sister put fake nails and lipstick on her anymore. With her sister becoming the embodiment of what Ashley saw as the "fast" black girl, she began to socially distance herself, saying: "To that day, I wanted to be the exact opposite of her." Being sexualized by the officer and Ashley's attempt to make sense of it subsequently impacted the siblings' relationship as Ashley sadly told me that her sister "always wondered why" their relationship had changed.

Everyday Policing and the Reproduction of Intersectional Domination

Through listening to black women's stories of police gender-based and sexual violence, I came to more fully understand how definitions of police violence play a critical role in everyday policing. Defining violence involves identifying actions that cause harm—making it possible for people to name their experiences to themselves and others. From these identified actions, they ground recognition in a shared awareness that others in our social worlds will also see these acts as harmful. From this shared recognition, violence definitions legitimate experiences and prompt empathy toward those also made visible as victims. From this empathy and legitimization, people are incorporated into our politics of whom and what are worth fighting for and given support. Efforts are also made to protect them from further violence. Importantly, violence definitions and ensuing processes of recognition and social action are not apolitical. They reflect the viewpoints and beliefs of those with power and resources to define harm—dictating how some police interactions are named and addressed while others are made "missing." As such, violence definitions reveal the lines drawn and redrawn, therein becoming sites where people struggle for recognition from institutions and others. Thus, definitions of violence can lift veils and they can also reinforce them. In reflecting on the persistent question "How are you defining violence?" I came to wonder: Are disciplinary demands for definitions an issue of gatekeeping or are they grounded in care and the prevention of harm for black women and girls? The question "How are you defining violence?" often felt rooted in gatekeeping, in protecting the lines drawn around what "counts" as harm from the police in our social worlds. And what doesn't "count" as violence constituted a distinct vulnerability to black women and girls as officers could leverage the space between—or the lack of protection and recognition of their stories—to inflict numerous types of gender-based and sexual violence with no accountability.

Drawing and Redrawing Lines of Exclusion: Knowledge Production, Protection, and Vulnerability

Exclusion from knowledge production processes in different spaces mirrored and reproduced vulnerabilities. In particular, the "missing-ness" of gender-based and sexual violence from understandings of police violence served as a resource for officers to target the margins. *Here*, officers relied on and exploited the lack of recognition around black women and girls' disclosures and legal estrangement within systems of reporting. They could maneuver around these gaps in politics to inflict violence with impunity. Black women subsequently described their journeys through the dissonance to name and legitimate what others would not recognize. Over time, many of them became aware of "missing-ness" as an active social process that constituted a distinct vulnerability to harm. In their journeys, some developed a multiple consciousness, calling out, during our interviews, the simultaneous exclusion of black women and girls along with their stories.

Drawing and Redrawing Lines Through Coerced Inclusion: Between Pathology and Politics

Many of the black women I interviewed had multiple experiences of police gender-based and sexual violence throughout their lives, wherein they learned and recognized their intersectional exclusions. Thus, Robin explained: "I mean, I went to a police officer, and I expected there to be, like, concerns, or take a report, or something, but he didn't do anything." Pointing to her legal estrangement and why there was no reason to report, Gina explained, "He's just gonna be right back out here." Veronica emphasized that she was excluded for several reasons: "I was black. I was poor. I was queer." Black women's stories also show how their absence from official and unofficial accounts did not mean that these harms didn't happen in front of others. Oftentimes, they occurred in public spaces as people watched and did nothing to intervene. "Missing-ness," then, is grounded in the relationship between exclusionary politics of protection and protectionism in which black women and girls become visible when viewed as deviant. And *here*, between pathologies and politics, the multiple veils provided cover for the police to target the space between.

Normalization of Intersectional Inequalities: Dissemblance, Self-Protection, and "Missing-ness"

For many black women, the preliminary survey indicated that their experiences were included in the studies' conceptualization of police violence. Still, dissemblance as self-protection was apparent in interviews as black women questioned me about my police encounters before sharing their stories. Through this questioning and storytelling vetting process, they worked to ascertain my politics as well as the norms and sanctions I brought to bear as a listener and a sociologist—or more specifically, whether I would engage in everyday policing of their stories. *Here*, I found that providing my lived experiences was integral to them deciding if they would lift the veil of dissemblance and share their accounts. Yet, even after answering their questions, many continued to engage in dissemblance as self-protection, going back and forth about what they would disclose and checking in around how it would be perceived. When black women chose to share, most defended their character and explained their behavior. They felt the need to justify how they were dressed and why they were in certain spaces. In this way, black women demonstrated dominant gender socialization that posits a relationship between gender-based and sexual violence against women and their attire, character, and behavior.

They also showed how resisting everyday policing can become an internalized, entangled process of navigating and adopting the silence matrix. For Ashley, resistance and self-protection meant adopting respectability frames to understand what happened to her and to prevent it from happening again. To protect herself, she ultimately engaged in the everyday policing of her sister and herself. Thus, she made sure to never dress in a way that could legitimize "asking for it" in the eyes of others. Veronica protected herself by recognizing that school was not a safe place, but rather, a hostile social environment. To ensure her safety, she started isolating, missing class, and avoided school altogether. This meant that she ended up missing so many days that her mother had to go to court, further entrenching them within criminal-legal institutions. Robin attempted to advocate for herself in both of her encounters with the police, requesting mental health support and reporting that she was sexually assaulted. In the former situation, she was taken to jail. In the latter, she was mocked and ridiculed. To protect herself moving forward, Robin decided to not disclose the assault and future incidents to police ever again. For Nema, she resisted by trying to get more information, calling her mother to listen in on the officer, and eventually challenging him about her case. Finally, Gina resisted by confronting the officer, letting him know that he couldn't gaslight her about the sexual assault. She also recognized the broader conditions and discourses on sexual violence, and thus, she strategically chose to not report. From her place, receiving protection from the officer who assaulted her was better than no protection at all.

In my interviews, I found that social class structured black women's frequency of contact with the police. Black women who grew up in, or currently reside in, highly surveilled, low-income neighborhoods shared how they had frequent, often daily contact with officers in different contexts. Those raised in, or who now lived in, middle-class neighborhoods had more sporadic police contact. However, their stories revealed that less frequency did not constitute an absence of police encounters and violence, and more, the similarities in their stories reveal the expansive ways officers exploit the margins. For example, stalking and coercion as well as persistent sexualization, harassment, and bullying were more likely to come from officers who had constant access to a particular context, such as school resource officers, those who patrolled specific neighborhoods, those following specific cases, and community liaison officers. As shown in the next chapter, this also includes police officers as family members.

Age was also an important factor in disclosure. The earlier these encounters happened in black women's lives, the more difficult it was for them to name them. This created a distinct vulnerability for black girls as those who were children and adolescents at the time of their encounters struggled at first to name and understand what was happening to them. In these instances, black women expressed *feeling* the harms that they did not yet have the words to name. This dissonance also meant many initially gravitated toward readily available gendered respectability norms as well as sexual violence discourses that blamed victims to understand their encounters. These frameworks of re-spectability often were articulated by people they knew—family, community, and people in leadership positions. Resistance, in these cases, often came with adopting the silence matrix as a form of self-protection. While some black women tried to report, self-protection often meant self-isolating and opting out of relationships and institutions that constituted different social worlds. Others sought alternative means of support from friends and social services as they got older.

"he's just gonna be right back out there"

"i expected there to be, like, concerns, or take a report, or something, but he didn't do anything"

"he just—[*pause*] he just—[*pause*] he just didn't do anything,

he was just, like, 'oh, you're being stupid,' or whatever"

"i wasn't supported by anyone in the community"

"i wasn't guaranteed any safety"

"i can't even put into words, honestly"

"but i won't stop talking!"

"and i know your mouth, too. and you need to sometimes don't even talk back"

"i was a snitch or something"

"you just created this whole mess for no reason"

"i didn't report the bullying because it was normal, honestly"

"i was kinda scared to report it"

4

Devin

A mutual contact first introduced Devin and me. We texted back and forth for a few days, trying to find a good time to meet but never quite settled on a day that worked for both of us. Our communication tapered off, and months passed by with no contact. Then, one day in my field site, I met a black woman at a pool, and we chatted while watching our children splash around and play. She told me about her work. I told her a little about mine. But mostly, we talked about our kids. Wanting to stay in touch, she and I exchanged numbers only to find that my contact information was already in her phone. Shocked and laughing at the coincidence, we quickly realized that she was Devin, and I was the person she had been texting several months ago about the research project. Jokingly apologizing for "ghosting" me, Devin explained that she thought I was a "white Shannon" doing a study on black women and the police. Now having spent more time talking casually, she changed her mind about participating in an interview and quickly set a date for the following week.

In her late thirties, Devin is a black, multiracial, light brown-skinned, queer, cisgender woman. The temperature outside of the café where we were meeting was well into the high 90s, so the outdoor tables sat empty while the inside was cooled, packed, and loud. Arriving a few minutes before Devin, I was just about to call to suggest a different location when she walked in. Standing in line to order our drinks, we intermittently made small talk about our mornings in between her greeting several other people she recognized in the crowded coffee shop. Once it was time to find a table, we sat on the outdoor patio, despite the heat, so that we could have some privacy.

From our conversation, I learned that Devin was very politically active on various social issues and comfortable talking about the police. She saw police as a modern extension of slave patrols, definitively describing them as "problematic" and referring to them as the "gentry for the colonial." She emphatically stated, "I don't have great feelings about them." However, her views differ somewhat from her familial conversations about police growing up. Back then, her father was a police officer, so some family members had "a different vision" of the police than others, viewing his position as a good "blue-collar job" and a "respectable career for people of color." Yet, she mentioned that her other family members weren't fond of police and considered policing a "shameful" job for a black person to have. Whether the job was viewed as "respectable" or "shameful," they all agreed that when you encounter police, "just do what they say whenever they tell you to do something—listen."

Her mother eventually separated from her father and married her stepfather, with whom she was very close. With him, there were "more critical" conversations about the police. Nevertheless, like other black women I interviewed, even as Devin participated in the discussions, the focus of them tended to be the vulnerability of boys and men to police abuse. "The way that he talked to my brother was different than I think the way he explained things to me." For example, with her brother, her stepfather stressed that "the police ain't no different than us, but that they can—they walking around with a gun, so you gotta be careful." Her stepfather was adamant about having these conversations with his stepson as he was, she said, "trying to keep my brother safe." With Devin, however, there was no direct talk as her stepfather, she said, "thought I would be okay."

"How did you feel about getting advice?"

She paused and eventually shared, "I didn't think about it until maybe just now when you asked me. I think it's interesting because I'm the one that has had the most intense, I think, interactions with police." I asked Devin what she meant by that, and she disclosed that an officer sexually harassed her in retaliation for speaking out at a community meeting. "The property management invited up our community liaison [officer] to our neighborhood meeting . . . because they wanted to implement a neighborhood watch program." Devin "wasn't feeling it" and was angry that the manager didn't check with residents beforehand. She and her neighbors didn't want to collaborate with the police. They were still reeling from all the high-profile cases of police violence across the nation. And as a community, she said, "we were dealing with our own shit" because police continued to harass them for speaking out after an officer recently shot and killed someone in their community not long before the meeting. Being an active leader in her neighborhood, Devin decided to attend the meeting and voice her community's concerns.

Upon hearing them, the community liaison officer, who was black, "got really angry and yelled at me and went off on me in this meeting" for "pushing" them not to implement the watch program. He didn't stop there. Furious at Devin for speaking out, he followed her outside and started "hitting on" her in front of her kids. She felt increasingly uncomfortable and tried to leave. But he repeatedly blocked her from doing so while yelling at Devin that "You need a man, and, like, you need some dick!" insinuating this would make her docile and quiet. Devin's fear turned into anger as she challenged him, screaming that she "don't do Uncle Toms!" At this, the officer escalated, saying "more crazy stuff," including calling the residents in her neighborhood "thugs" who "just need to follow the law," and that the person recently killed by the police "got what they deserved." He then blamed Devin and other activists for why officers don't protect them or come when they call for help, saying that speaking out and "bring[ing] up race, that's why people [read police] don't come and back them up when they call for backup." Before leaving, he told Devin that she and the people in her predominantly black and Latinx neighborhood "were roaches" and "needed to be exterminated."

Devin was terrified. Even though he eventually let her go, her fear stayed with her for a long time because he was the community liaison officer and had unrestricted access to different spaces in her neighborhood. To protect her family, "that night I made my kids sleep in my room with me, 'cause— he just seemed crazy. He just seemed like he wasn't right." Fearing retaliation, she strategized ways to prevent him from having contact with her children as well, telling me that he was "teaching this anti-gang curriculum" at her daughter's school, "and I wouldn't let her attend. [long pause] I didn't let her go." Despite her fears and concerns, Devin didn't report the officer. She had reported an officer before for misconduct and "it took them forever to even respond." She also said that with the way the reporting system is set up, police were able to get access to information, and thus, "the issue is that people don't, [pause] they don't feel safe to say anything, and there isn't anything that keeps them safe or keeps people from retaliating." Here, in the space between speaking and retaliatory harassment, days turned into weeks and months of seeing him in different spaces throughout her neighborhood, fearing he would retaliate again against her or her children next time. So, Devin decided it was best to stay quiet. In the view from her place: "I was kind of scared to report it because he knew where I stayed."

"I Was Kinda Scared to Report It"

THE SPACE BETWEEN SPEAKING
AND INTRACOMMUNAL
BACKLASH AND POLICE RETALIATION

Black women disrupting "missing-ness" by speaking—or disclosing, challenging, and reporting violence—is not a simple choice or action. Officers and others mete out "swift" punishments for breaking through the veils that hold our social worlds together. Yet, despite the potential police retaliation and intracommunal backlash, some black women, like Devin, spoke anyway. She and others, however, also strategically chose silence when the difficulty of speaking quickly turned dangerous in the face of sanctions. The resulting dissemblance, or work to produce and remain behind the cover of veils, was a critical decision some black women made to protect themselves during and after encounters. Dissemblance, in many cases, was also an effort by black women to sustain their longer-term ability to live, resist, and build safe conditions. Still, for others, a return to silence signified the adoption of the silence matrix's politics, norms, and sanctions. From there, some black women, like Laura, whose story is to come in this chapter, actively engaged in everyday policing.

Whether imposed, chosen, or strategically deployed, black women's stories reveal how the purpose and meaning of silence changes with shifting power dynamics and consequences. Therefore, this chapter examines when and how black women decide to talk about violence, or what comes next in their stories after they speak. *Here,* I reengage some of the questions posed in the book's introduction: When is silence suppression? Resistance? Both? Or something else altogether? Wrestling with these questions, I analyze the nuances in the push–pull dynamics of black women's attempts to challenge and lift multiple veils others work to keep in place.

Karen

Karen and I planned to meet one Saturday at a Starbucks café. It was early morning and not too hot when I arrived, so I waited outside for her under the green umbrellaed shaded deck. Watching the cars line up at the drive-thru and snake around the parking lot, I periodically checked my phone to see if Karen had texted. Ten, fifteen, then twenty minutes go by, and still no Karen. After almost thirty minutes, I wondered if I should send a follow-up text or consider her a no-show. Deciding to leave, I packed my things and headed inside to order a drink. At that moment, a medium-brown-skinned black woman with dark red hair timidly walked up, waving her hand to get my attention.

Leaning in toward me and speaking in a low voice close to my ear, she quietly asked if I was the researcher doing a study on black women and the police. When I said I was, she smiled, visibly relaxed her shoulders, stuck out her hand, and introduced herself as Karen. A medium brown-skinned, black, African American, bisexual, cisgender woman in her mid-twenties, Karen informs me that she was not actually late for our interview. Instead, she had arrived almost twenty minutes before I did and sat in her car for nearly an hour, intently watching each person walk into the coffee shop. A little surprised to hear this, I asked Karen what took so long for her to decide to come in. She told me she was "nervous." She hoped the researcher would be a black woman or woman of color but didn't know who would show up. So, she said, "I was taking time, almost not trying to go."

We moved outside of the cafe and sat on the patio for privacy where I asked Karen if she had any questions before we got started. Shaking her head to indicate no, she leaned back in her seat while sipping her frappé but then stopped me from asking the first question. "I do wanna say," she warned, "I don't have any—I don't feel like I have any personal experiences to tell you." Instead, she wanted to have a space to talk through her views and opinions about police violence, as she felt "some type of way about it."

Karen's perspective about the police evolved over time. As a kid growing up in a small, rural town with her mother and grandmother, "I wouldn't say we talked about [police]; we didn't have conversations like that." She was advised on how to deal with people generally being suspicious of her, especially in stores where she might be accused of stealing. For example, as a little girl, her mother and grandmother taught her "little things," like "don't touch that thing in the store." Yet, as we talked more about her childhood, Karen recalled how they would "go back and forth talking about it," remembering how important it was to "ride with the car lights on" at night so police can easily see who is in there. When she got a little older and started driving, her mother and grandmother stressed that to her that "even if I is wrongly pulled over," it was important to "don't try to argue" with the police. Instead, she should "comply" and say, "Yes, sir, no, sir, yes, ma'am, no, ma'am." Most importantly, Karen was advised never to advocate for herself, learning there should be "no 'I know my rights' type stuff." Altogether, Karen learned from these conversations to show immense deference so you "won't provoke them," because once that happens, "we all know where that goes." She summed up her perspective now by saying the best "preparation is [a] smile."

Karen also knew early on that she needed to fear the police. To emphasize her point, she shared a story about when she and her brother ran into an officer in a store. Walking out of a store, "as soon as we got out, we saw some cops, and the first thing we did was put our hands up." Karen was five years old at the time. And "looking back at this," it "just shows you at such a young age, it's already instilled to be afraid." Shocked by their reaction, the officer tried to assuage Karen and her brother's fears by giving them stickers and telling them he was "here to protect" them. Ultimately, Karen remembers this interaction— both the fear and the officer's response—as a "good" childhood encounter, even now as she held conflicted feelings about the police.

When I asked Karen if she would reach out to the police now in an emergency or if she needed help, she responded, "I don't feel comfortable, but I'd do it, you know what I mean? 'Cause who else is gonna help?" She disclosed that she reached out to an officer at school for help after a high school classmate sexually assaulted her. As Karen described, she was entering puberty and "blooming" when a guy at school "literally shoved his hand down my shirt and got a good grip on my boob." She "obviously felt violated" and went immediately to report it to the principal and the school officer. They appeared to take the assault seriously and "obviously there was a corrective action taken."

After initially feeling confident about her decision to advocate for herself, Karen quickly became confused after she became a target at school after reporting. She explained, "Ever since then, him [and] his friends, they bullied me and made fun of me." Karen "questioned" herself and wondered whether she had done something wrong. Looking for answers, she turned to a friend and classmate for support and guidance and asked her, "What was I supposed to do? Was that wrong? Was I not supposed to do that?" In response, Karen's friend told her that if she had been the one sexually assaulted, "I wouldn't have said nothing."

Ostracized and isolated by peers who disapproved of her decision to report the assault to school authorities, Karen explained how she started to feel "horrible" and "degrading." The assault and peer reaction to her reporting made high school "a bad experience." Even as Karen reflected on what happened during our conversation, she was unsure about whether she regretted reporting the assault to the principal and school officer. Although reporting felt to her like "the right thing," advocating for herself came with consequences, in-cluding "him and his whole crew that were just against me for it." Labeled a traitor by her peers at school "because I stood up for myself," she said in speak-ing from the space between: "I was a snitch or something."

Laura

Laura invited me to her apartment for our interview, which gave us some pri-vacy and also allowed her to wait for a maintenance appointment. A black, African American, heterosexual, cisgender woman in her mid-twenties, Laura grew up in a small, segregated town. When she was a child, she did not receive any advice about avoiding the police, "not like you [read adults] have to have the talk now with your kids." For her, there was "never" a conversation because police violence was not an issue back then, not like "with how things are now . . . especially . . . you click to see videos." Laura said as a young child she learned "nothing bad" about the police nor was she given any of the messages such as "'Hey, you need to watch out.' None of that." Instead, she was taught "if you have an issue, call the police" for help.

As she grew older, however, Laura started observing officers in her small town noticed "everybody have their own section they're supposed to be in." Police made sure they stayed there. She also overheard some people in her community complain about how the police "don't do their job." What she overheard overruled what she was taught about the police being "here to help," as Laura made sure to limit her interactions to "always on an emergency-only basis." Yet, she went back and forth about whether she would actually call the police in an emergency because, she stated, "I don't trust them at all" and "look at all of them sideways." Yet, depending on the type of emergency, she felt that she would have "no choice, but to call," especially because she had "nobody else to call for emergencies." Ultimately, Laura wished that black communities could "help take care of our own selves instead of depending on people," like the police, to intervene.

To give an example of what this could look like, she immediately transi-tioned to another incident that involved a domestic dispute between her cousin and his girlfriend. Laura shared her story, revealing along the way how she participated in the backlash directed at her cousin's girlfriend. She began by making it a point to tell me, "My cousin has an anger problem. We all know he has an anger problem. He knows he has an anger problem. We just do what we can to—" She stops midsentence when there is a knock at her door. The maintenance staff arrived, and he and Laura spent time talking before he headed to the back of her apartment. Once back in the living room, Laura immediately returned to her story. She and her family had been at a community drive all day and were getting ready for a family dinner that included extended kin. Then, the dispute happened. "When he pulled up, him and his girlfriend pulled up. They got out of their car. I already knew them two wasn't vibing. I could tell. He didn't try to act like it, but she had it all over her face, so I was 'no, like, not getting into that.' You all either gonna help with this coat drive or whatever."

Noticing the girlfriend's discomfort, Laura and her family also tried to stay out of it and focus on the event. But the couple kept "arguing," and the girlfriend got back in the car while Laura's cousin stayed out. Then, a loud "boom." Her cousin had hit the car window, shattering it to pieces. Although his girlfriend was in the car when the window was smashed, Laura quickly noted, "He, like, barely tapped her window," so she didn't understand why the girlfriend called the police.

Angry with her cousin's girlfriend, Laura yelled at her. "My first issue was, what'd you call the police for?!" To which the girlfriend replied, "I was scared of what he was gonna do." Knowing that the police would be coming, Laura's family mobilized, first scolding the girlfriend. "We're like, you know, well—you know he's not gonna put his hands on you." Trying to get her to understand his anger issues and why he was upset, Laura's family explained to her, "You know he's upset about our grandma being—he was upset our grandma being dead, and you know that's the reason. Our grandma being dead doesn't go back to him putting his hands on you."

Frustrated, Laura told me, "She called the police. The police came. By this time, he's upset so he's walking with my other cousin." Her cousin left before the police arrived. The responding white officers told her family they must arrest him for vacating the scene. Pleading with officers and letting them know "we're trying to get him back," Laura's family was very afraid of what might've happened. They frantically called around. "We're trying to get him back, calling, calling. Calling his other brother [and] was like, look, this is what's going on. See if you can call him and get him back so nothing happens." Eventually, her cousin returned, and the police immediately arrested him. Worried for her cousin, Laura "got aggravated, so then I start mouthing off." She questioned the officers, "You feel good about yourself, putting him in jail? That gets you off, just arresting people?" Attempting to de-escalate the situation, an officer uncuffed her cousin and took him aside to let him know he "understands you going through a situation." Laura distinctly remembered the officer empathizing with her cousin about domestic abuse; he told him, "Me and my wife was going through a situation" similar to her cousin's, so he understood.

Ultimately, the girlfriend decided to not press charges. As Laura relayed this detail, this seemed to make her angrier. Scoffing, she said, "The girl didn't press charges and crazy. . . . They drove here together, and they drove back." Reflecting on this conversational exchange with the girlfriend, Laura said, "I was like, why you call the cops in the first place? You did all that, and you still drove back together? [. . .] You're still with him. If you were so scared of what he gonna do, why you still with him? 'Because I love him.' That's your safety and security." In the view from Laura's place, the girlfriend was to blame for the entire situation, as Laura said to her: "You just created this whole mess for no reason."

Kerry

It's midafternoon, so Kerry and I were at one of the only two occupied tables at a restaurant that's usually loud and crowded for lunch. The outside patio and after-lunch lull provided the privacy needed for our interview. When the waiter left with our order, Kerry apologized profusely for pushing back our lunch and informed me that she may not have much time to speak. I let her know that I understood and that the interview could be as long or as short as she wanted. Nodding and smiling, she shared that she usually would not participate in something like this but felt comfortable talking with me because I was also a black woman.

At the beginning of our conversation, we realized we both grew up in predominantly black cities and spent twenty minutes chatting about what that was like. Although our lunch together was casual, I noticed Kerry became nervous when we transitioned to the more formal part of the interview. Going over the topics we would cover, I asked Kerry if she had any questions. She responded, "You can answer those." She wanted me to answer all the questions from the interview guide first. *Here*, Kerry began to interview me, asking me the questions I had prepared for our interview, and more, she questioned me about my previous research and my future goals and plans for the project. Only after answering all her questions was Kerry ready to begin answering mine.

A dark brown-skinned, black, African American, heterosexual and queer, cisgender woman in her late twenties, Kerry grew up working-class in a large, urban city in the South. "Everybody on my block, for the most part . . . was black." While she remembered her family having "real hard times" as a child, especially after her mother's divorce, she now considered herself to be upwardly mobile and middle class. No one talked to young Kerry about the police. They didn't have to, as almost everyone in her family was a police officer. As such, she learned how people interacted with police by watching some of her relatives who weren't officers shift their demeanor when they interacted with her police family members or other police, describing it as, "for a lack of better words, slave and master." For example, when officers approached her older brother, "he would be like, 'Oh yes, officer. Whatever you need, officer. I ain't doin' nothin', officer.'" From watching these interactions most of her life, Kerry said it "made me feel like that's how I'm supposed to be around the police." From there, she learned to "adopt" a "very subservient" attitude toward them. "This is the role that I need to take on. Because, when the police are around, we need to be somebody else, to be different. We need to be harmless. We need to let them know they got the power. 'Cause they do."

These roles permeated almost every aspect of Kerry's life, as several police officer family members had a "sense of authority even [when] they had on their uniform or they didn't have on their uniform." It didn't matter if they were on duty or off duty. As Kerry remarked, "They always came with 'I know what's right. I'm above reproach.'" To further emphasize her point, she joked, "They was an authority on going to the bathroom—everything." As we talked more about what it was like for her to grow up surrounded by so many officers in her family, Kerry became extremely cautious and uneasy. Her discomfort was visibly acute when discussing her stepfather. She expressed concern about retaliation from him and others during the interview, asking several questions about the recorder and the anonymity process. After explaining the protocol again, I reminded Kerry that she did not have to tell me anything that she did not want to and that she could always stop the interview.

Kerry decided to continue. Wanting to tell her story, she informed me that this would be one of the few times she had told anyone about the domestic violence that happened in her home. She shared that her "first memory" of the police was with her stepfather when she was about seven years old. "I just remember the authority that he had and the temper that he had." Reiterating his "sense of authority" numerous times, Kerry detailed how he used his authority to make sure that "I always knew I wasn't his child." He psychologically and physically abused her, often picking her up from elementary school and other places, handcuffing her in parking lots, and making her sit in the back of his patrol car like a suspect.

If he would come and pick my brother up in his cop car, he would sit in the front, and I would sit in the back. Stuff like that. Or he would play "hand-cuffs" with me and stuff like that. That has just always been, [*long pause*] I don't know . . . He never called me by my name. He always called me "*Thing.*" That was his nickname for me. [*long pause*] My brothers, they had real names. They didn't have nicknames . . . He would be like, "*Thing*, you gotta get in the back." Like, "*Thing*, you gotta get in the back." My brother would get in the front, and then I would get handcuffed, and I would get put in the back.

Kerry paused for a long time and would continue to do so at different points while remembering these and other interactions with her stepfather. She oscillated between how it felt as a kid and how it felt now as an adult. For example, as a child she sometimes thought it was "fun" and "exciting" to "ride around the block and all that other stuff." As an adult, she said, "I just know that, as an adult, I look back and I was, like, that was inappropriate." Kerry took her time as she continued to tell her story, walking me through the shifts in her understanding of her experiences with her stepfather. "You know how sometimes when you're a child, you don't realize certain things like there's micro- or macro-aggressions and blatant disrespect and stuff like that. Some-times, you trust adults, or you believe adults and stuff like that. As an adult, I was like, 'That wasn't okay.' As a child, I was like, 'There's nothing wrong with this, or whatever.'" Over time, Kerry picked up on the fact that he never be-haved that way with her brother. "You didn't think he would think that was fun or appropriate or acceptable. I'm not held to the same standard as my brother because I'm not your child."

When I asked her how she coped with it all, she replied, "I was really young , . . A lot of make-believe. [*pause*] Yeah. I would say that. [*pause*] I would say a lot of make-believe, a lot of pretending things weren't as they actually are." Because she was so young, Kerry said she had difficulty understanding what was happening to and around her, saying, "Some stuff, not even fully understand[ing]." But "It's another thing when I *know*." In other parts of our interview, Kerry shared that she was close with her grandmother and would talk to her about many things. But when I asked if she spoke to her or anyone else about her stepfather's abuse, she laughed as she told me, "You know black people don't talk about stuff. Black people don't talk about anything." After I nodded to let her know I understood what she meant, Kerry smiled and em-phatically stated, "I would say, 'no.'"

She disclosed that her mother and stepfather "had some family-dynamic stuff" happen. Alluding to additional forms of abuse, Kerry said that her mother finally left her stepfather. This period in their lives was extremely dangerous as her stepfather used his "power to basically gain custody of my brother." In relaying to me the legal battle and retaliatory harassment that occurred, Kerry first made it a point to describe her mother's character. "Mom worked a lot, but she was a very, very plain mama. She never smoked. She never drank. She was like, 'I go to work, and I come home.' She was very, 'I just take care of my children.' To this day, my mama is literally—my mother never smoked a cigarette. She's had a sip of beer, and she's like, 'Oh, I'm woozy.' She doesn't do any of those things. That's just who she is."

My appreciation of this point was important to Kerry because, during the legal battle, her stepfather made "false allegations" about her mother to intentionally tarnish her reputation. To make matters worse, friends of her stepfather, who were also police officers, harassed them. "My mama was being arrested constantly, so they constantly was going through the judicial system." She described the toll this harassment took. "They didn't have any charges that stuck, but it made it easier. Like, 'Okay. Well, I'm constantly having these legal issues that I can't afford to really put effort in. I'm missing work. I can't really afford a lawyer. This court-appointed one really don't mean much or whatever if I get a court-appointed lawyer depending on what the charge is.' Anyways, so it made it easy for them to gain custody of my brother."

Ultimately, Kerry said her stepfather being an officer "made it easy for him to use his power, and he did . . .'cause he had that type of power. He had judges behind him. He's been with the police department for twenty-five, thirty years, or whatever." Never talking publicly about their experiences, Kerry said some family members who weren't police discussed these incidents among themselves. In those conversations, they spoke of "how crooked they were" and "how they're able to wield their power at times." And while she didn't feel comfortable talking with her grandmother about it, she said to me, "I will tell you, now that I look back on a lot of things, when I was younger, a lot of shit just was accepted as the norm." From these experiences, Kerry learned that her stepfather and other police are "above the law" and "above reproach."

Now that Kerry was an adult and had moved away from her hometown, she felt more comfortable challenging her stepfather. If she saw him, Kerry refused to be intimidated by him or let him call her "Thing." However, she noted that neither she nor her family ever reported her stepfather or his colleagues for retaliating against her mother for her leaving him. In the space between: "You can't do anything about it because they have the whole judicial system backing them. And, if one crumbles, then they all crumble."

Ella

Ella and I first connected at a local protest, and we met a few weeks later to do our interview over lunch. A medium brown-skinned, black, African American, heterosexual, cisgender woman in her mid-twenties, Ella spent the first twenty minutes asking me several questions about my background and the project. She had "anxiety speaking on this issue," and let me know almost immediately that she "had debated speaking to [me] for a while." When I asked her why, she replied with a cryptic statement: "I won't say anything 'cause it might come up with the questions." I nodded, and we moved on to discuss her first memories of the police and early childhood conversations. She quickly confided, "I just always remember being scared of police officers because of learning that my father was killed" by a white police officer when she was a baby.

Losing her father to a police shooting when she was so young deeply impacted Ella and her entire family. It hurt her that she barely remembered him. However, she vividly recalled the moment she learned about his death from her grandmother. "I remember it like yesterday. I was playing, having the best time, and my granny stopped me randomly, [*pause*] I don't know why, [*pause*] and was like, 'You know, your father was killed by a police officer, a white police officer.' It was just the most random thing to me." Looking back, Ella said the way this information was dropped on her without much of a warning or more conversation and explanation "kind of traumatized me, the way that I was told." Afterward, there wasn't really space for Ella to ask questions. "I think that that's one thing that I hated was there was all these questions I had that nobody would even—[*pause*] As a kid, you don't just—[*pause*] I wasn't the type to just go ask and get the answers I wanted. You expect the adults to come tell you, 'This is what happened. As a result of that, this is why your father died in this way,' or 'This is what's going on in the world.'" Instead, "nobody would talk to me about it." Ella pointed out that she understood why "because it was traumatizing for them to talk about" and that "still, to this day, my granny, my father's mom, she just can't even—nobody wants to . . ." She didn't finish her sentence.

Unable to cope with this information alone as a child and unsure of what it all meant, Ella developed an immense fear of the police, saying she had "so much anxiety when I'm around law enforcement." Her father's murder and the subsequent way it was disclosed to her, she said, "shaped my whole view of law enforcement." It impacted her daily life. "When I'm driving down the street and a police officer gets behind me, I get anxiety 'cause I'm like, if they pull me over, I don't know what I'm gonna do." Ella made it clear that she tried to avoid the police as best she could since even the sight of them gave her anxiety attacks.

I asked Ella how she now coped with her father's murder and her fear of the police. Her voice got faint as she responded, "I don't think I ever did." She attempted several times to convey to me exactly what it felt like to deeply miss someone you don't necessarily remember. First, growing up, "I didn't realize I didn't have a father," and she rhetorically asked me if this makes sense. Making another attempt to express what these feelings were like for her, she said, "For me, it was like, I got my mom. I have my grandmothers. I didn't realize there was a person that should have been there that wasn't. So, when that happened, I think it made me sad. It made me resentful towards police officers. Now, as an adult, I'm really angry. I have a lot of resentment toward law enforcement and the current climate and all the black men dying." Ella named several emotions, including anger, sadness, anxiety, and resentment. To move through them, "I think I'm just now coping with it, honestly," by speaking with a counselor. While this was helping, she "still has so many unanswered questions about my father's death" and was determined to get them.

Ella explained that her father's death was why she wanted to tell stories. She wanted to "investigate his death and provoke change through writing, videography, and photography." She spent a lot of her free time researching "all of the documents" she could find about her father's case, saying that "my life goal has been to tell his story." *Here*, in our interview, Ella shares the details of her father's story with me. Afterward, she described how difficult it had been to speak about his story more publicly and how it had taken "a toll" on her mentally and emotionally, saying it "just, [*pause*] it hurts. I can't even put into words, honestly." Even though going deeper into his case was upsetting for her, Ella shared that working on the story was also critical to how she coped and healed. She went back and forth between "avoiding" the story and feeling "cathartic" by continuing to work on it.

When we spoke, Ella was in an "avoiding" phase. She was trying to take some space and had "just been sitting" on the story. Pausing for a long time and appearing anxious, Ella explained that one reason she was avoiding speaking about her father's story was because she had been recently approached by someone close to the police department who "knows the politics." Wanting to protect Ella, this person told her that "if you write this story, you're going to make it really hard for yourself." In response to this warning, Ella "left the story alone" because she was "scared of retaliation."

Although she was currently "sitting on it," Ella emphatically stated that she was still determined to tell her father's story and the stories of her family—those left behind to grieve their loved ones. But because, she said, "I just don't have the capital . . . don't have the experience," Ella didn't feel safe to tell her family's stories now. For her, silence was a part of a longer-term strategy to "make sure that I'm at the right place" and felt safe enough "where I can really speak out and tell the truth." In the space between, she confessed that she thought about her father's police killing every day: "I think about it literally every day. There is not a day that goes by that I don't think about my father or police brutality."

The Conditions of Silence:
Rippling Codes of Silence and Cultural Betrayal

The meaning and purpose of silence fluctuated for black women as they navigated shifting visibility conditions, power relations, and contexts. Faced with the risk of police retaliation and intracommunal backlash, they had to make strategic decisions about whether it was safe and worth their effort to speak about violence. I therefore situate their choices to speak about violence, from the police and others, in the interrelated police and community codes that promote and enforce silence.

———

Police training emphasizes danger and socializes cadets into seeing themselves as protectors. With the militarization of police departments across the United States, officers often conceptualize their daily work as engaging in "warfare."[1] Assuming this role means bringing others into view as threats and being aggressive toward certain communities. In the process, officers show loyalty to one another, which is commonly referred to as a "blue code of silence."[2] Behind this "blue wall," officers follow unspoken rules that equate silence with loyalty that is best conveyed through a refusal to report each other's misconduct. If individual officers break this code, or speak out against another officer, they can be labeled a snitch or a rat within the department.[3] This labeling has professional and personal implications as officers fear their own exclusion from protection, or that others on the job will not have their back and seek out retribution.[4] Importantly, this code extends to other actors in the legal system, including prosecutors and judges, and in many ways, is enshrined in qualified immunity policies that make it extremely difficult—if not impossible—to charge officers for violence.[5]

Reporting officers to police departments, then, means confronting the blue code of silence. Specifically, it means navigating the relational, institutional, and policy barriers to holding officers accountable. Consequently, reporting police violence opens oneself up to the risk of police retaliation. This is especially risky given that a third of citizen complaints are not sustained by police departments and there is often little to no follow-up or reprimands for officers.[6] Further, in police training, cadets are explicitly made aware of this reality, learning that they are not likely to face severe consequences stemming from citizen complaints.[7] These conditions impact people's willingness to speak out against police violence and report encounters, with legal estrangement encompassing the broader conditions under which marginalized communities have limited power to hold police accountable.[8] Community policing models, in many ways, are designed to address this barrier. To do this, departments strategically place officers in neighborhoods to cultivate trust and meaningful relationships with residents and act as liaisons between communities and police departments.[9] This type of reform gained momentum in the public after Ferguson and again during the 2020 uprisings, with the expectation being that trust helps increase community cooperation with police departments to address crime and that officers reduce the use of force against residents with whom they have built relationships. However, Tony Cheng demonstrates how officers can respond to complaints with perfunctory scripts or literal silence.[10] Further, Victor Rios and colleagues also show how community policing models fracture social worlds, providing protection for some residents and mobilizing community members to surveil each other.[11] This stratification process breaks down social relations and increases departments' ability to police communities, separating those who collaborate with the police from those who don't.[12]

Alternatively, black communities develop their own codes in response to policing, of which silence is integral. These codes explicitly dictate that people should refrain from talking to officers and outsiders. The codes also center around respect and cultivating reputations, a critical part of which is making sure that others in their intracommunal social worlds are afraid to speak out and challenge them.[13] Specific sanctions for speaking to officers or those considered outsiders include exclusion, being labeled snitches and rats, and violence.[14] As detailed in the previous chapters, black women are socialized into an intracommunal loyalty that is best displayed through a refusal to speak about violence to the police as well as outsiders to their nuclear families. From this place, cultural betrayal is grounded in black women's felt experience of intracommunal violence alongside pressures to remain silent and sanctions for speaking.[15] Thus, this chapter traces Devin, Karen, Laura, Kerry, and Ella's stories through the silence matrix while considering the everyday relationship between the police and intracommunal codes mandating silence.

The Silence Matrix:
Politics of Protection and Protectionism

Police retaliation is a sanction against people for speaking out, reporting, or engaging in political activities that conflict with officers' personal interests and police politics.[16] This type of violence aims to put people back in their place for crossing the lines and challenging police power. In Devin's story, the officer explicitly draws on pathologies to retaliate and demarcate the lines in police politics of protection. For example, after she spoke out at a community meeting, the officer followed her outside and proceeded to call her and the black and Latinx residents "thugs," and said that their neighbor who was recently killed by the police "got what they deserved." The officer further described how police neglect, or failure to provide protection, constituted an intentional form of retaliatory violence toward those who speak out—stating how people who keep "bring[ing] up race, that's why people [read police] don't come and back them up when they call for backup." Drawing upon an extensive history of police and state dehumanization of black people and other people of color as "animals,"[17] he then described Devin and her neighbors as "roaches" that "needed to be exterminated."

Kerry and Ella's stories further demonstrated how officers' loyalty to one another, or the blue wall, can be mobilized to intimidate those who speak out and engage in political activities—including their own families. To my knowledge, there is no sociological research on police domestic violence against black women and girls. However, Kerry's experiences with her stepfather gives insight into how officers can use their broader institutional authority in their private social worlds to retaliate against family members and intimate partners. Growing up, Kerry's experiences of childhood abuse and witnessing violence in the home taught her that it didn't matter if police were on duty or off duty as they could draw on their power or "sense of authority" at any time. Research on domestic violence already indicates that exiting a relationship can be one of the most dangerous moments for women.[18] And when Kerry's mother decided to leave, she confronted the blue wall and her stepfather's twenty-five to thirty years of building relationships with officers, prosecutors, judges, and others in the criminal-legal system. Excluded from police politics of protection, Kerry's stepfather leveraged these relationships to effectively terrorize her mother as she was "arrested constantly" and "constantly . . . going through the judicial system" to make her appear as an unfit mother. Kerry explained that he "had judges behind him," which "made it easy for him to use his power" to gain custody of her brother. Terrified to speak and, given the complicity of other officers, unsure whom they could even report him to, her family remained silent. As Kerry concluded, "You can't do anything about it because they have the whole judicial system backing them. And, if one crumbles, then they all crumble."

In Ella's story, police retaliation was used to silence those who speak out about police killings. After learning, as a child, about her father's murder at the hands of the police, Ella spent a significant part of her life trying to honor him. She had many questions about her father's death and started investigating what happened. Yet, as she looked more deeply into the case, someone from the department who "knows the politics" reached out to her. They let her know that "if you write this story, you're going to make it really hard for yourself." The politics of police protection were clear—if she continued to talk about her father's case, there would be consequences. *Here*, police protection was an officer telling her to stop looking for the truth or risk police retaliation. "Scared of retaliation," Ella went silent and "left the story alone" to protect herself. However, she explained to me that her silence was temporary. She was waiting until she had the experience and social capital to be in "the right place" that could offer her some protection so she could more publicly share her father's story.

Intracommunal backlash is a sanction for people speaking out and violating the beliefs and practices within the intracommunal politics of protectionism.[19] This type of violence aims to put people back in their place after crossing the lines that uphold black heteropatriarchal social worlds. Importantly, these politics are partially grounded in black communities' legal estrangement and distrust of officers due to historical and present-day experiences of police violence. Thus, Laura explained that she "don't trust them at all," Devin shared how community members were "dealing with our own shit" after a recent police killing in her neighborhood, and Karen knew from "such a young age, it's already instilled to be afraid." Resultingly, black communities create their own politics of protectionism to provide some sense of safety from broader violence and pathologizing. Yet, as shown in the previous chapters, protectionism politics did not include black women and girls, elevated black heteropatriarchal viewpoints and vulnerabilities, and shielded perpetrators of intracommunal violence. Thus, when Karen immediately reported being sexually assaulted by a peer at school, the politics of protectionism are mobilized against her, not on her behalf. As Karen described, "Ever since then, him [and] his friends, they bullied me and made fun of me." In Laura's case, she and her family first ignored the encounter and actively worked to make "missing" the domestic abuse between her cousin and his girlfriend. Left alone to deal with domestic violence, his girlfriend eventually called the police for help. It is at this point that her family acknowledged the situation and mobilized protectionism politics on behalf of her cousin.

Importantly, intracommunal backlash constitutes cultural betrayal against black women who speak about and report intracommunal violence. For Karen, this backlash didn't let up as she was labeled a "snitch" and bullied throughout high school, explaining how "him and his whole crew that were just against me for it." Feeling "violated" and confused, Karen turned to a friend for support in naming what was happening, asking, "What was I supposed to do? Was that wrong? Was I not supposed to do that?" In response, her friend stated that if she was in a similar situation, she would have remained silent. Bullied into isolation, Karen questioned then if it had been worth advocating for herself when she experienced sexual violence. She still asks that question. In Laura's story, we see how black women can engage in the politics of protectionism against other black women during domestic violence incidents. Her cousin's girlfriend was excluded from protectionism politics and only made hypervisible as the problem for violating them, with Laura exclaiming, "My first issue was what'd you call the police for?!" She was ultimately framed as "crazy," left isolated, and treated as disloyal for reporting the abuse.

The Silence Matrix: Norms and Sanctions

Working alongside norms, sanctions included ostracization, blame, and violence. In Kerry's story, gendered norms of respectability were mobilized against her mother as retaliation. With legal institutions pathologizing black single mothers, her stepfather intentionally targeted her reputation and made "false allegations" to consistently arrest her and gain custody as a punishment for ending the relationship. Deeply aware of the controlling images that shape visibility, Kerry worked in our interview to protect her mother's image. She wanted me to know that despite the campaign her stepfather waged against her mother, she was an ideal lady and mother who didn't smoke or drink and only went to work and came home to care for her kids. In Devin's story, the community liaison officer yelled at her for speaking out and explicitly showed how black women remaining silent is a gendered norm that signals respect and a heteropatriarchal presence in their lives, insinuating that if Devin had "a man" and "some dick," she would know how to be quiet. In this way, the officer illustrates how gender-based and sexual violence can be used to sanction black women and girls who challenge heteropatriarchal authority.

At the same time, Laura's story demonstrated how norms and sanctions simultaneously bring some people into view through pathologization while alternatively excusing others' behavior. Hence, during the domestic dispute between her cousin and girlfriend, Laura quickly noted how they "all know he has an anger problem." Throughout telling the story, Laura consistently worked to minimize the incident and excuse his behavior, telling me that the girlfriend should just "know he's not gonna put his hands" on her and understand that "he was upset our grandma being dead." When he hit the window, shattering it with his girlfriend inside the car, Laura excused it again: "He, like, barely tapped her window." She directed the full brunt of her anger at the girlfriend, whom she blamed for her cousin's police encounter. She subsequently ostracized and shamed the girlfriend for the domestic abuse, for not having empathy for her cousin's anger, and for reaching out to the police. Even though the girlfriend told her that she called the police because she was scared, Laura held her primarily responsible. She let the girlfriend know that she "just created this whole mess for no reason." Through the silence matrix, we can see how Laura simultaneously empathized with her cousin's behavior while blaming his girlfriend for hers. The officer too empathized with Laura's cousin around the domestic abuse, explaining how he understands what it means to be "going through a situation." He then revealed that he, too, had experienced domestic disputes in his intimate relationships, saying, "Me and my wife was going through a situation" that was similar. At no point did Laura describe the officer or anyone else checking on her cousin's girlfriend. She only became visible through pathology and incurring sanctions for violating the politics.

Last, in Ella's story, norms around silence also corresponded to age and position within the family. Ella shared how she was further traumatized by not being allowed to ask questions when, as a child, she learned of her father's police killing. She wanted to know what happened and what it all meant, but, she explained: "Nobody would talk to me about it." Ella had immense empathy for her family members' silence due to trauma around his murder. However, she shared that the silence was extremely anxiety inducing at such a young age. "I think that that's one thing that I hated was there was all these questions I had that nobody would even—[*pause*] As a kid, you don't just—[*pause*]. I wasn't the type to just go ask and get the answers I wanted. You expect the adults to come tell you . . ." Living with the fear of the police without anyone to talk to about it, Ella said that from a young age, "I just always remember being scared of police officers because of learning that my father was killed."

Everyday Policing and the Reproduction of Intersectional Domination

Black women speaking from the space between was no easy feat. Learning silence and having it enforced throughout their lives, they had to figure out how to navigate hostile visibility conditions and name their experiences of violence on their own. Once black women were able to develop a lexicon, they quickly found that officers and others sanctioned speaking because it violated multiple politics and disregarded norms around silence. Thus, through black women's journeys in deciding if, when, and how to speak about violence, we can see how officers and others engage in everyday policing.

Drawing and Redrawing Lines of Exclusion: Ignorance, Politics, and Domination

Black women speaking out about their experiences with the police and others who inflicted harm undermined their epistemic and literal exclusions—absences that buttressed white and black heteropatriarchal social worlds. Sharing their stories, then, not only illuminated "missing" violence, but also challenged the beliefs and practices within these worlds. Therefore, sanctions were used to reinforce the veils holding these worlds together. Resultingly, officers and others could maneuver around them for the cover to inflict violence, evade accountability, and retaliate against those who speak out against them.

Drawing and Redrawing Lines Through Coerced Inclusion: Weaponizing the Silence Matrix and Supporting Heteropatriarchy

Officers were distinctly positioned to understand police loyalty, reporting policies and mechanisms, and which harms are taken seriously. They knew how difficult it was for people to report, along with how dangerous it could become if they persistently try to hold them accountable. From their place inside police departments, officers could weaponize the silence matrix against those excluded from multiple politics and mobilize the "blue wall" to evade accountability. In Devin's case, the community liaison officer—an officer put in place through reforms designed to build relationships, promote more accountability, and reduce police violence—was able to sexually harass her as punishment for speaking out with little to no fear of being reported. Although there are mixed results on the efficacy of this reform in decreasing police lethal and physical violence, there is little to no sociological research on how community liaison officers shape experiences of police sexual violence and reporting.[20] Importantly, Devin's "missing" encounter challenges how we understand these policies and their impact. In retaliating against her, the officer framed Devin speaking as emblematic of her lacking a heteropatriarchal figure in her life to keep her quiet. His access to her community also directly shaped her willingness to report the encounter because "he knew where I stayed." Eventually, Devin was silenced. However, she also chose to protect herself and her family.

For Kerry, her stepfather called upon his fellow officers to repeatedly harass her family, and specifically, her mother. His retaliatory harassment mobilized multiple actors in the police department and criminal-legal system; through their positions of authority, they obscured and participated in his abuse and discrediting of Kerry's mother. Further, given his position and Kerry's race, gender, and age, he was able to publicly abuse her throughout her childhood. Kerry and her family were terrified to report him and the other officers. They, too, chose silence after being silenced. In Ella's story, someone warned her about the potential retaliation for researching and talking about her father's killing. With her father's death ever present in her family, these consequences felt all too real for Ella. Thus, silence was again forced and chosen.

Others close to black women also evaded accountability by mobilizing the intracommunal politics of protectionism. They, too, were uniquely positioned to understand these politics—how racial loyalty to one another is masculinized, which harms are taken seriously, and how speaking to officers and outsiders incurs sanctions. They knew how difficult it was for black women and girls to report, along with how dangerous and isolating it could be to pursue intra-communal accountability. From their place within communities, they could weaponize the silence matrix to inflict harm on those excluded. Karen was bullied after being sexually assaulted at school, and the teen who assaulted her was also able to mobilize support from their peers, which brought Karen into view as a snitch for reporting the incident to school authorities. Her sexual assault was made "missing," and the focus became her disloyalty. For Laura, this meant deriding and isolating her cousin's girlfriend during a domestic dispute before and after she called the police. Her story showed how the girl-friend's experiences of domestic violence were rendered invisible through protectionism politics until she crossed through the veil by way of pathology and became hypervisible for reporting—both of which made her "missing." From their side of heteropatriarchal veils, protectionism politics framed the backlash as a defense of her cousin from the police while also excusing his domestic abuse toward his girlfriend. Importantly, the officer also empathized with Laura's cousin about domestic violence, once again showing the link be-tween the politics of protection and protectionism around heteropatriarchal violence. While this incident also demonstrated how veils can thin through empathy (*more on this process in the next chapter*), it also showed that empathy within the politics of protection and protectionism is grounded in heteropa-triarchy. This type of protection serves perpetrators of abuse and disregards black women and girls as victims of violence.

Normalization of Intersectional Inequalities: Safety, Dissemblance, and "Missing-ness"

In the space between speaking, retaliation, and backlash, silence took on many meanings as black women navigated shifting visibility and searched for safety. Thus, the meaning of silence cannot be fully interpreted without the experi-ences, perspectives, and stories of those subjected to consequences for speaking. While Devin spoke at several points—at the meeting and challenging the officer afterward—she quickly recognized that silence may be the best way to protect herself and her children. *Here*, deciding whether to speak was a constant evalu-ation between the risk of violence and the potentiality of accountability, and as such, speaking shifts to silence and back to speaking again, depending on when and with whom black women feel safe and see a pathway to justice. Karen re-ported the sexual assault, but because of the consequences she faced for doing so, she was unsure if she would speak if she was assaulted again in the future.

Here, speaking was followed by long silences, thus showing how backlash is a form of punishment that produces dissonance for black women as they internally consider the risk and rewards of advocating for themselves throughout their lives. Kerry did not speak as a child but eventually came to challenge her stepfather when she saw him as an adult, refusing to let him call her a "thing." *Here*, long silences were followed up by speaking later as an adult, as she shows how black women's memories and imaginations can hold their stories in the space between for long periods of time. Ella worked to tell her father's story later in life, speaking to others about it when she could, researching the details, and waiting until she felt safe to share it. *Here*, silence was a short- to long-term strategy with a vision for publicly speaking one day, and as such, it can be a long pause that holds space for black women to speak when they feel ready. Laura did not share how her cousin's girlfriend felt and what happened next in her story. The girlfriend, in many ways, was rendered "missing" in Laura's retelling as speaking about intracommunal violence was still considered deviant when we met. *Here*, it cannot be assumed that someone is a safe person to listen to black women's stories just because they share an identity.

Black women carried these lessons about silence with them throughout their lives as they learned when, where, and whether they would share their stories. The interview served as a site through which to observe these evaluations as many were hesitant to lift the veils around their "missing" experiences. Thus, the storytelling vetting process that many put me through at the beginning of our interviews (*and throughout*) was to ascertain the risk of their stories being subjected to the consequences discussed in this chapter: shame, blame, ostracization, backlash, and retaliation. As such, Devin initially ghosted me and was not trying to talk to a "white Shannon." Karen was late, telling me, "I was taking time, almost not trying to go," as she sat in her car to make sure the researcher was a black woman or woman of color. While Laura was comfortable and didn't have many questions, Kerry made me answer all the questions on the interview guide before I could ask her anything. Last, Ella shared that she "had debated speaking to [me] for a while" because she had "anxiety speaking on the issue" of police violence.

"i was kind of scared to report it because he knew where I stayed"

"i was a snitch or something"

"in the smallest ways, I do so much to make sure that you are being seen as an entire human, and for you to turn around and toy with my emotions and play me for weak is fucked up!"

"you can't do anything about it

because they have the whole judicial system backing them"

"i think about it literally every day"

"i'm desensitized to most things. music is . . . [*pause*] that's the emotion part side of me"

"you just created this whole mess for no reason"

"i'm getting used to talking about difficult things

in order to work towards freedom"

"when we gather"

5

Simone

It was early in the afternoon when Simone and I greeted each other with a hug at the coffee shop. I first met Simone, a dark brown-skinned, heterosexual, cisgender woman in her early thirties, at a community event a few days prior. As we stood in line, we talked casually about what it was like for both of us to spend time as black girls in the rural South. While the nostalgia from sharing a few childhood memories gave way to some sense of familiarity, the energy quickly shifted when we transitioned to the formal part of our interview as Simone became anxious and reserved. She quickly informed me that she didn't want to be recorded and preferred that I stick with handwritten notes. Wanting to talk freely, she worried that an awareness of a recorder would make her too nervous and self-conscious. She was also concerned about how she would feel after our interview, letting me know that while some of her black girlhood memories were fun and sentimental to reflect upon, others remained difficult to speak about even decades later.

When it came to the police, Simone definitively told me that "the uniform is all that matters." She considered all officers untrustworthy. By "witnessing conversations" about the police in her childhood, she learned how important it was to "avoid them at all costs." Overhearing talks between caregivers and the boys in her family taught Simone to put "your hands where you can see them." She understood that the focus was making sure they were aware of the risk of getting killed by the police. Simone would never "tell a person *not* to be afraid," believing that black children "need a little fear." To her, "a healthy case of cultural paranoia is important for survival."

Simone also received a separate talk in which her mother discussed police sexual assault. To avoid this risk, Simone was told by her mother she "don't [need to] be out at certain times of night." She was also warned that as a black girl, and specifically, a dark brown-skinned black girl, "You are going to have to work harder." So, that's what Simone did. However, the harder she worked and tried to excel, the more she learned that others "saw my curiousness and intellect as defiance." Her attempt to be excellent brought her into view as a troublemaker, and she received a lot of criticism whenever she tried to speak up. Over time, Simone explained that she "internalized and learned the rules of whiteness to survive." To survive in her own community, a similar rule applied. She was basically expected "to be seen and not heard." Simone reflected more on the expectations of silence and the consequences of speaking while sharing multiple stories of police and domestic violence throughout her life.

Simone described how, as a child, she closely watched how people responded when black women and girls in her family pushed back against violence. From watching an aunt report domestic abuse, Simone learned that "black women are less trusted by institutions than black men" and "got a sense of what being devalued as a 'thing' and not a person was early on." Understanding the risks associated with speaking and that "people don't trust the word of girls," she had kept most of her childhood stories to herself. She pointed out that our interview was one of the few times she had ever talked about some of her numerous experiences with violence.

To protect herself as an adult, Simone tried to ignore the police as much as possible. She refused to call them in emergencies. She also took mental health days by "calling in black." This self-care practice was especially important to her when high-profile cases of police violence went viral on social media. She needed to work through her grief. These tragedies also triggered memories of past encounters and made her confront her own personal risks and the vulnerability of those around her.[1] In these moments, she took time for herself because the last thing she wanted was to interact with "white people [who] ask her stupid questions about how she feels."

Toward the end of our interview, I asked Simone where she goes to talk about her feelings and where she was comfortable discussing black women and girls' stories of police violence. She paused. Sitting on the back café bar stools, facing a large window overlooking the street, so much time went by as she peered outside that it seemed she may never answer the question. I turned to look out the window with her. More than a few moments passed as we silently sipped our drinks while watching cars drive up and down the street. Eventually, she turned back toward me and started listing all the places where she felt *uncomfortable* discussing police and other forms of violence against black women and girls: "open spaces," "churches," and "the coffee shop where we are currently sitting and talking." We both looked around and laughed. In places where others are present, others who are not black women, Simone said there was "too much crap to wade through." Turning back toward the window, she and I continued watching the cars pass by as we sat together in silence.

Here, I do not know how long this pause lasted. Yet, at some point, while still facing the window, Simone finally shared where she felt comfortable talking about her experiences—only among other black women, "when we gather."

"When We Gather"

THE SPACE BETWEEN LIVED
EXPERIENCES AND SELF-DEFINITION

Black women desired spaces to speak openly about police violence and other forms of violence in their lives. Without these spaces, most struggled to make systemic connections between their encounters and the "missing" encounters of others. If unaware of these connections, black women felt alone in their journeys through the spaces between and questioned if they were to blame for violence others would not name and recognize. The interviews, then, served as a rare space for black women to speak aloud, bear witness to, and reflect upon their stories that had before been silenced. And it is through their accounts that we glean how the silence matrix not only created a gulf between black women and those around them, but also forged a space between themselves and their own lived experiences.

From this place, Collin writes how "naming becomes a way of transcending the limitations of intersecting oppression," and that self-definition is about black women reclaiming the "power to name one's own reality."[2] Harnessing this power is essential to developing knowledge that aids in physically and psychically surviving domination. Thus, black feminist thought is knowledge created by black women in the space between, which provides clarity on shared and diverse lived experiences at the intersection of anti-blackness and patriarchy that others make "missing" from information about our social worlds.[3] While everyday policing uses the master's tools to put black women in their place, creating this knowledge requires a different set of tools. It requires an ethic of care and dialoguing about encounters, wherein emotions and empathy signal that someone indeed understands these experiences.[4] From *here*, accountability closes the rift between people, connecting them through the knowledge they create together. Hence, black feminist thought disrupts the veils supporting domination in our social worlds, providing ways of seeing, knowing, connecting, and building with one another. This chapter then asks: How do black women create black feminist thought regarding policing and violence in their daily lives? What does the development of this liberatory knowledge reveal about the everyday conditions for safety, solidarity, and building alternatives to the police?

While Simone initially listed several places where she felt uncomfortable sharing her story, she went on to note that the only space in which she felt safe enough to name her experiences and explore their meaning was with other black women, "when we gather." Drawing from Simone, this chapter focuses on the safe spaces in black women's lives to gather and move from the margin to the center of their stories.[5] A counter to everyday policing, *gathering* connected the literal with the liminal, wherein the center for recognition was not a fixed, static place. Instead, the center expanded and restricted through relationality, through valuing people and their stories. This valuation formed the basis of solidarity and the creation of alternative pathways to legibility and safety in everyday life. In particular, I examine the experiences of black women who gather—or those who convene people in their communities to have conversations about policing. I also analyze the experiences of black women who've been gathered—or accessed and built spaces with people in daily life to self- and collectively define. Together, I theorize gathering as an epistemological and literal process of growing a relational center that recognizes and values people and their stories. While I show the promises of gathering, I also explore its challenges and how this relational center could quickly give way to everyday policing.

Audrey

"I'm pouring your tea for you, and I'll give you a heads up or ask you," Audrey said as she poured us a midafternoon cup of tea in the café where we met for our interview. She had spent the past twenty minutes asking me very detailed questions about my background and journey to the project. A dark brown-skinned, black, African and Afro-Caribbean, bisexual, cisgender woman in her mid-thirties, Audrey was politically active in her community and organized spaces for people to have conversations about racism and the police. Now that I had answered her questions, she peered over her steaming cup of tea, gesturing with a wave of her hand that it was okay for me to turn on the recorder and start our formal conversation.

"I mean, that is an interesting choice of topic."

"How do you feel knowing that we're gonna be talking about police today?"

"I imagine this might be a relatively difficult conversation, or it might bring up uncomfortable feelings—or not uncomfortable, bad memories, basically. [But] I am getting used to talking about difficult things in order to work towards freedom. Yeah, I'm all right with that."

"What does freedom mean to you?"

"Well, shoot, either it could be in terms of activism and organizing and making sure that my community is alright, so having to have those conversations or—to work on racism type space. I have to put out energy to do those things 'cause I'm an introvert, but also personal freedom as well. That's more related to my own internal balance and balancing my life, mind, body, work, nonwork, stuff like that, community, and all of that. Yeah, freedom can be a few things."

"What are your general views about police? Or what do you think of them?"

"As an organization, or a construct, a social institution maybe, I don't like it at all. I don't like them. People who are police can be great, or they can be assholes. And that's on a person-to-person basis like everyone else. The institution? When I think separate from the people, so I can like a person who is a police officer. But the institution? I am not comfortable with, will never be comfortable with, I don't think. It puts power in the hands of the wrong people and gives them guns and lets them run around communities and terrorize communities is the thing. This is everywhere in the world."

Audrey then started telling me about her childhood growing up in the Caribbean where she didn't talk much about the police. However, she recalled a traffic stop with her father that "definitely made me not feel like police were safe people." She recounted other cases of police violence where officers would be "running around terrorizing people." Back home, she said, the "problem with the police was the arrogance and the power tripping." But she didn't fear for her life. Audrey explained that as an immigrant, she had to learn more about anti-black racism and police violence when she moved to the United States, where the "problem with police is that I'm afraid they would kill me or somebody I love for no reason, and that's different." Moreover, she said that developing different views of policing based on one's experience was the entire point and strategy of the institution. Audrey went on to explain:

Policing started as a slave-catching organization, and that still exists. It's an unbroken line of that institution, and so it is very clearly associated with race. And different races have different experiences and understanding of what police are for. Police is not for protecting and serving everyone. It's protecting and serving white people and protecting and serving capitalism, not anyone else or anything else.

Audrey learned how she should interact with the police in the United States by watching black people around her "code-switch." From them, she determined that she needed to be "a very pleasant citizen and not escalate the situation." With disdain she noted that it was "fine being nice to people [but] would prefer to not feel like my survival is contingent on being nice to people." Thus, she felt that showing "civility" when interacting with officers was "a hostage situation for my life and well-being in the moment" when she interacted with officers.

Since immigrating, Audrey has had several encounters with the police and witnessed others' encounters. As someone who was politically active in her community, she made sure to film the police as a "matter of safety."[6] She also worked to support others after their encounters, helping them find lawyers and mental health resources. And she facilitated community conversations for people to share stories and receive communal support.

I asked Audrey if she felt comfortable sharing her own encounters or talking about black women's experiences with police in these spaces that she organized. She replied, "Not really. I feel like I can't talk about that with black men."

"Why is that?" She explained:

Because then they wanna talk about how much more black men experience police violence. The fact that black men don't advocate for black women—they advocate for themselves. Black women advocate for black men. [*pause*] I don't get into those conversations. I don't get into them with black men because then it becomes a competition of who is more oppressed by police, and that's not what—[*pause*] If I'm specifically wanting, for whatever reason, to talk about black women's experiences, let me talk about black women's experiences. It's not oppression Olympics. I feel like black men feel—often feel threatened that their story—[*pause*] they want to feel like the most oppressed group. When black women start talking about their intersections, black men are unwilling to listen.

Audrey then went on to describe her specific fears of police violence as someone who is an activist. She worried about police sexual violence. She worried that if she were killed by the police, no one would care enough to demand answers because she was a black woman. She reflected more on what it meant to be a community advocate and facilitate space but not have the space to talk about her own anxieties and experiences. Audrey said, "Black men very rarely are willing to listen to black women or talk about the experiences of black women without centering themselves." After saying this, she began to cry. She cared about black men, emphasizing that when they "get pulled over, because their lives are really in danger, they could get shot." Her fears for them were also her fears for herself and other black women.

> I also don't want to interact with police because, yes, we could get shot. We could also get arrested and killed mysteriously or die mysteriously, like Sandra Bland and others. She's not the only one black woman who gotten arrested unnecessarily and was found dead in her cell. It is not the only situation; it's just the most publicized one. That could happen.

Terrified of being killed mysteriously and that no one would know what happened to her, Audrey explained that this was one of the main reasons she didn't talk openly in activist spaces about her mental health. She didn't post anything online, either. This was also because people excavated Sandra Bland's posts after her death and found ways to blame her and support their theories that she committed suicide due to mental health.[7] As a consequence, Audrey states, "I stay off of Facebook, as in I don't post very much because I'm also dealing with, probably depression. I don't want to post a status that if I am found hanging in a jail cell at some point, will people pull up and say, 'Yes, she was suicidal.'"

But, as Audrey pointed out, she "wants to be able to talk about my mental health in a open space to give other people permission to talk about that, because I think it's important for health, the health of all people." However, that people would "assume that" and not look more into it because she is a black woman was painful for Audrey. She emphatically stated "I want people to investigate why the fuck I'm in a jail cell and why I'm dead!" She had "to override that desire to encourage discussion about mental health" in her community in ways that included herself because, as she said, "I keep being afraid that if I'm found hanging or found in some other—a lynching situation, that people will assume that it finally got me, and I committed suicide."

Despite not feeling safe enough to openly discuss her police experiences, Audrey still had a need to share her story. For solace, she turned to poetry, "a good release" that "helps me express things that I could not express in statuses or blog posts." Through poetry, she wrote about "social situations," "social justice," "relationships," and her "perspective as a black woman." While she didn't trust other spaces, Audrey emphatically stated, "I trust my poem instead." Poetry helped her share her story and learn that she was "valuable" and that her experiences were "valid." Poetry gave her a safe space to say things that "need to be heard." From her place, "I mean, some things I haven't said through my mouth before."

Individual Gathering: Poetry, Imagination, and Creative Expressions

Poetry is the way we help give name to the nameless so it can be thought. The farthest external horizons of our hopes and fears are cobbled by our poems, carved from the rock experiences of our daily lives.

—AUDRE LORDE, "POETRY IS NOT A LUXURY"[8]

The silence matrix made it difficult and dangerous for black women to speak about violence. Alternatively, poetry and other forms of creative expressions are essential tools for black women to name their experiences and define themselves. It helps them move from the nameless in the space between, and as Lorde states: "toward survival and change, first made into language, then into idea, then into more tangible action."[9] Journeying through several spaces between, some black women turned to their imaginations and creative expressions to gather or reflect on their lived experiences along with the broader conditions and lines that shaped their lives. These tools helped them resist the internalization of everyday policing, to reclaim the power to name and self-define their realities without significant pushback and retaliation. For some, this creativity was a gathering of one.

As a communal gatherer, Audrey organized spaces for people to talk about police violence, their mental health, and connect with resources. Yet, while she worked toward building alternative pathways to the police, she did not feel comfortable naming her own fears and experiences in these same spaces where she intracommunally confronted protectionism politics. These politics often restricted the center of recognition and valuation to black heteropatriarchal viewpoints and black men's experiences, leaving little to no room for black women to share their stories. As Audrey put it, "Black men very rarely are willing to listen to black women or talk about the experiences of black women without centering themselves." Indeed, black women and LGBTQ+ activists organizing around policing share her concerns, struggling in their community work to build and expand a relational center and bring into view the policing of gender and sexuality.[10]

At the same time, Audrey worried about being murdered for speaking out against police violence. Remembering the media discussions of Sandra Bland's mental health after her death, she understood how the police and others could weaponize her story. She feared that if the police ever retaliated, they would use her mental health posts as a way to bring her into view and blame her.[11] She was terrified others would believe them, and, given how police and intracommunal politics share a framing of black women as deviant, she feared no one would care to question her death. Unable to access safe spaces to trust with her story, Audrey intimately told me she "trusts my poem instead." Through poetry, she resisted the internalization of "missing-ness," alternatively named what "needs to be heard" and taught herself that she was "valid" and "valuable." As an individual gathering space, poetry helped her bear witness to her experiences that others would not recognize. From *here*, it helped her in creating knowledge and "getting used to talking about difficult things in order to work towards freedom."

Audrey was not the only one in the space between who turned to her imagination and creative expressions. In chapter 1, Sadia used her imagination to envision different talks that acknowledged and addressed her vulnerabilities. This envisioned talk named how her "experiences were gonna be different" as they would be made "missing," so, she needed to "be mindful of those experiences." Later in our conversation, Sadia shared how creative expression helped her reclaim the power to name her reality: "If spells are words, and there's power in the tongue, then what are we manifesting in ourselves when we say, 'I am this?'" Thus, she used multiple creative expressions to name herself and her experiences, sharing how even though she lived in a world where "you call me whatever you wanna call me," creative expressions have been critical in her journey toward sharing her story and naming her fluid gender and sexuality outside of the gender binary and heterosexuality. An effort to resist everyday policing, Sadia's imagination and "allows for me to stay true to myself."

While Toya's experiences were not shared in the previous chapters, she, too, explained how poetry and music helped her cope with being physically assaulted by the police as a teen and witnessing neighborhood violence. A dark brown-skinned, black, African American in her early twenties, she describes her gender and sexuality as not conforming to a binary or typical categories. In sharing her story, Toya explained how, as a child, "I couldn't read, but— [*pause*] I couldn't read, but I could write." So, she wrote poems and rap lyrics to name her experiences others would not recognize. "I just really, really like music. I just feel like for the most part, I really don't—[*pause*] I'm desensitized to most things. Music is . . . [*pause*] that's the emotion part side of me." Music and poetry helped Toya tap into her emotions, bridging the space between her experiences and self-definition. This, in turn, helped her narrow the gulf between herself and others in her neighborhood:

> Everybody on the block used to come to our house. We had a set-up. My mom had got us an *American Idol* game for Christmas. It came with these microphones you put in the Play Station . . . We ended up mixing up—we had mixed—we would mix tracks. We were rapping, all the kids on the block would come. It was our own little studio. We would record songs and everything. That probably was it right there. [*laughing*] We always used to have rap battles and everything.

Toya, Audrey, Sadia, and other black women I interviewed used their imaginations, poetry, and creative expressions as tools to individually gather, navigating the space between themselves and their lived experiences. In the process, many developed a multiple consciousness, or their "perspectives" around experiences that were unnamed by others in their lives.

Quita

"Did you have any questions before we start?"

"I don't think so. Everything was pretty straightforward."

"How was the survey for you?"

"I felt I didn't have enough information for it. I felt I did a bad job at it."

"How so?"

"I don't know. I don't know, I was just like nope, nope, no, I don't know. I felt it missed me in a weird way."

Quita is a dark brown-skinned, black, African American, heterosexual cisgender woman in her late twenties. With a bachelor's degree and working several odd jobs, Quita was able to get away from work so we could meet for lunch at a coffee shop for our interview. She was "nervous as hell" about participating. "I think it's [that] I normally communicate on my own terms. I'm reserved until I'm ready to introduce myself to people. Deciding to participate in this put me in a situation where I don't know what was gonna come up, so I'm nervous as fuck right now." She decided to participate only because we were first introduced through a mutual contact in my field site.

She then told me that the survey missed her because she "was safe" as a kid. This safety, she explained, was grounded not in a lack of harm, but in having people to talk to about her experiences and address them head on. When we started to discuss her childhood, particularly her relationship with her mother, she visibly relaxed. As a child, Quita grew up in a low-income neighborhood in a large city. Despite the neighborhood's negative reputation, "I appreciated my childhood" there. In the predominantly black space of her neighborhood, "I didn't have to think about race a lot as a child" and is "grateful for the fact." Around others in her community, Quita felt "safe to explore and just be an individual as a child." When it came to the police, she observed other's en-counters and learned that "everybody around me just not really fucking with cops." From "shit I picked up" over the years, Quita learned how to interact with the police. But her main teacher was close to home: "I learned everything I know about interacting from my momma."

Quita was taught early by her mother about "taking care of yourself," because as a black girl, "if you don't nobody else will." By constantly stressing "you gotta do it first," Quita's mother let her know that she may not receive validation from others. She learned that this is because, in terms of violence, black women and girls are taught "it's our duty . . . to withstand so much of it, like a sign of strength or something." Her mother told her that this belief had been "enforced in us for a long time." Reflecting on her mother's resistance to these gendered norms, she said, "I'm really lucky. My momma is amazing. She hasn't really had tolerance for stuff, but she also has really clear boundaries about everything or everybody." From her, Quita stated, "I don't think it's true at all" that she had to tolerate violence.

I asked Quita if she would feel comfortable calling the police during an emergency. She replied,

> No. I'd call my momma and then we'd figure it out from there. I'm like, Ma, you know, and I'll just call and tell her. She's so quick that we'll figure it out. I don't have time 'cause I worry that cops will get called up and they, like, weird, preconceived notions. I don't trust they decision-making. Personally, because that's what I've done in situations before. I call people that I trust instead of calling the cops every time.

Quita gave the example of how, when she was a child, she dealt with the domestic violence between her father, who was a prison guard, and step-mother. Instead of calling the police, "I called my momma on my daddy" whenever "he's done some shit that I felt was out of line." In these moments, her mother would say, "Give him the phone." Quita could hear her mother "cussing him out and then five minutes later she was outside" to get her. As she got older, Quita would protect herself during domestic disputes by putting up a boundary and telling her father, "I don't have nothing to say to you until you get your shit together."

Another example of how Quita learned about the relationship between self-care and boundaries was that her mother would give her a self-care day as a child, which allowed Quita to decide for herself when she didn't want to go to school. Importantly, her mother would stress that she did not need to explain her reasons why. "We got one day a school year where we could just decide we didn't wanna go to school. Every year we had one day where I could wake up and I could do it as late as that morning. I could be like, 'Momma, I don't want to.' She'd be like, 'Okay, this is your one.' It's like, 'Okay.'"

Quita also remembered being taught how to advocate for herself, and how her mother would support her by reinforcing her daughter's boundaries with other people. For example, her mother helped Quita leave situations when she felt uncomfortable without providing an explanation.

> If I went to somebody house to spend the night, but then I got uncomfortable at 3:00 in the morning and I wanted to go home, I could call my momma and she would come get me and I got to go home. She was just always really there for us. We didn't need a reason. It was just like, 'Momma, I don't want to.' She'd be like, 'Okay,' and she would come get me.

This helped Quita feel confident to advocate for herself when others crossed her boundaries. "There have been times where other kids' parents would be like, 'No, it's okay. Just stay the night,' and whatever. I'm like, 'No, I'm gonna call my momma. She's not gonna be mad at me.' She was never mad at us for doing it, so I know that was important."

Another lesson Quita gleaned from her mother was how to make interconnected, relational decisions, or how to see and consider other people in her decision-making process. Specifically, Quita learned to see and value her mother's labor and resources as a single parent. "Her rule with extracurriculars was we could quit before she spent money. That was her rule with extracurriculars. That was the point where I was like, 'Try running track.' I was like, 'Okay,' and I did it and I hated it and she was like, 'Okay.' It was always if she ain't spent no money yet, we could quit, but if she spent money, you had to finish out whatever she had paid for." Through this lesson, Quita learned accountability, or how to balance finishing things she had committed to while also having the space to change her mind. "It's [how] she held us accountable, and she taught us decision-making. I feel I made really thoughtful decisions because of the way that her rules were set up." Finally, Quita said she developed an understanding of how important trust was in relationships. "The only thing I ever got in trouble for was lying . . . Anything else, it was a conversation, but if I lied about something, she was pissed."

Together, these lessons helped young Quita navigate the domestic violence between her father and stepmother. This particularly helped her resist gaslighting as she watched how her father abused her stepmother and was able to "hide it from everybody else." Within the home, "we are the only two people who see it. It's me, her, and my momma." Watching her stepmother be gaslit deeply impacted her. "It fucking sucks. I found myself having heart to hearts with my daddy's wife, [pause] because he's been treating her like shit and only me and her know this particular brand of crazy from him because he hides it from everybody else. He doesn't remember stuff. You'll tell him some shit that he did, and he'll look at me and tell me, 'I would never do that.'"

Given their conversations, Quita's father intentionally tried to keep his daughter and wife from talking with one another. "It's crazy. I ended up on the phone with his wife and she told me, she was like, 'Quita, I'm convinced that he intentionally keeps a wedge between us because he don't want *this* to happen.' She was like, 'I'm sure if he knew I was on the phone with you right now, he would be pissed.'" In this situation, "this" was speaking with one another and developing a shared understanding of his abuse. Quita grew even more angry when remembering her father's gaslighting and how he tried to prevent her and her stepmother from talking. She stated that in "black communities, you still have to deal with misogyny," and referred to black misogyny as her "least favorite brand." About her father, she specifically said, "In the smallest ways, I do so much to make sure that you are being seen as an entire human, and for you to turn around and toy with my emotions and play me for weak is fucked up."

When Quita needed support or to talk through experiences, she continued to turn to her mother. Even now, when she gets anxious about putting up boundaries and protecting herself, "I still have to call her to get that reinforced because society does such a good job in making you feel bad for it." She laughed, recalling her recent conversation with her mother and how she always brought Quita's awareness back to herself, asking her, "What do *you* wanna do?" If Quita was unsure, her mother responded by walking her through the space between. "'Okay, well, we could do it like this or what if we did this? Or what if maybe you did it like this?' You know, whatever, whatever. Then me and her just spitball ideas until something sticks." In the view from her place, Quita explained that she learned from her mother that "I am worth being taken care of."

Relational Gathering: Talks and Alternative Pathways

> The extended family is a good place to learn the power of community. However, it can only become a community if there is honest communication between the individuals in it. Dysfunctional extended families, like smaller nuclear family units, are usually characterized by muddied communication. Keeping family secrets often makes it impossible for extended groups to build community.
>
> —BELL HOOKS, *ALL ABOUT LOVE*[12]

According to hooks, clear communication about lived experiences is necessary for community building, whether that community is the nuclear family, extended family, or others. Throughout their lives, black women searched their various relationships to have "honest communication" about violence. Some created and found such spaces later in their lives, wherein they learned to name their early childhood experiences. However, long before these journeys, many black women I interviewed first turned to their mothers for help with naming what was rendered "missing." Instead of receiving support, many often confronted the silence matrix in their relationship with their mothers, wherein they had to navigate respectability, exclusionary racial loyalty, and black heteropatriarchal politics. But, a few, like Quita, shared how their mothers relationally gathered them—dialoguing with their daughters and guiding them through the space between toward self-definition and safety.

Most black women who relationally gathered with their mothers did so when they got older. In these conversations, mothers and daughters learned to name and define their experiences together. For example, Kristen from chapters 1 and 2 discussed how she and her mother discussed violence both outside and within their home as she got older:

> I specifically, I talk a lot with my mom. I talk with my mom a lot about different sorts of violence. . . . How violence can just manifest itself in so many ways that I didn't know or I didn't recognize or that—[*pause*] at a different time in my life I wouldn't have called it violent, I might have called it

something else—[*pause*] and now that I see it, like, "Oh, this is violence, this is harmful, this is detrimental to me and my well-being and my health." We talk about violence a lot. Not only the violence that I've experience but the heaps and heaps of it that she deals with in her own space.

Importantly, these talks occurred in private, away from Kristen's father and other family members. Indeed, having these conversations under the veil of dissemblance was common among black women who grew up in two-parent heterosexual households where the center of recognition and valuation was primarily restricted to black men and boys. Talks that expanded the center to include black women and girls were more likely to occur away from black heteropatriarchal nuclear family structures. These familial conversations typically happened within nonheteronormative family structures, such as black women with single mothers, lesbian mothers, and othermothers, including godmothers, grandmothers, aunts, and fictive kin.

Within these gathering talks, black women very explicitly engaged in black feminist epistemology—sharing stories, dialoguing about their lived experiences, expressing empathy toward one another, providing care, engaging in accountability, and creating alternative pathways to safety.[13] For example, while Quita's mother didn't use the term "everyday policing," she described to her daughter how violence and silence worked together to put her in her place. She provided Quita counternarratives and practices, teaching her early on the importance of "taking care of yourself," explaining that "you gotta do it first" because "if you don't nobody else will." Naming and recognizing the spaces between, Quita's mother also let her know that her caring for herself and prioritizing her safety would likely not be validated by others. According to her mother, this was because black women and girls are taught that withstanding violence was a sign of strength. Thus, her mother effectively challenged and resisted the internalization of the silence matrix by naming violence and the conditions that shape black women's place. From her mother's relational gathering, Quita learned to see and resist the process of "missing-ness" and knew that she was worth being protected.

While Quita and Kristen had conversations with their mothers, other black women turned to othermothers. Kerry, from the previous chapter, had conversations with her grandmother. "I just talked to her about everything. She was able to help me cope when my brother was moving out of the house and my mom was always working." In *Grandmothering While Black*, LaShawnDa Pittman talks about how grandmothers work to ensure their grandchildren's physical and psychic survival in the broader world as well as within their own communities.[14] For Kerry, her grandmother helped her deal with her mother's disinterest in exploring alternative approaches for navigating the world. Kerry described her mother as "not very open to multiple things," explaining, "She's very much how she was raised. She doesn't be like, 'Okay. Well, maybe I need to unpack this and not carry this all.' She's like, 'It worked for me,' or whatever, 'And I'm gonna keep repeating that.'" Thus, Kerry described how everyday policing could become internalized, and then used to intergenerationally reproduce the space between family members. Kerry was encouraged by her grandmother to not simply do as she was told. Her grandmother would tell her, "'Okay, you don't need to take on everything that your mom is feeding you.' She would be, like, 'Let's unpack this. You can take this piece, and you can take this piece, but, if all of this has got served, you don't have to eat everything on this plate.'" Relationally gathering Kerry in the space between, her grandmother taught her to be critical of the politics, norms, and sanctions that dictate her place. She encouraged her to sift through the messaging she received and to carefully choose knowledge that reflected her lived experiences and that would serve her. Thus, she taught Kerry how to create black feminist thought:

> She allowed me to slowly start to figure out what serving or not or whatever and what I want to hold onto and what I don't want to hold onto. Because a lot of times, as a child, you're a sponge. You just absorb and absorb and absorb. You hold it all. For her to teach me, "Your mom is your mom. She's wonderful, and she's lovely. She's all of these things, but she's a product—." This wasn't her words, but she's a product of her environment or whatever. "You don't have to be about that." She helped me process those type of things.

Importantly, while Kerry's grandmother disagreed with her mother, she did not pathologize her. Instead, she taught Kerry to see the conditions shaping her mother's life and to take in information that was useful and disregard the rest. Thus, through relational talks, black women learned to include themselves in the center for recognition and valuation while practicing empathy and care.

Quita's story also demonstrated how trust is a critical part of the self and relational process linking care to accountability. As Quita noted, her mother encouraged her to practice freedom but expected honesty: "The only thing I ever got in trouble for was lying." Her mother also taught her self-trust and to be comfortable establishing boundaries. Learning to speak up for herself when she felt uncomfortable, Quita also trusted her mother to be a lever for power, or someone who would use their access and resources to support her in a crisis. She knew her mother was "not gonna be mad at me" if she reached out for help.

Notably, when I asked Quita who she would call for help in an emergency, she was one of the few black women I interviewed who consistently had an alternative to the police, explaining how she would call her mother or other people she trusted. Building this trust is a form of black feminist theorizing as well as a practice of abolition. Battle and Powell detail how survivors of violence may not use the language of abolition but will often describe police failures and their desires for alternatives.[15] Quita does not use the language of abolition, but nevertheless sought alternatives to the police among her relationships, as when she "called my momma on my daddy" as a child to access protection during domestic violence between her father and stepmother. Further, when we met, Quita and her mother's conversations were ongoing, as her mother continued to relationally gather her, walking her through the space between her lived experiences and toward self-definition and alternative pathways to safety.

Last, while Quita, Kerry, and Kristen turned to their mothers and othermothers, other black women relationally gathered with their friends. Krystal, a queer, light brown-skinned, black, African and multiracial woman in her early thirties, whose story of police sexual harassment and coercion was not shared in the previous chapters, described how she and her friends struggled early in their lives to name sexual violence. "I don't think we had the right words for it. I don't think we had the right—[pause] yeah, our lexicon was not there." Krystal explained in the course of gathering with her friends, the meaning around sexual harassment shifted as she developed the words to describe interactions from her perspective:

> I think it was more like, "Oh, this guy thinks I'm cute," you know that kind of stuff but then we talk about how they flirted with you or something. Then, you realize just how incredibly sexist it was. Later on, you think like, "Oh, no. That was awful." He shouldn't have said those things and comments about clothing and things like that, not even to say that I wore revealing things. Again, it doesn't matter.

Danielle from chapter 2 also had conversations about police violence with a close friend of hers who was Latina. These conversations helped her navigate the space between as well as see the similarities between her and her friends' experiences with the police. "One of my best friends, she's Mexican. She gets it. I find it hard talking about it with my white friends. I just felt it's been a lot of teaching. I don't wanna teach right now, but I feel for our friendship to work, you need to understand where I'm coming from." What helped Danielle feel comfortable talking with her friend was that they had shared experiences with the police. In relational gathering, shared experiences became one of the foundations for building solidarity—it made it easier to disclose and expand the center of recognition and valuation. However, with her white friend with whom she did not share experiences, bringing each other into view and expanding the center required additional labor. Yet, Danielle went on to describe how they bridged the gulf between them through storytelling, ongoing conversations, and empathy:

> It's been a lot of teaching. I think it's been helpful. One of my friends, she was like, "I truly didn't understand." She's like, "I will never understand how this will be. I do get a picture of when you're talking to me that can't be from my experience." I'm like, "You really just have to listen to what I have to say. It's how I'm feeling and be there for me." Hold that, yeah. She's like, "When you used to talk to me, I tried to put myself there and try to feel it. I realized I can't." I'm like, "I appreciate that." I appreciate you taking the time to listen to me and just hear me bitch about it.

Through listening, Danielle and her friend developed an understanding that they were not treated the same by the police. They also realized through the process that one did not have to relate to build community; they could simply listen and be supportive. Relational gathering, then, served as a site for self-definition and solidarity, as black women built relationships with themselves and others across shared and unshared lived experiences.

Alexis

"Just in your own words, what are you doing?"

Sitting down in the back corner booth of a semi-crowded restaurant, this was not the first time Alexis and I met. It's also not the first time we talked about my study. A week prior, we met at a local event on policing and schools. We sat next to each other and chatted about her activism and the interviews I was having with black women about the police. A medium brown-skinned, black, African American, bisexual woman in her late twenties, Alexis locally organized against police violence in her neighborhood. She facilitated community conversations and was especially passionate about removing cops from schools. This was because, as she would share in our interview, she remembered what it was like to have the police patrol her school every day in the working-poor neighborhood in which she grew up. She remembered the police "arrest[ing] people and doing whatever."

Alexis now wanted me to explain the purpose of the project again. She wanted to know my story and how it related to the study before continuing the interview. After listening to me share parts of my story, Alexis decided she was okay with sharing hers:

> My interactions with police stem from the school environment. It was usually friends or being in educational spaces and seeing police officers getting called and slamming kids and doing all of that and knowing—okay, I'm black. I'm not trying to fool with that . . . those are my first recollections of interactions with police.

As a teenager, Alexis had her own police encounters. Arrested by an officer close to her school for breaking curfew and loitering, she described what it was like to be handcuffed and forced to sit on the side of the street.

> That was my first interaction with the police to where I was like, "I don't understand why this has to be the outcome. My mom can't afford that. We can't go to court. My bad. I will go in the house." We're sitting there having that conversation, and it's like, "Y'all wasn't even worried about us. Y'all over here patrolling the elementary school. We're not doing nothing. We're not bothering nobody." It was that whole back and forth and vouching for your life. I feel like I'm vouching for my life. Please, just let us go home. Why do you gotta do all of this? Can we get a warrant in? Something.

She compared her encounter to those of her white peers who also skipped curfew and "know for a fact Sarah from around the corner . . . got caught out the house and went home. Ain't nobody had no tickets. Ain't nobody go to court. None of that happened." Despite having witnessed police violence on several occasions, being arrested let her know that her place was different from Sarah's. "That was a moment where I realized I don't have grace like that."

Alexis and her parents went to court. The lawyers and judge treated her parents poorly. "They weren't even trying to hear them." This was because, as Alexis explained, her mother was a single parent and her father was disabled. She felt a lot of shame about the experience, for her parents having to go to court, and having to face the reality that they couldn't afford the ticket. She felt she put her mother in an awful situation because "my mom is a felon, she was in and out of jail." She hated that her parents had to go to court for her. "Ah, she got to be in front of these people. I know we don't got this. I really feel disappointed in myself for putting us in this situation."

Alexis's encounter and the family's court experience prompted a police talk. Alexis's mother questioned her, "What if something would've happened to you 'cause somebody would've did something to you?" She explained how the situation could've turned out differently and that "police also could have been a danger to you." Her mother emphasized that Alexis would not get the same chances as some of her peers. In the end, the police encounter and court appearance made Alexis feel like she was "in a bad dream." These talks continued, and her mother shared what it was like to deal with the police and be incarcerated. In turn, Alexis shared with her mother what it was like to watch this growing up. "I've been that child," she explained to me about her and her sister. "We've been overtly aware of what's going on around me and the emotions of the women in my family."

The conversations in her family continued and expanded over time to include herself, her sister, her mother, her father, and her stepmother—her mother's partner. Recalling one of the talks, Alexis critiqued how she was called an "old soul" as a child. She explained to her three parents, "No, you really just ended up having to mature way faster 'cause no one had the capacity to pay attention to you. [*nervous laughter*] I felt like a burden otherwise as a child, and putting those types of behaviors into my adult life is to just stay in my zone." Her mothers would listen and "always tell me to think if something's in my best interest." Alexis laughed as she described the questions her mothers would ask her:

"Is this in your best interest? Even if you wanna respond, is it in your best interest?" She said, "Replace asking yourself would I, could I, should I, and ask yourself is it in your best interest, regardless of what you know you should be able to do." I was like, "That's really great advice, Mom. Thank you."

Alexis's father also imparted advice, explaining to his daughters that "I just don't want you in the wrong place at the wrong time" and to "just be aware of your surroundings." Her father's advice made an impression, as Alexis always had "Pops in my head anytime police come," and tried her best to "avoid police."

Altogether, Alexis's father and mothers were "very open and candid." Her mothers, in particular, were "pretty awesome in that way." Now, "we're having these conversations that we never could have as kids or even as a adolescents," explaining, "We reflect a lot together." These conversations shifted her perspective of her one mother's experiences with the police and time in prison; she saw them "in a completely different light." Alexis explained that these talks were also "humanizing my parents" and she "wishes it for every black woman is that you get that experience," to "work on those relationships . . . they need a lot of repair."

I asked Alexis where she felt comfortable having conversations about police violence against black women. Outside of her parents, she, too, only felt comfortable with other black women, "'cause it's not healing otherwise." This doesn't mean she doesn't talk about it. She broke down how she otherwise disclosed her story in a way that gave off the illusion of vulnerability without actually being vulnerable.

> I'm a soapboxer. I've learned to share my story in a way to where it isn't actually healing for me, but it's testimonial, almost. It's like, "Oh, okay, da, da, da, da." I know how to share enough to share, but really not enough to work on myself. The reason why I do that is 'cause I'm just really guarded as a human. I think my space is with other humans that I feel I can relate to that experience.

As Alexis explained, she was only comfortable with other people who could *feel* her experiences:

> When I'm with black women, that's what gets me is this type of thing. I can talk about this, 'cause I feel like, you know, I'm not tripping, right? You know I'm not crazy. You're not gonna let it out, and you can relate, and we can move forward. If I gotta have that conversation with someone I gotta explain some shit to at any point, then it's like, "This feels like work. This feels heavy, and it feels pointless. You could've went online and read that this is a real thing. Now, instead of hearing my experience, you're challenging it." I don't wanna deal with that. That doesn't feel safe.

When she did get a chance to gather with black women, sharing her story felt different, explaining how it "felt so good."

> We're all in here crying. [*laughter*] What's going on with you? Let it out. Let it out. Let it out. Let it out and puttin' love on each other and just really having that understanding that we have this experience. That's why I'm reading *Sisters of the Yam*. That's why I was like, "That's my answer." When I'm around black women, I get healed. When it's just us, when we can just talk about whatever, it's a great experience for me.

As much as Alexis felt comfortable talking with other black women about their shared experiences, she nevertheless felt uncomfortable talking with some about black queer women's experiences. She recognized that among some black women, the center became exclusionary and did not expand to include black queer people's testimonies. Thus, Alexis talked about police violence against black queer people only with other black queer people. In those spaces, time was mostly spent discussing "the violence that other black people have on our queer black bodies . . . It's just the anti-gay experience that black people have inherited and they hold onto. It's just -isms. You don't wanna deal with all those -isms, so you gotta find you somebody to hate." She pointedly asked me, "You in sociology. Y'all have to read Paulo. Didn't y'all?"

"Mm-hm."

"Yeah, it's literally like that. [*laughing*] The pedagogy of the oppressed in action."

"How does that feel?"

"It feels like a mouse fricking running on a wheel, right? It's like, argh. We're just oppressing each other. Come on. We gotta stop this shit."

When I asked Alexis how she coped with intraracial violence, she responded, "Not well. I respond pretty angrily, honestly. [*laughing*] I don't think in a healthy way. I'm just about it. I'm just like, 'Shut the fuck up.'" Alexis got especially angry growing up when watching her mothers navigate homophobia in black spaces. "I don't have healthy response or coping mechanisms . . . They've been together for eleven [years]. That's mama one and mama two." She shared that when her grandfather died, he was "a traditional black type, and so his stuff was at a church."

> We had to go to the funeral, and then we had to sit in the church and listen to the pastor they chose rail about black gay people ruining the black family unit. I'm sitting there with both of my moms, and it's like, "This is so fucked up. I'm sick of this shit." [*laughing*] I wanna tell you to shut up. We're strong because of my moms. You're directly shitting on our family unit, and I don't got time for it. Yeah. I'm not in a positive, healthy response way at all. I just be ready to throw all the curse words [*laughter*].

Alexis drew from this anger and her conversations with her mothers and father to organize and disrupt communal spaces around policing in schools that did not include black girls or LGBTQ+ youth's experiences.

> I'm that woman. That's also why I was interested [in the project], 'cause I'm the woman who's always correcting black men when they say, "Man, black

men, da, da, da." I'm always like, "It's all of us. It's not just you. You get to be the poster child for black criminalization, but all black kids are getting criminalized." At first, I used to have a lot of resentment and anger in that messaging. Why do I gotta explain this to you? I think now just having a real-world understanding of the impacts that masculinity have on boys in general and learning and taking all those experiences and put them together—it gives me a lot more patience with black men in that way. I first think you probably just don't know, and that's it. You just aren't aware of the experiences that black women have, because we have conditioned ourselves not to share those experiences and to put your healing before ours.

But from her conversations with her parents, Alexis learned that having these "uncomfortable" conversations and sharing stories people wouldn't otherwise hear was "a part of my healing process." She called herself "a positive disruptor," and we talked back and forth as she explained to me what she meant by this.

"What is that?" I asked, "What does that mean, a positive disrupter?"

"Some disruption is positive, and it garners long-term positive responses. In the short-term, it might feel uncomfortable. You might feel disrupted, and you might feel mad, even. In the long-term, this disruption was positive."

"Hm. I've never heard that before."

"It was needed. It was necessary. It was important for me to say it, even if it sucked to hear it, or even if it sucks to be the one that has to say it. It was important to be said. Yes, it's a disruption, but how else are we gonna recognize that we need change?"

"I like that. I've never heard of that before. I feel like I'm gonna use that. I'm gonna put it in my back pocket."

We laughed together. "Yeah," Alexis replied. "That's why I put it in my pocket. I was like, 'Okay, this is me.' I was like, 'Oh, my God.' That's me, 'cause I'm always having to deal with being reprimanded for saying something. I'm like, 'But wasn't we all thinkin' it?'"

"Isn't it, though?" [*We laughed.*] "That's always my thing. *We all thinkin' it.*"

"Yeah!"

"Why you mad 'cause I said it?"

"Exactly! So, it's choosing to be in a space of discomfort and being okay with it and being like, 'I'ma be whatever. I'm gonna be uncomfortable anyway, so I might as well say what I'm gonna say.' . . . We got a lotta experiences as black women, and I don't feel like we talk about it."

Alexis took these "positive disruptions" into different spaces with her as she moved throughout her day. She took them to her organizing against school police and to her home. For example, during a recent conversation, someone disregarded black girls' experiences with police.

> But what about the black girl who's getting frickin' rubbed up on the side of the road when she gets pulled over? She's not coming home and telling you, 'cause she don't think you can handle it. Now, I'm walking around with this type of hurt and baggage, and you get to say you the only one getting hurt?! I'm still able to be resilient. It's this resentful type of dynamic. It's like, they treat me like shit, too, bro.

Disruption, for Alexis, can be healing. "Part of my healing process is to make sure you're aware of what you're doing to me . . .' Okay, you feel uncomfortable. This is gonna be a two-way street.' I have a lotta conversations like that."

Having uncomfortable conversations in her community and family gave Alexis hope. "But then, I even sometimes resent the hopefulness. It's like, [*laughter*] why am I feeling hope? Look at this shit [*laughter*]." Organizing community conversations also helped Alexis cope.

> I know that I need to put myself in spaces where I can try to break my perception that's making me sick. It's making me sick to feel this way, and so I try to put myself in spaces and be active and talk about my—this is how I cope is to put myself in spaces where I don't have a choice but to face it, talk about it, see police officers as humans. I don't got a choice. I gotta sit in a circle with you. I gotta do this and realize that—step outside of that, taking classes, and just trying to really understand where everybody's coming from.

For Alexis, uncomfortable conversations and accountability are necessary for healing and social change. "I just feel like systems of accountability are the only way that we can expect a system that was never made for us to not hurt us. I think you just have to constantly be engaged, because it's not for us. It's the same way for the schools." For her, an accountable space was "that safe space."

When asked how she coped with her experiences, Alexis replied, "I don't know if I'm coping with it or not. Maybe I'm not. I'm not sure, and I don't know if I'm doing it right or doing it healthily. I'm just doing the best I can." She then turned the interview back around on me again, laughing as she asked: "How are other black women coping? If I could get a matrix [*laughter*] or a list of real intentional ways *you're* coping with police violence. How are *you*—are *you* having conversations about it?"

Collective Gathering: Abolition Feminism
and Positive Disruptions to Everyday Policing

An ability to look both inward and outward, to meet both immediate demands
and confront broad systems of injustice, and to think in complicated and
layered ways about abolition represents a feminist approach to change.

—ANGELA Y. DAVIS, GINA DENT, ERICA R. MEINERS,
AND BETH E. RICHIE, *ABOLITION. FEMINISM. NOW.*[16]

Abolition feminism is a praxis of looking outside and inside communities to
address violence—in all its iterations and connections—to build new worlds
grounded in care and relationality.[17] Thus, Ruth Wilson Gilmore refers to abolition as "life in rehearsal," which involves practicing each and every day ways
of being, relating, and building alternative pathways to legibility and safety
grounded in shared recognition of humanity.[18] As a communal gatherer, Alexis's activism focuses on addressing police violence at the intersection of
schools, neighborhoods, and families. This work is grounded in her lived experiences, particularly in growing up watching the police assault her peers at
school and her own police encounters. One specific encounter as a teen led to
her and her parents going to court. This prompted a talk in her family about
the police being a "danger" to Alexis, with her parents emphasizing that officers
would treat her differently than her white peers. Within these conversations,
her family—including her mother, stepmother, father, and sister—began to
collectively gather, expanding a relational center of recognition and valuation
through sharing stories about their lived experiences and providing support.
Moving together toward self- and collective-definition, they rehearsed a different way of being from talking openly, explaining how they "reflect[ed] a lot
together" and that this has been critical to "humanizing" one another and repairing their relationships.

For some of the women I interviewed, engaging in this collective gathering
in other spaces, however, had proven far more difficult. Some, like Alexis, practiced dissemblance as self-protection or "learned to share my story in a way to
where it isn't actually healing for me." Confronting everyday policing in her
organizing spaces, she explained how sharing her story "feels like work" and
more an intellectual exercise rather than community building. Going through
the motions, she learned to appear open in spaces "that doesn't feel safe" to
guard her privacy. These unsafe spaces included schools, churches, and grassroots organizations, wherein she and others faced challenges to expanding the

center to include their stories about sexism and homophobia in addition to racism. However, Alexis often spoke anyway, framing herself as "a positive disruptor."[19] Disrupting the silence was critical to her gathering and creating alternative processes. "Part of my healing process is to make sure you're aware of what you're doing to me." On the other hand, Alexis also described how "with other humans that I feel I can relate to that experience," she could more easily move through the dissonance to self-define and create black feminist thought: "I can talk about this, 'cause I feel like you know I'm not tripping, right? You know I'm not crazy. You're not gonna let it out, and you can relate, and we can move forward."

While Alexis was able to collectively gather in her family, other black women described their desire to collectively gather to build alternative social worlds as a pathway to organizing, activism, and other daily forms of political mobilization. In these journeys, they highlighted how the ability to share their stories and produce knowledge about their lived experiences was tied to the creation of safe spaces and real alternative pathways to protection. Thus, Veronica from chapters 2 and 3, explained how she felt she couldn't collectively gather in black churches where she was excluded from the center because of her gender identity and sexuality. "Even if it was a good organizing space for black issues, I couldn't receive the benefit to that because I was queer." As a result, Veronica took her desire to collectively gather elsewhere and worked to build safe spaces to share her story, develop knowledge, and mobilize action:

> We created our collective because we don't feel accepted in a lot of white organizations because they don't recognize the issues of—[pause] we don't feel accepted in a lot of LGBT organizations because a lot of them are predominantly white, and they don't address the issues of systemic racism and racism in general and poverty and classism and all of those things. They don't really address those. Then we didn't feel safe in black spaces because they don't acknowledge that LGBT being a member of the LGBT community also makes you a target for racism. We developed our own space to where we can push our experiences and try to help improve the lives at all intersections of our identity.

Everyday policing reproduced exclusions along many lines, and through her search for safety and recognition, Veronica developed a multiple consciousness of these lines in different contexts. To collectively gather among black women, Veronica stated it was important for black cisgender and transgender women to engage in dialogue, care, and accountability as a way to build solidarity, and that there needed to be "education on both sides of the issues." Also needed is "validation on both sides of the issues." Veronica underscored how black cisgender women engaged in the everyday policing of black transgender women, reproducing the silence matrix that can make it difficult and dangerous for them to share their stories and collaborate in alternate world-making. As Veronica explained:

> A lot of cisgender black women see black transgender women as not women. They, again, think that they're just gay men or whatever. They're belittling their lives and they're undervaluing who they are as people.

In similar ways to how cisgender black women described the labor of "teaching" across differences in race with white women and gender with black men, Veronica also discussed the labor of teaching black cisgender women about black transgender women and gender-nonconforming people. Noting she was "trying to be really patient with people who are trying to learn," however:

> I would advise cis black women to not learn directly from trans women unless they're offering experience. It's still really annoying when a cis black woman, or a cis woman in general, is asking me a bunch of questions about transness or why this matters or why non-binary people are weird. They're asking me all of these questions, and it's not like I—I don't have the time always to teach them. If they cared, I would say read about it from trusted resources and educate yourself before engaging with a queer person just so that everyone's on the same page or something . . . We all need to be aware of where we're at and what needs to be changed, and to do that, we have to all educate ourselves.

For relational and collective gathering, Veronica and other black women explained how knowledge is situated and how people in a position of ignorance needed to take personal responsibility for their political education when working across lines to build solidarity. Specifically, educating oneself before engaging in dialogue was for Veronica integral to creating solidarity and safer spaces as it reduced the labor of sharing their stories.

Last, Devin, whose story was shared in the previous chapter, discussed how the imaginations of those who experienced police violence and incarceration were a critical resource in collectively gathering and envisioning alternative worlds. "Yeah, there's a lot of work around the country around police abolition, prison abolition. I think there are models around the world to deal with violence in our own communities, and quote unquote, crime in our own communities. I think it's hard to imagine living outside of a carceral system for people, because that's all they know." To do her organizing work, Devin mobilized love in the spaces between. "One of my mentors is always like, 'You can't do this work out of anger cause it just fizzles out. You got to do it out of love.'"

Devin's commitment was fortified by the moments when she witnessed black women engage in self-definition, or observed them stepping into their power by sharing their stories and pushing back against the veils that render them "missing." Giving an example, she shared the story of a friend whose baby tragically died in childbirth while she labored incarcerated. She was afraid to speak out about her experiences because of the grief and potential for retaliation, saying she "didn't want to say nothing cause she was scared." Over time, Devin and others relationally and collectively gathered with her each day, "call[ing] in to check on her" and providing resources while they organized on her behalf. Devin intimately shared that one of the most powerful moments was witnessing her friend practice self-definition, and then publicly sharing her story:

> The biggest thing that came out of that, fuck all the rest of that stuff, was whenever my friend—'cause for a long time she couldn't get up there and address these folks. I would just go and hold her hand and tell the story. By the end of it, she was telling her own story to those people, and they had to look at her and listen. That was probably the most powerful moment I've ever seen . . . She was able to hold people accountable, and not—[*pause*] she stepped into her power, just like, straight stepped into it.

Everyday Policing and Gathering: Linking Black Feminist Thought to the Conditions of Safety

Policing works to stratify people, or, as Audrey states, create "different experiences and understanding of what police are for," and then engenders a "missing-ness" around their stories. As we saw in the previous chapters, black women were explicitly taught to see their mouths as a source of deviance and cause for punishment. While everyday policing pathologized speaking and pushed black women, girls, and their stories to the margins, gathering linked storytelling about experiences and the co-creation of knowledge with the everyday work of building safety and solidarity. To gather meant to, as Alexis states, 'positively disrupt' the silence and develop black feminist thought in daily life. It meant to, as Collins writes, "question not only what has been said about African American women but the credibility and the intentions of those possessing the power to define."[20] Engaging in this questioning—whether individually, relationally, or collectively—was a direct challenge to everyday policing. It encompassed what historian and organizer Nicole Burrowes describes as "the potential power of struggling together."[21] In reflecting on the lessons learned through Sista II Sista's organizing around black and Latinx women's experiences of police and interpersonal violence in New York in the 1990s and 2000s, Burrowes describes the power of questioning and naming, to "push open more space to be expansive in how we think about change and respond to the huge challenges that face us today . . . if we can truly see each other, if we recognize and have the space to name the differences in our experiences of oppression—and to demonstrate how messy it actually is."[22] Importantly, gathering was not some idealistic one-time conversation, but a commitment to ongoing processes that embraced the messiness of everyday life and addressed people's experiences of violence. While sharing people's "missing" stories may make people, as Alexis describes, "feel uncomfortable" in the short-term, these accounts needed to be heard for longer-term social change, for what Threadcraft calls people and world-building.[23] In their day-to-day lives, black women gathered to build safe conditions, explicitly engaging in black feminist epistemology to dialogue about their experiences. Among them, empathy, care, and trust were essential tools for navigating the space between and building alternatives to the police. Gathering linked the ability to listen and learn from people's stories with the development of accountability systems and protection in everyday life.

Given the silence matrix, black women discussed how they had few, if any, safe spaces to gather and share their stories without the fear of sanctions. As a result, most individually gathered through poetry, their imaginations, and creative expressions. These articulations gave them a safe space to name what was unnamed, work through their dissonance, and clarify their perspectives or standpoint. Some also found ways to connect the knowledge they created by themselves to others who had shared them as well as those who did not share their lived experiences. In this way, relational gathering occurred when the center of recognition and valuation expanded from the self to include other people and their stories. When the center contracted, the exclusions illuminated unsafe conditions, wherein people were unwilling to listen and address violence on the margins. Yet, within many intracommunal unsafe spaces, black women were expected to listen to, empathize with, and humanize black heteropatriarchal viewpoints.

Thus, broader societal and intracommunal relational gathering in everyday life often took place under the cover of dissemblance, outside of (*or in between*) white and black heteropatriarchal institutions and structures. Among the black women I interviewed, intracommunal relational gathering mostly occurred with their friends, othermothers, and in some cases, mothers when they got older. Within these conversations, shared experiences became a foundation for care, accountability, and linked understandings of the social world. For example, Quita was able to share stories, develop trust, and reliably access her mother as an alternative to calling the police during domestic violence disputes.

Ultimately, black women consistently used the word "healing" to describe spaces and people with whom they could relationally and collectively gather. This healing involved the thinning of veils through sharing stories, listening, humanizing one another, repairing relations, and building a collective politics of protection. For black women, safe spaces were where and with whom they could engage in this process to create everyday alternatives for safety. Thus, in the first chapter, we learned from Kristen how conversations with her mother helped her learn "how violence can just manifest itself in so many ways that I didn't know or I didn't recognize." Audrey also individually gathered through her poetry as a way of struggling with difficult things in order to "work towards freedom." Similarly, Quita's relational gatherings with her mother helped her challenge her father's abuse and find safety. Further, Alexis's relational and collective gathering among her family gave her the tools and confidence to positively disrupt everyday policing and say what needed to be said. Black women also discussed how spaces could easily shift from safe to unsafe. Importantly, black women who gathered discussed how power was not static, but rather, relational, contextual, and based on the many lines shaping our social worlds.

a gathering poem:
the space between black women participants and an outsider-within[1]

"i don't like to talk about other people's business"

                                     "the people that death leaves behind is very difficult"

"but she's had some experiences. i'll say that"

"it has affected her"

                                                          "it has"

"she's been through a lot of stuff"

                             "she's been warring ever since"

"she doesn't speak on it much"

                           "because with war there's wounds"

"we live in a society that individualizes us as well as makes us feel like who we are and what we are don't belong to us. now i think that i'm the only one who's being abused. so, i'm alone in this part. i feel like i'm the only one. So, if i feel like i'm the only one, then i'm gonna do only-one things. i'm gonna think no one can help me through this. no one knows what this is like. i can't talk to anybody"

"who am i gonna talk to?"

"can we just talk? i don't understand"

"can we just meet up once a month?"

"if i do talk to them, what is that gonna look like?"

"i don't know"

"i think humans, in general, tend to not deal with their emotions or where
they stem from or understanding the bigger concepts that force themselves
on their lives as individuals. i don't think people want to think about that.
i think it's easier to just . . . [pause] . . . i don't remember your question.
i know that i'm babbling"

"let me know if i'm talking too much"

"i know this is a lot"

"let me know if i go on a tangent"

"i got, like, three decades worth of stories"

"the stories"

"i mean, i would be interested to learn more stories"

"i think the individual stories are always helpful"

"it just feels like black girls need more stories about it being okay
to listen to themselves"

"the stories of the women who—black women who had their stories shut down"

"whether it's because they passed away or because they were 'got in that way,' or maybe
the media snuffed out their story for a bigger one"

"those stories need to be told"

"it's happening every day, but you're not gonna pick our stories"

[loud silence]

"there's negative stereotypes against black women
that make people think that black women . . ."

".. . they deserved what they got"

"or how did they contribute to the heightened
violence against them for some reason?"

"were they doing something?"

"they agitated the situation"

"were they saying something?"

"they had a bad attitude"

"were they acting a certain way?"

"they escalated it"

"i think that black women have this cloud over them that so many people believe . . ."

[*long pause*]

".. . to combat that is very difficult"

[*long pause*]

"we shouldn't have to be saints to survive"

[*long pause*]

"last night, i was under so much stress"

"we think that what we do doesn't affect the other being in any way"

"other people can do all kinds of shit"

"but God forbid you do even half of those things"

[*break from fieldwork*]

"was there any question that was difficult for you to answer?"

"mmm, i think any time you ask me how am i coping with anything"

"i don't know"

"it's difficult to answer"

"why do you think that is?"

"i don't know"

"well, how do you feel like you coped with everything?"

"huh?"

"what was the question?"

"i don't"

"it just is what it is"

"i try not to think about it honestly"

"there's not really—just try to not think about it"

"honestly, how i coped is by not really thinking about it"

"try to think about something else"

"my mind is racing"

"i can't manually turn it down and center"

"oh, lord, it was hard"

"just really trying to focus on other things"

"and thinking of it as this like a one-off"

"i just push through"

"it's just your everyday life"

"i guess you move on with your day"

"my whole moving-on-type-thing"

"i don't think i have good coping mechanisms"

"you know, i was really young"

"so, a lot of make-believe"

"i don't even know"

"i would say a lot of make-believe"

"a lot of pretending things weren't as they actually were"

"i don't think i do"

"i'm trying to find my way around it"

"i think i'm just now coping with it"

"i turned a lot of my feelings off"

"the coping is really hard because it's a thing where, like, you know that this happens"

"you know that this happens"

"you can't do anything about it"

"nothing is going to happen or change"

"i just was apathetic"

"it was the only way that I could be 'there.'"

"cause otherwise it was very painful"

"i feel things"

"feeling that pain is like—"

"i'm just angry a lot"

"i don't think i really—i get angry"

"i get real angry"

"there's like this kind of impotent rage."

"rage inducing"

"it's fucked up"

"also, if you go around angry all the time; white people may come up and be like:
'you're just angry all the time'"

"you know, i'm going to go to jail if i express this anger to these people"

"i wanted a place that would recognize my anger"

"a place where everyone was just yelling and screaming"

"i'll cry sometimes"

"sometimes, i cry"

"i remember one day i just cried, and cried, and cried, and cried, and just slept"

"i was going through this spiral"

"drinking"

"i drank"

"i felt like i was powerless"

"i'm not going to lie, i've done fucked-up things"

"i did fucked-up things because i was traumatized"

"we're just dwelling on something that is awful"

"i literally get depressed and i just wanna stay in bed all day"

"it brought me into a depression"

"i was feeling really anxious"

"i would get so anxious"

"just a weird cycle of selective forgetting"

"i put a lot of dreams on hold and assumed that they wouldn't be possible"

"i wasn't able to ever effectively communicate"

"i pray"

"girl, i talk to Jesus a lot"

"i just hope God sees"

"i tend to hold my breath during the day"

"a lot of breathing"

[*loud silence*]

"i have to tell myself i'm not in my head, it's not just me, this is a thing"

[*loud silence*]

"it feels like my choices and just something's being taken away from me as a person"

[*loud silence*]

"your place is to be invisible"

[*loud silence*]

"i just don't think there's a lot of spaces"

"to talk about what was going on in our life"

"i don't think there's a space for black women to talk
about our issues generally, unless they relate to children"

[*long sigh*]

"i feel like a lot of times black women are forgotten"

[*long sigh*]

"i wouldn't even know who to go to"

[*long pause*]

"i don't have, like, a set person to go to, like,
'hey, this happened, what can I do about this?'"

[*long pause*]

"i think we're just afraid to speak"

"and no one is going to follow us"

"we're afraid that we're not going to have a strong voice"

"and no one is going to listen"

"i just tried to tell the truth and just make sure everybody knew how i felt"

"we're afraid no one is going to listen"

"even with my situations to where i didn't speak about it
because it's like, whatever, nothing's gonna happen"

"nothing is going to happen anyway"

"who do you feel uncomfortable talking with
about police violence and black women and girls with?"

"umm . . ."

". . . white people"

"why?"

"white people are tired of hearing about
black people being killed by police"

"i feel like with my white friends on campus,
there's so much performance . . ."

"if i told my white friends or some white coworkers that,
they'll be like, 'oh, what's the big deal? don't worry about it.'"

"i'd be like, 'no, you don't understand'"

"i just felt it's been a lot of teaching,
i don't wanna teach right now"

[*pausing*] [*fidgeting*] [*looking away*] [*whispering*]

"i did look into counseling. i told them i don't think i want anyone white,
either, 'cause i need to be sure someone can relate to what I'm talking about."

"then the very first person they give me was a white, old, country woman"

[*laughter*]

"i'm not surprised"

"i was just, like, no"

"so, i never went"

"i didn't feel safe talking there"

"so, i didn't even go"

"we're not there for people to gawk at us,

write notes,

and figure out how they can better connect with their clients of color"

[*long pause*] [*fidgets*]

"and also, around black men"

[*long pause*][*looks around*]

"people want to say things like,
'oh, it's harder for black men, you know'"

"nobody really thinks about how black women
are the fastest-growing prison population"

"but black men"

"but that's not what
I'm trying to talk about right now"

"but black men"

"but there's a lot of conversations
already being had about police violence and black men"

"but black men"

[*pause*]

"it happens in conversations honestly anytime
that i try to talk specifically about black women"

"when black women start talking about their intersections, black men are
unwilling to listen"

[*pause*]

"it's like when you talk about black women
all people hear is the absence of men.
but, when you talk about black men,
people are less inclined to inquire
about the absence of black women"

[*pause*]

"we're conditioned as black women to allow everyone to come before us"

"it feels like an uphill battle"

"i feel like they both carry burdens"

"it could be any of us"

"a lot of cis black women see black trans women as not women. they, again, think that they're just gay men or whatever. they're belittling their lives, and they're undervaluing who they are as people" "it could be any of us"

"people read her—
the police read her as a man,
especially at night.
i know that she's been in situations
and will be profiled.
i don't know,
i think queer folks just catch hell"

"if i'm specifically wanting for whatever reason,
to talk about black women's experiences,
let me talk about black women's experiences,
it's not oppression olympics"

"it's still really annoying when a cis black woman,
or a cis woman in general,
is asking me a bunch of questions about transness or why this matters
or why non-binary people are weird"

"i know black trans women are some of the most vulnerable folks out here
when it comes to violence"

"at some point, we can't keep on saying that we want different results and we
continue to utilize the language of the oppressor.
labels—it's a very white man's oppressive way"

"why must we conform to these boxes?"

[pause]

"some disruption
is positive,
and it garners long-term positive responses.
in the short-term,
it might feel uncomfortable.
you might feel disrupted,
and you might feel mad, even.
in the long-term,
this disruption was positive"

[pause]

"we would all love to move beyond the conversation, but we can't move beyond the conversation *until* the conversation is settled"

                    "how is change going to go about if we can't even discuss it?"

"what would you want to say?"

    "it's just the anti-gay experience that black people have inherited and they hold onto.
                    it's just -isms. you don't wanna deal with all those -isms,
                    so, you gotta find you somebody to hate"

"i mean, i think that it would be important to note that there's more to this than just them versus us. I don't know how you would word it, but I think that that's an underlying factor that needs to be addressed. once that's addressed, then maybe we can move forward with positive relationships. but I think that's always blocked us"

"i would advise cis black women to not learn directly from trans women unless they're offering experience"

"you just aren't aware of the experiences that black women have, because we have conditioned ourselves not to share those experiences and to put your healing before ours"

"i don't have the time always to teach them. if they cared, i would say read about it from trusted resources and educate yourself before engaging with a queer person just so that everyone's on the same page or something"

"i just felt it's been a lot of teaching.
i don't wanna teach right now"

                    "because if we're teaching black men these things
                    and we're not teaching black women, that's a disconnect to me"

"it's a process of popular education, i think that's what wrong with the way we teach. it's very from, 'oh, you are you, and i am the one with the knowledge and i will pour that into your mind.' instead of taking people's experiences, connecting the dots, interjecting some information, doing an action and revisiting, the praxis of it all, right. we start to internalize on it, violence and all that shit whenever we can't spread it"

"are there spaces where you do feel comfortable
talking about black women's experiences of violence?"

[*pause*]

"i started using dating sites to find black women"

"i was like, i don't know where y'all are at,
but I need—i realized this is what's missing in my life"

"so, i started meeting friends on okcupid"

"bumble has a bff side, so you find friends,
specifically, so you don't have to be the awkward person
being like, i don't wanna date you but—"

"it just sucks that i don't have that person to relate to. i literally just two days
ago met with someone off of bumble because i'm looking out there for a
black homegirl, just so i can have someone to talk about this with"

"i feel for the friendship to work,
you need to understand where i'm coming from"

"last night we were talking about our experiences of being labeled as the
angry black woman"

"we were able to talk about it, and it was such a relief to have that"

[*sigh*] [*pause*]

"i'm having a good time just being regular with you right now,
like shit, just being chill"

"i think that's really all you have is your community and your network" "what advice do you have for other black women?"

"if you can handle by yourself"
"if you can try to not call the police"
"if there is anything you can do, do not call the police"
"try to avoid them"
"do not call the police"
"there is no reason to call the police"

"it was just that other fucked-up person's problem"

"when you go through that violence, you lose a piece of yourself, and you try to find that piece in everything and everybody"

"you have to understand that you never lost it"

"don't recreate this narrative of you being incomplete"

"that keeps you searching"

                              "searching for something outside of yourself"

"all the time"
                    "all the time"

                                   "all the time outside of yourself"

"when really, you just need to be still with yourself"

                                   "you realize you ain't never lost nothing"

"how many women have experienced some sort of violence—black women—towards their bodies and never talked to other black women or their daughters about moving through and healing from that trauma and not going through the same rabbit hole of what it means to not love yourself?"

   "... be very open with your experiences. . . . all experiences aren't just your experiences . . ."

"now has she been taking care of herself?"

"if we can take care of ourselves and each other the way we take care of white people or black men . . . and have all of that protection for us . . . and save some love for us . . . i think that we can do amazing things . . ."

"i think you should definitely own your power"

"that you are loved, i don't think they get that enough, that you're allowed to put yourself first"

"i know we talked about coping,
but like, how do you heal from all of it?"

"people don't understand. when you're traumatized, you have a lotta unlearning to do"

"i had to heal through my trauma"

"allowing myself to see it. I feel like maybe it was some defense mechanisms. i don't see this, if I repress this, or if i don't see this, because if you do think about it, it's hurtful and it's mean"

"i try to put positive things out"

"i take a lot of photos of black people in positive things"

"what does that do for you,
putting positive things out there?"

"well, sometimes i feel silly. but i think mostly, i think it's helped out in the
way i personally cope. it doesn't get rid of everything, but i think it definitely
does help just getting through it 'cause it's not gonna go away"

"it's not gonna go away"

"it's gonna take a lot to make that kind of stuff go away"

"what do you do to take care of yourself?"

"i have a therapist"

"i honor and respect her for it"

"dance in the sun"

"yoga"

"nature"
"i love being outside"

"i could sit outside all day"
"i like food"

"hanging out with people who are lovely"

"amazing people that add to my life"

"journaling"

"ceramics"

"woodworking"

"painting"

"checking on people. that's all"

"it's like walking up a hill
for five minutes
and then i can—[*deep breath*] i'm okay,
i'm less anxious and I can focus on stuff"

"i think building, carpentry is therapeutic for me cause it's slow and i have a hard time" "we have to build it"

"i'm an advocate"

"i started a nonprofit"

"i'm active and involved"

"i do all their photos and flyers"

"by being active"

"that's really how i've been coping with it 'cause instead of just being surprised and sad, try to better the lives of a couple of people so that they never have to deal with something like that or that I had to go through"

"that's where my realization that the work is not done—that i cannot climb into the hole and just be"

"i didn't want people to throw me away, so why would i throw people away understanding that they too have experienced trauma?"

"let me not pressure myself to save everyone"

"again, i think finding community, that was, is the most important here because it's harder to ignore twenty voices speaking about police violence than it is to ignore one. involving yourself with people that support you is probably the only way that you can really deal with police violence"

"i just want black people to live and not die and not get killed for no reason by the police"

"what gives you the energy to keep doing that work?"

"i don't have no energy to keep doing it"

"it's hard"

"i try"

"but it's hard"

"you can't do this work out of anger
'cause it'll just fizzle out"

"because it's intense"

[long pause]

"you start to move through it"

"by taking my time and trying to just do it"

                                       "and not pushing myself too hard and being nice to myself"

"you realize how you have the capacity for humanity that other people don't have"

                                                      "like empathy and compassion"

                                       "i have to be intentional about how i express myself"

"i've been having to really find my voice about stuff"

                                  "the stories"

"'cause for a long time she couldn't get up there and address these folks. i would just go and hold her hand and tell the story. by the end of it, she was telling her own story to those people, and they had to look at her and listen. that was probably the most powerful i've ever seen"

"why do you think it was powerful, what made it powerful?"

"well, shit, she was able to hold people accountable, and not—she stepped into her power, just like straight stepped into it"

"you got to do it out of love"

field note memo: healing encompassed their embodied gathering journeys in the space between their lived experiences and themselves as well as with others . . . moving from margin to center of their stories and forming connections and building safe communities

"all of my advice is about really taking care of yourself. because if you don't, nobody else will. you gotta do it first"

"we live in a world that says that black women should never take the time to be with themselves"

"the world
will slow down
for black women"

"honor and love themselves"

"i feel like i—i mean, like, i have love to give,
but i certainly don't feel like I have any advice to give"

"i'm just getting to a space where i can be like, 'i'm a valuable person. i am
not a burden.' yeah. i'm just hittin' that, literally"

"i think i flourished very dramatically. . . . what i'm learning, it was the
community"

"it was the support of the community that i needed to thrive"

"my family . . . couldn't really assist me in that way. once i started getting
around better people, my life started to start shaping up, and started to
finally be able to accomplish the things that i'm most passionate about. i
guess i would say to my younger self, the people that you around are not the
only people that will be in your life always. try to move around. try to get to
know other people and try to find some trusted people. try to find people
that you can trust. i didn't feel like i could trust anyone at the time"

"i tell people i'm a combination of black women's prayers, faith, and some love"

[*long pause*]

"i feel much better"

"shannon, i hope you're taking care of yourself, too"

"thank you, [*long pause*] what do you want to see from this?"

"a vision"
"imagination of radical love and healing"
"a world where things are—people are fully human"
"people realizing their full humanity"
"making sure that my community is all right . . . but also personal freedom as well"
"yeah, freedom can be a few things"

Conclusion

"Missing" to Whom? Listening to Build Something Better

For four years, I listened to black women's stories: the ones "missing" from the databases, headlines, and intracommunal talks on policing. Many black women intimately relayed their willingness to share their personal histories as a praxis of hope that it would somehow help with "building something better" for themselves and other black women and girls. Indeed, in our interviews, they point to how black storytelling—even about the hardest moments in our lives—can be life affirming if we are committed to listening, learning, and changing conditions.[1] Yet, for those who had spoken before, they described the ways people in their lives unlisten. Specifically, they shared the challenges in reporting to school authorities and police departments; the shifting obstacles in trying to confide in their families and friends; the internal and external struggles talking about domestic violence, along with how these intimate encounters led to encounters with the police; and the pressures to keep their stories to themselves within grassroots and civic organizations dedicated to addressing police violence. Throughout all these different institutions and social relations, black women shared what happened when they pushed through the silence—detailing how they were often met with significant pushback, deflection, and punishment.

In the book's introduction, I posed the question: "Missing to whom?" And in sitting with this question since 2017 (*and much, much longer*), black women's stories make visible how "missing-ness" maps onto shared institutional and interpersonal investments in the dominant order, the one intersectionally built and rebuilt everyday through policing. Thus, this conclusion shifts us away from how difficult and dangerous it is for black women and girls to speak about violence in their daily lives and toward what can be learned if we listened to the stories shared in these pages: How does listening transform the way we understand the social problem of policing? How does listening transform the ways we conceptualize and track police violence? How does listening transform the ways we approach the creation of safety in everyday life?

How Does Listening Transform the Way
We Understand the Social Problem of Policing?

Black women's stories demonstrate that policing is too often treated as an isolated institution that enters people's lives at their worst moment and swiftly leaves. Their accounts push us to consider policing beyond the bounded and isolated institution, beyond the spectacle, and toward the way people in and out of uniform engage in policing everyday as a social process to regulate personhood and stories about violence. While violence creates schisms, silence moves in tandem with violence, breaking and bending black communities, social relations, and interior life into a complex web of social control. The silence matrix, consisting of the politics, norms, and sanctions that make it difficult and dangerous for black women and girls to speak about violence, lifts and analyzes multiple interconnected veils to allow us to see this process. In doing so, it brings into view how policing transitions from the institutional to the intimate in everyday life. It illuminates how coercive silences can take root within strategic silences and be used to mask or rationalize violence against those differently situated in systems of inequality. Indeed, it makes visible how the police as an institution requires the adoption of policing as an everyday social process to construct, reproduce, and normalize an intersectional, dominant order. Everyday policing, then, is how officers and others use violence and silence to build and rebuild their social worlds by withholding recognition, asserting dominance, and enforcing their interests and realities.

Excavating the elisions around policing, black women's experiences reveal how exclusions form protection and knowledge production about violence are inextricably linked—a connection that is integral to the maintenance of the dominant order in different social worlds. The African American Policy Forum's #SayHerName report calls out the public exclusion of police violence against black women and girls from media, organizing, and research.[2] In listening to black women's stories, I trace how these public exclusions are mirrored in intracommunal conversations and everyday resistance practices around policing. These exclusions obstruct our ability to see and hear experiences, revealing how what Richie describes as the violence matrix aligns different contexts through shared views and practices that make black women and girls vulnerable to public and private violence.[3] The silence matrix allows us to identify the linked circular process that draws lines and veils experiences of violence in everyday life, wherein: protection is grounded in beliefs about vulnerabilities; beliefs are created through the sharing of stories and inclusion in processes of co-creating knowledge about violence; and this knowledge shapes our practices of protection. The omission of black women's stories is critical to maintaining this closed loop, wherein veils took the epistemological place of black women's stories—forming the grounds by which others claimed to know and unknow their experiences. This distorted knowing and unknowing seeded an atmosphere of pathologized difference and indifference. It created an evolving and dynamic cover,[4] ushering in a vulnerability officers and others could leverage to target black women and girls with little to no pushback or accountability in multiple contexts. *Here,* police violence is not just about perceptions of racial threat and danger. Officers strategically leveraged the vulnerability of black women to target them, particularly in cases of police gender-based and sexual violence. Others in black women's lives were also able to mobilize exclusions from the intracommunal politics of protectionism to inflict various types of domestic and communal violence. Thus, black women came to recognize throughout their lives that they were not guaranteed protection from police, nor from their families and communities.

Looking into the silences around policing, black women's experiences show how, despite their differences, exclusions made them collectively vulnerable, as protection and non-pathologized legibility were scarce resources on the margins. Black feminists scholars of policing and violence, such as Treva B. Lindsey, Sarah Haley, Kali Gross, Christen Smith, Brooklynn Hitchens, Amber Joy Powell, and many others call attention to the race and gender lines etching out this place, as well as the other lines creating distinct vulnerabilities. Thus, while exclusion was encompassing at the intersection of anti-blackness and patriarchy, black women's experiences also bring into view the other lines co-constructing the margins and how distorted stories operated specifically— creating shared and distinct vulnerabilities to violence. Intersecting with race and gender, these other lines, of heteronormativity, social class, and disability simultaneously shaped black women's vulnerabilities and constructed pathways from the space between to legibility and inclusion within the dominant order. As Cohen and Grundy note, respectively, in *Boundaries of Blackness* and *Respectable*, pathologies and deification lined, expanded, and contracted these pathways, making them restrictive and coercive.[5] These pathways to legibility constituted unique conditions under which black women experienced violence, as they required people to adopt everyday policing as a social process of regulating others as well as aspects of themselves to achieve inclusion and rebuild their social worlds. Thus, specific pathways involved conformance to heteronormative gender roles, racial loyalty, the gender binary, the pathologization and deification of other differences, and silence around gender-based and sexual violence. Embedded in all of these pathways is what Carlson calls a politics of vulnerability, which entrenched certain standpoints and hierarchized people and their stories based on an intersectional social order.[6]

Here, officers oscillated between pathologizing and excluding black women from protection based on race, sexuality, gender identity, class, and disability. Officers used black women's multiple exclusions to inflict violence, especially sexual harassment and coercion. In the latter cases, officers would sometimes offer the protection and leniency within the broader carceral system that black women and girls do not receive in exchange for silence around inflicting these harms. While the Task Force on 21st Century Policing pushes police departments to diversify and mirror the racial demographics of communities as a way to address violence,[7] officers who shared a racial identification with black women would sometimes empathize with racial injustice in policing and express racial loyalty to gain black women's trust—strategically maneuvering around the cover of the veils to inflict sexual violence.

Also *here* were the ways Gómez points to how black women were culturally betrayed, or pushed to remain silent to protect their abusers while their experiences of intracommunal violence remained unaddressed.[8] As Richie notes, this entraps black women in cycles of abuse, with adherence to black heteropatriarchal ideals and submission to this order seen as pathways to legibility and protection.[9] Along with being framed as disloyal for calling the police, black women also described how officers empathized with abusers in their responses to heteropatriarchal violence. Some officers would even disclose how domestic violence existed in their own interpersonal relationships as well. Such gestures were less about empathy and more an effort to appear relatable while abusing their power as officers to sexually harass black women. Excluded from intracommunal protection and conversations on policing, black women were often left with no community-sanctioned pathways for seeking safety.

Thus, peering into the absences brings into view how the silence matrix worked alongside the violence matrix to normalize power asymmetries—putting and keeping black women in their shared and distinct places.

Importantly, black women's stories demonstrate that while white ignorance is a modality of power that works to erase and distort experiences of people of color,[10] ignorance is not just white—it's also patriarchal and heteronormative. Seeing ignorance intersectionally elucidates how certain standpoints leverage a politics of vulnerability in different spaces to make themselves fixed reference points for understanding social problems. Everyday policing created an atmosphere wherein black women had to face the realities of their vulnerabilities and experiences alongside the persistent public and private erasure of their stories. Consequently, many reflected on what it meant to name and unname, be confused by and understand, and speak about and hide their encounters with officers and others throughout their lives. Similarly, Garcia-Hallet describes how the carceral state can produce an embodied dissonance between ideals rooted in social control and people's lived realities and circumstances.[11] From *here*, dissonance and ignorance were resources that officers and others used to reproduce intersectional domination in everyday life.

Listening to black women's stories, it was clear that dissonance constructed a pathway for the internalization of everyday policing. Some black women coped with the lack of recognition and valuation by gravitating toward readily accessible loyalty, pathologizing, and respectability frames—everyday policing themselves and others. As such, silence—as the difficulty and danger associated with speaking about violence—did not constitute the absence of an encounter. It signaled unsafe conditions. It mirrored societal distinctions in ignorance, apathy, dissonance, and rationalizations for and investments in violence. Still, many black women eventually came to resist silence, journeying through dissonance and into knowing about their lived experiences others would not recognize. In their journeys through these conditions, black women developed what King describes as a multiple consciousness as a form of resistance that linked the systemically unnamed with the systemically experienced.[12]

While all of the black women I interviewed encountered everyday policing, their differences shaped how they were surveilled, targeted, and the frequency of police contact in daily life. Police officers were a constant presence for black women who grew up in highly surveilled low-income or working-class communities of color, particularly in inner cities where officers were fixtures in schools and neighborhoods. When we met, some of these black women still lived in the same highly surveilled communities from their childhood or in similar neighborhoods. Others had experienced economic mobility and detailed how they relocated to mixed-income, middle-class, white, or suburban environments where they had less daily contact with officers. Yet, as Boyles argues, officers also heavily patrol the borders of privileged spaces to ensure the maintenance of the many lines shaping our lives.[13] Thus, while black middle-class women were less likely to discuss the police as a constant presence in their daily lives, the similarities in their stories demonstrate that any space where officers had access to them—home, school, work—constituted a risk of police violence. Further, officers' consistent access to spaces conditioned experiences of police gender-based and sexual violence and retaliation. Social class distinctions correlated with prevalence of police contact tied to highly surveilled contexts. Regardless of social class and the degree of police contact, black women were targets of silencing and violence. Yet social class did play a role in how black women sought help to address violence. In domestic violence cases, class distinctions emerged around willingness to call the police, wherein black middle-class women were less likely to reach out to the police or others for support, and black working-class women were more likely to engage in what Bell describes as situational trust and call officers in a crisis.[14]

Stories about sexual deviance, sexuality, and gender pathologies work to legitimate violence against black LGBTQ+ people. Black women's stories show how these narratives permeate the broader social world as well as black intracommunal conversations on violence. I found that threats and acts of violence against black LGBTQ+ women were most likely to be verbally legitimated by multiple people and in different contexts. Officers used transphobic frames to pathologize black trans, nonbinary, and gender-fluid women. These frames undergirded police trans-exclusionary practices and failures to provide protection. Officers and others also used homophobic narratives to bring black lesbian, bisexual, and queer women into view, and sometimes made claims that they would know their place or how to stay silent if they were heterosexual or in submission to a heteropatriarchal order. From *here*, violence against black LGBTQ+ women was the most consistently public, revealing how scholars call attention to how public and explicit pathologization is linked to exclusionary politics of protection and public violence.[15]

Police responses also exacerbated mental health crises. In line with preexisting work on policing disabilities,[16] the black women I interviewed described how officers ignored their pleas for help and psychiatric support. Using criminalization narratives to bring black women with disabilities into view as deviant and dangerous, officer neglect often coincided with arrest. Lastly, age materialized as a significant distinction as black women were targeted as young girls.[17] As girls, they did not yet have frames to name their experiences, especially without pathologizing themselves. This is similar to how the Combahee

River Collective stated that as girls: "we had no way of conceptualizing what was so apparent to us, what we knew was really happening,"[18] As such, they were distinctly vulnerable to dissonance, the internalization of everyday policing, and the normalization of encounters over time. From *here*, officers and others could leverage the wide-spread delegitimization of black girls' testimonies to groom them for further violence that was often minimized and ignored. And as black women's stories teach us, what gets minimized and ignored, gets normalized in everyday life.

How Does Listening Transform the Ways We Conceptualize and Track Police Violence?

Social science methods filter people's stories through predetermined categories, based on certain reference groups' experiences—often white, masculine, and heteronormative.[19] Resultingly, most data on policing centers black heteromasculine standpoints, as well as what Lindsey refers to as spectacular police violence—mainly shootings and physical assaults.[20] This reliance on pre-existing categories and definitions methodologically distorts the realities of those whose experiences lie outside or between them. Using black men and boys as a fixed reference point for understanding black women and girls' encounters not only marginalizes the latter's accounts of spectacular violence but also obscures how gender and race ideologies intersect and result in experiences of slow, soft, and everyday police violence.

Many black women confronted how dominant narratives about policing did not recognize their experiences. They encountered these narratives among those they wanted to trust or sought support and recognition from, whether family members, community members, fellow activists, or public discourse and scholarship. As a result, black women relayed their embodied journeys to develop a lexicon around their encounters. These journeys were not linear. Thus, methodological approaches aiming to examine and address black women's experiences of police violence must account for these journeys around and between the usage of black heteromasculine reference points in everyday life. As such, life-history or life course methods can be uniquely suited to account for subjective shifts in understandings of violence that are often "missing."

Importantly, social science investigations into social problems must take seriously epistemic violence, or the ways our beliefs, methods, and measures quiet black women's testimonies. As Menjívar notes, lived experiences provide a window into the social world between fixed reference points and categories used to investigate social problems.[21] On their own terms, black women's stories provide a window into the social world of policing outside of dominant and intracommunity categories and conversations. *Here*, black women's accounts further reveal how misrecognition is an active means of domination weaved into the very data and frames meant to demonstrate the impact of police violence. Taking seriously epistemic violence and investigating what has been "missing" pushes researchers to seek more methodological precision when conceptualizing violence while also embracing evolving imprecision in our measures. For example, black women did not just encounter officers in roadside and pedestrian stops used in many databases and surveys to estimate rates of police violence. They encountered police in schools, neighborhoods, malls, parking lots, community meetings, work, college campuses, and homes. They also encountered various forms of police violence and abuses of power outside of spectacular violence. They were subjected to police who wielded their power when they were off duty. Whether officers were on or off duty, accompanying or justifying their policing were discourses that are particularly targeted at black women, such as black women being "bad mothers" or "fast" and asking for violence.

With a reliance on media accounts, convictions, and department administrative data, these experiences are often "missing" from how sociologists track police violence. Yet, tracking black women's experiences has implications for how we understand the problem of policing, not just for them, but also for other populations and society overall. As such, black women's stories shine a light on many remaining questions: What is the prevalence of police sexual violence among black women, nonbinary people, and men, as well as other social groups? What is the scope of police violence when we consider off-duty encounters? How pervasive is police violence when we account for contexts outside the pedestrian or traffic stop? How widespread is police violence if we include police domestic violence and the ways officers wield their power against their families and intimate partners? How do officers take advantage of people and groups' structural vulnerability to impose themselves in people's lives or commit violence, sometimes under the guise of care or empathy?

It is imperative to underscore that officers used the cover of multiple veils to inflict harm beyond how violence is often conceptualized in the data. In this way, preexisting definitions that are nonadaptive and exclusive can produce vulnerabilities to harm as frames about risk and social problems transition from research to policies and everyday life. Thus, conceptualizations of violence must remain grounded in the experiences of those impacted: *Marginalized populations, their experiences, and their stories must be their own reference points*. This is especially critical if claims will be made about their encounters to illustrate the presence, prevalence, or lack thereof of a social problem. As seen in black women's reactions to the pre-interview survey, grounding measures in their experiences dispels the dissonance and legitimates their accounts that have gone unrecognized. Given that power is not static and moves, methodological inquiries into violence must also embrace imprecision and evolve. Embracing imprecision in measuring violence, as Collins notes, is to be attuned to the reality that the same power dynamics that condition vulnerabilities also shape the development of measures—as literal violence is tied to epistemic violence.[22]

Finally, seeking precision and embracing imprecision necessitates what feminist scholars have directed our attention to for some time: The emotions of those on the margins are an epistemology for naming the unnamed.[23] While "missing-ness" connected black women across different contexts and intersections, their stories remained very much alive and a critical part of their interior. *Here*—in the space between, developing a lexicon and multiple consciousness—black women felt violence as their emotions often alerted them to the harms they could not name or were unsafe to speak about. Thus, their emotions mapped onto the linked power dynamics between violence and knowledge production in different contexts. As such, black women embodied knowledge about their experiences that were not yet reflected in definitions, databases, talks, reports, and headlines. Black women's interior worlds, then, inherently existed as an archive about experiences of violence that have been made "missing" in their intracommunal and broader social worlds.

How Does Listening Transform the Ways We Approach the Creation of Safety in Everyday Life?

The black women's stories presented in this book urgently remind us that abolition feminism calls us to remember that along with abolishing policing and prisons, abolition always and also includes unlearning internalized policing logics in private, intimate, and in-between spaces.[24] Abolition feminist world-making offers a vital counter to everyday policing, which uses violence and silence to build social worlds based on domination. Battle and Powell describe abolition feminist world-making as "identifying and dismantling oppressive institutions and collaboratively (re)envisioning how to build communities that center care while grappling with nuanced everyday needs, fears, and concerns."[25] Listening to people's stories about violence is essential to abolition feminist world-making calls to action. It's an invitation into a new world built through wrestling with and learning from people's stories—recognizing the alternatives we seek are in the space between lived experiences and radical imagination. As Mariame Kaba and Andrea Ritchie point out in *No More Police: A Case for Abolition*, victims' stories form the basis of a black feminist politic that is "focused on ending all forms of violence experienced by Black women—and all other people."[26]

In this vein, Threadcraft emphasizes that black storytelling is essential cultural work in building not only the world we want, but the people, relations, and knowledge that sustain it.[27] Indeed, black feminist thought is not just knowledge created by black women about our place in the social world. It's also knowledge with the potential to disrupt this world and the systems of domination that support it. It's a guide for building new worlds, ones with alternative systems and different ways of socially relating to one another. Thus, at its core, black feminist thought is a product of abolitionist modes of knowledge production in everyday life, which require listening to and valuing stories on the margins, harnessing wisdom, and promoting life within structures that currently cultivate black death and disposability.[28] It is no surprise, then, that a world dictated by policing is held up by the same social conditions that make black women and girls vulnerable to violence and our stories "missing."

Importantly, calls to listen to black women can come from outside and inside the house. Black women's "missing" stories make visible how the presence of officers in public spaces do not equate to public safety. They also show how the larger carceral landscape can be leveraged in private spaces to further make black women and girls unsafe. To navigate the space between, some black women described how mothers, othermothers, and friends acted as guides for naming their "missing" experiences of violence. And as seen throughout their stories, these guides many times also operated as intracommunal levers for creating and accessing protection outside of the police. Despite some of these forms of support, most of the black women I interviewed still desired more alternatives from within their communities that were not the police. *Here*, they wanted their kinship ties, friends, and neighbors involved in creating pathways to safety, providing protection, and responding to crisis.

For those who did not trust their communities to build these pathways, some considered police reforms. Nevertheless, they, too, still pushed for more intracommunal resources around violence. Ultimately, most black women were less concerned with police reforms and desired intracommunal transformation and community-sanctioned alternatives to the police that made reaching out to officers unnecessary in cases of community and domestic violence. They wanted people in their lives to listen to them and co-develop frames to recognize each other's experiences and address them. As long as the police exist, they wanted their social relations and communities to be responsive to the realities of their vulnerabilities—to not gaslight them about their experiences within and outside their communities and engage in vulnerability politics in ways that reproduce restrictive notions of social problems and solutions.

Additionally, black women's stories illuminate how many of the alternative pathways we seek are not futuristic, but that some already exist in their day-to-day lives. As such, they described developing unofficial peer safety practices at school where they collaborated with other kids to deescalate fights so that officers were not needed, neighbors watching out for each other and creating community-engaged pathways to safety, and trusted network ties responding to domestic violence and sexual assault. These efforts are examples of what Gilmore refers to as life in rehearsal.[29] Each of these alternatives, as rehearsal, were grounded in the recognition of people and their stories.

Such storytelling disrupted everyday policing, creating a space for talking about lived experiences and expressing empathy around collective and distinct experiences of violence. This storytelling often happened when black women gathered, whether in conversations between mothers and daughters, between friends, or in community spaces. And sometimes, it happened between them and themselves. Importantly, the center expanded based on mutual recognition, trust, and accountability as they worked with those around them to create alternative pathways to legibility and safety. Gathering saved lives—it thinned veils and created a relational center that included the valuing of black women and their stories.[30] However, gathering could also easily give way to everyday policing across differences in sexualities, gender identities, social class, and ages, as it, too, had to stay attuned to shifting power dynamics. Thus, growing these alternatives, as Ruha Benjamin, Philip McHarris, and others note, demands the transformation of social relations, as these relations and the meeting of essential needs are what catches people in the space between.[31]

Finally, one lesson that I personally take away from listening to so many black women's stories is that speaking about violence is dangerous to the lines carving out our social worlds. The dominant order—whether outside or inside a community—needs "missing-ness" to obstruct mutual recognition, care, and relationality. It needs to regulate both personhood and stories because story-telling develops our ability to see shared vulnerabilities and care about distinct ones, determining our social and political priorities. It needs silence because building alternative pathways in daily life is difficult, if not impossible, in the face of it—or as these black women's stories show, we cannot build something better to address experiences we do not name.

This conclusion, then, does not offer any policy recommendations for re-forming the police. There are no shortage of books and research for interested readers detailing the intricacies of different police reforms—often without black women's accounts taken into consideration. These accounts include the reality that, even when they did not describe themselves as abolitionist or were not part of movements to defund or abolish the police, many black women wanted approaches to safety that did not involve the police. Yet many policing reforms are grounded in a praxis of unlistening, whether to the layered ways people experience violence or their expansive vision of safety that rejects a world built on domination and policing.

Thus, after listening to black women's stories, I am also suspicious of an abo-litionist politic that does not include them, that pathologizes or deifies black women and families to distort experiences, that does not speak to violence in intimate relations and communities as well as from the police, that does not address everyday life and spaces between. While this is one lesson learned from sitting with black women's stories, a dynamic aspect of black storytelling is that someone different could read the stories in these pages, listen, and learn something else—something I missed, didn't get quite right, or maybe even wrong that could help keep us safe. Embracing this instability, the contradic-tions, and adjusting as we go is necessary part of abolition feminism, to build-ing and rebuilding something better.

Veronica on 2020 (*and some final thoughts on unlistening and the space between*)

What happened was it was a lot of things, right? It was police racism. It was misogyny. It was anti-LGBT. All of those things happened at once. It hap-pened in front of a bunch of people that maybe didn't seem to see these things that happened in front of their face.

I think a lot of people want to talk about what happened and want to talk about why what happened, happened. A lot of the reason why these things happened is because the police are racist. The police hate women. The police don't like wild women. The police don't like black women. The police don't like gay, black trans women.

There's a lot of things that happened. Unfortunately, people sitting there—fortunately, people care now, but again, I think that also at the time, seeing people wanting to defund and abolish police. What happened to me was a proof of all the intersectional issues coming together at once. [*pause*] It's nice being able to talk about it. It is a little exhausting, actually.

"How do you take care of yourself?" I asked.

I'm on the team of abolishing police. I think the whole system needs to be reworked. Most of the people that I work with don't like that kind of language, so I have to really monitor myself a little bit.

"What do you think that is—them not liking that language?" I asked.

It just makes them uncomfortable. People don't know what life would be like without police. They think that society would crumble automatically. I don't think that's the case at all. I think abolishing policing as is and creating something new to support and protect the community to replace it would make dramatic improvements in every neighborhood, in every neighborhood. If there was literally someone just to control—maybe like a community counselor. Just someone who can show—or a community social worker. Just show up and just be like, "Hey, what do you need? What is going on? Do you need a job? Do you need this?" Just to find out exactly what these people are really needing instead of punishing them for being in need.

Then people just are—they can't have the conversations on how to fix the community because they don't know what the world would look like without police. It's really weird, but I don't know. I've certainly thought a lot about what police do and society, and, so, I'm very pro—I'm already done with the idea of reforming police or fixing police. I'm just like, no, no, no, no. Why don't we talk about a better system in general? I'm already over that. Let's just start actually working on building something better.

The officer killings of Breonna Taylor and George Floyd in 2020 catapulted the United States into the space between a world with state-sanctioned policing and a possible new world with what Veronica calls "a better system." In this collective liminal space filled with economic precarity and mounting uncertainties brought about by the COVID-19 pandemic, people took to the streets in unprecedented numbers to protest anti-black police violence around the world. News outlets prominently featured debates parsing through what it meant to reform policing versus defunding the institution. Communities openly had conversations about alternative pathways to safety, and at the height of the summer, two-thirds of adult Americans supported the #BlackLivesMatter movement.[32] It is during this time that I interviewed a cautiously hopeful Veronica, who was encouraged by what seemed like a tipping point toward a new world without the police.

But she was worried. Grateful that "fortunately, people care now," Veronica nevertheless feared that this sentiment would not last long enough for people to seriously consider and implement alternatives. She was anxious people would return to a dependence on the carceral system, to the story that the police are critical to ensuring public and private safety. This story—of police as protectors against dangerous "others"—has been used to crush dissent and push carceral expansion and reforms. This story, like other enduring stories, thrives on what Dotson refers to as epistemological resilience—or the stability needed to support us in sifting through, dismissing, and incorporating information in the space between what we know and what we have yet to learn.[33] All stories, according to Dotson, require this resilience because in order to craft new narratives, we rely on the durability of our previous ones.

> Resilience is just this adaptive capacity. Without such resilience, we would be unable to know anything about our worlds and, worse yet, we would be unable to detect noticeable changes or the need for significant changes within our epistemological systems. Stability, here, is the backdrop against which change can be measured and epistemic resources can be shared. Resilience not only enables that stability, but it institutes a new state of stability after significant disturbances. It is arguably a dynamic, yet, integral feature of our epistemological systems.[34]

The problem, then, she stresses, is not necessarily the durability of our epistemological systems, or the longstanding stories that shape our lives—in this specific case, the narrative that the police are guardians who provide safety and services in a crisis. Instead, the issue lies in our inability and unwillingness to incorporate information, to change our story when met with experiences that push us to expand our narrative or let go of it.[35] To hold onto our story and keep our frames and systems intact, we turn to silence to create an unknowing.

We turn to silence to unlisten. If to speak is to be socially and politically recognized, then unlistening is how we ignore and devalue people and their stories. We unlisten because listening to people's stories outside of what we are willing and able to recognize would initiate a process that makes us feel uncomfortable, disoriented, and afraid, even as it carries within it the potential to usher in a new reality, a new world.[36] So, when we find ourselves in the space between old worlds and new ones, we hold onto the stories that give us stability. In this case, people hold onto the story that officers are critical to providing protection and services, even though the origins of policing are rooted in domination and research persistently demonstrates that the police are harmful to communities of color. We unlisten, and we resist change.

To rationalize and justify our unlistening, we pick up the master's tools—we bring victims of police violence, those with different perspectives, and those who advocate for alternatives to policing into view through pathology. We see them as "untrustworthy," "unreliable," "biased," and "deviant." "Why were they acting like that?" "Why couldn't they just comply?" "Why would they be so disruptive?" "Do they actually think something else could work?" Feeling some stability in the durability in these views grounded in historical stereotypes, it becomes much easier to discredit the storytellers, as Dotson writes: "To those who believe their credibility to be compromised, those words will often sound like, at worst, lies and, at best, unreliable statements."[37] With the help of the master's readily available tools, we return to the lines that etch out the dominant order. These lines provide some stability in our social worlds, help us justify our attacks on the narrators, and ignore their stories. And so, we return to stability within the story that the police are the best way to conceptualize providing societal protection and services. We close the window to other possibilities.

Indeed, when we spoke, Veronica already felt the care waning and, with it, the window closing on people's openness to alternatives to the police. She felt it in the small changes, noticing the need to still "monitor myself a little bit" when working with people on various social justice issues. Analyzing some of the fear behind people's dislike of the "language" of police abolition, Veronica described how people become "uncomfortable" in liminal spaces. However, she and many black women whose stories were shared in this book had for their entire lives, been navigating the spaces between. They had already experienced the idea and reality of our commitment to reforming the police. Thus, their stories show the limitations of police reform policies in addressing experiences at the intersection of anti-black and patriarchal violence.

For example, in *Pushout*, Monique Morris parses through the reality of policies that increasingly placed officers in schools and its impact on black girls.[38] While they are twice as likely to be suspended than white girls, black girls stories are often "missing" from conversations on the school-to-prison pipeline.[39] In centering their place, Morris brings into view less discussed pathways to carceral confinement, such as alternative schools where Kristen from chapter 1 was tracked, and house arrest, in addition to juvenile detention centers and prisons. Through making these pathways visible, Morris, Connie Wun, and others allow us to consider how school resource officers are integral to making schools sites of social control, wherein black girls are subjected to physical, verbal, and sexual harassment.[40] Although police in schools have been touted as a way to protect children, we can trace the story back to the maintenance of the color line and efforts to address panic among white populations after pushes in the 1940s and '50s to desegregate.[41] Veronica and other black women's stories also provide further details on what it is like to live in the aftermath of policies making officers a staple in public schools across the United States. In chapter 3, she described navigating daily harassment from a school resource officer, which turned into assaults and death threats. Alexis, whose story is shared in the previous chapter, also detailed her arrest for breaking curfew and growing up watching officers assault kids on a daily basis, experiences that ultimately led to her organizing around the removal of cops from schools. Abena, whose story is shared in chapter 1, chose not to report her sexual assault to school police because she, too, grew up witnessing their daily abuses of youth.

In addition to school-based reforms, the black women I interviewed also lived with the reality of carceral feminist pushes in the 1980s and '90s to deepen collaboration with the police to address domestic violence. These reforms cemented officers as first responders to domestic abuse and ushered in a wave of state and local mandatory arrest policies that allowed the police to arrest both parties in domestic incidents.[42] Black women's stories in chapter 2 further contextualize these policies, showing how officers not only failed in many cases to provide protection but also physically assaulted and arrested them for self-defense. In some cases, officers leveraged these vulnerable moments to sexually harass and coerce them. Still, another reform, community policing, is widely touted to promote safety and decrease police violence in highly surveilled communities of color. However, Devin's story in chapter 4 makes visible how this reform puts black women at risk for police gender-based and sexual violence. Even more, she describes how black women are afraid to report violence inflicted by community liaison officers because they recognize how their stories are unlikely to be believed, and thus they are vulnerable to retaliation from officers who have consistent, deeper access to their communities. Collectively, their stories speak to how police reform policies intended to increase public and private safety failed to address violence in the space between and compounded their experiences of harm and marginalization.

And *here*, living in the aftermath of these reforms and the realities of different types of violence, black women expressed a need for different officer responses, resources, and real pathways to protection. In doing so, their stories push us to take seriously the connections between police, interpersonal, and community violence. Yet, in sharing their attempts to speak openly to these connections, black women illuminate a second way we unlisten: by refusing or being unable to learn shared tools for interpreting people's stories.[43] Dotson notes that this is particularly the case when we do not share people's experiences and have never heard stories like theirs before. From where we stand— clinging to our narratives about the police for stability—the disconnect between them and us starts to feel like a gulf we are not capable of naming and, eventually, over time, not even noticing. From this place, Dotson sums it up: "Convincing people that they are missing something integral when, in fact, they cannot detect such deficiencies is no easy task."[44] Some people return to unlistening. However, others notice the "missing-ness" and are willing to ease their grip on their story, recognizing that while officers provide protection and services to them, this is not the case for others. Moreover, they recognize that the police are integral to building and maintaining separate social worlds based on differentiated access to state protections. "But these people use different methods." "They have different ways of communicating, of creating and sharing data, of telling stories." From where we stand, on the other side of the space between, holding on to what we are able and willing to recognize about policing, it feels too challenging to learn new tools to build something better with other people's stories.

And in 2020—in the space between the old world with the police and the possibility of a new world without them—Veronica explained how many people feared that nothing would be there to catch them. "People don't know what life would be like without police. They think that society would crumble automatically." This crisis of imagination and remembering, of conceptualizing other ways of socially relating and providing safety, deepens people's fear. And overwhelmed by this fear, it feels much more stable to go back to the story that we need the police, to ignoring other people's stories and attacking the narrators. Indeed, the structures that make up the current social order facilitate this process: in our institutions, communities, and intimate relations. Using the master's tools to draw lines with "us" on one side and "them" on the other, Dotson explains how, at best, we interpret our inability to build something better with other people's stories as proof of the reliability of our epistemological systems, or in this case, our story: that we need the police. At worst, she warns, we interpret our inability to build something better as proof of the system's supremacy: There is no other way of providing protection and services other than the police.

Veronica, like other black women I talked with at protests and vigils during this time, worried that people would listen to their fear, draw lines, and return to "the idea of reforming police or fixing police." They *felt* the possibility of retrenchment. By September 2020, their concerns would prove to be right as support for the protest waned in ways that directly mapped onto the existing fault lines carving out our current social order. Thus, white people's support of the #BlackLivesMatter movement had dropped from 60 percent to 45 percent, while black people's support remained above 86 percent.[45] Our place within the lines, then, influences our perceptions of the problem of policing and, subsequently, whether and how quickly we desire a return to normal with the police.[46] Yet, as Phelps notes, black communities are not a monolith and have different responses to police failures, and without addressing poverty and having viable alternatives in place that people can easily access, even those who desire a better system will return to the old one.[47]

Many times, the story of needing the police has taken root and obscured our ability to see and even detect people's building of alternatives. Over time, people's stories—ones on the other sides of veils—appear fantastical. When a person speaks from another epistemological system, or from the space between, Dotson says, "her testimony of the experience may be rejected as nonsensical; they may designate her as a deceiver with dangerous ideas; or the conclusions she draws might even invoke ridicule and laughter."[48] In 2020, in this collective space between, standing on the precipice of what seemed like radical social change, Veronica expressed the sentiments of many black women organizers I talked with during that time when she emphatically stated, "I think abolishing policing as is and creating something new to support and protect the community to replace it would make dramatic improvements." However, from the other side, this appears dangerous, idealistic, and nonsensical. So, we unlisten. We go back to the structures that carve out our lives believing the story that we need the police.

Thus, a final way we unlisten is through our unwillingness or inability to loosen our grip on our old worlds. We may want to listen, learn new tools, and build something better with others, but our needs have not been met, and we deeply desire the stability embedded in the story that the police are critical for protection and services. From where we stand, even if the old world with the police doesn't work for many, it's predictable and stable. So, we are willing to shift and reform, but we run back to our old world when we realize that including different people's stories in our efforts to build something better is inherently transformative. It *requires* us letting go. While we were willing to expand, we are unwilling to fundamentally change. And if we listened and cared about people's stories from the spaces between, their narratives would change what we believe and know about our social worlds. Their stories would transform our reality: the way we recognize people and the purpose and function of policing. To listen to their stories, then, would mean facing how our reliance on the police as the only way we can conceptualize providing societal protections and services continues to cause harm. However—it would also mean we can envision safety as social relations and practices that challenge domination as the basis of our social worlds.

A Brief Note on Methods, Continued

The story does not simply describe, it demands representation outside itself. Indeed, the story cannot tell itself without our willingness to imagine what it cannot tell. The story asks that we live with what cannot be explained and live with unexplained cues and diasporic literacies, rather than reams of positivist evidence. The story opens the door to curiosity; the reams of evidence dissipate as we tell the world differently, with a creative precision. The story asks that we live with the difficult and frustrating ways of knowing differentially. (And some things we keep to ourselves. They cannot have everything. Stop her autopsy). They cannot have everything.

—KATHERINE MCKITTRICK, *DEAR SCIENCE AND OTHER STORIES*[1]

———

Sociologists tend to autopsy stories for the purposes of "proof" to demonstrate claims and arguments. However, black storytelling is a liberatory practice of livingness that affirms black humanity in the face of anti-black erasure, violence, and death.[2] It bridges the space between old worlds and new ones, guided by the sharing of our stories. This book, in centering black women's stories of policing that often go "missing" in hopes that it could help with building something better, is grounded in this praxis of black storytelling. Similarly, I'm going to take a step back and tell the story of this book in a way that affirms the humanity of the black women who chose to participate in this study, as well as my own humanity as a black feminist researcher doing something that many times felt impossible. It's somewhat of a long story. But I'll keep it as brief as I possibly can, starting with what I refer to as *epistemology-methods*.

As I understand epistemologies and methods, they are interrelated—as how I know is determined by what I already know and the varied ways that helped me come to know that.[3] As I understand them, they are embodied—as I cannot divorce who I am from what I know, how I know, and the many ways I choose to know more.[4] As I understand them, they are sociohistorical practices and ways of relating—as our personal biographies and collective histories shape our many ways of moving toward and away from each other (*and what we share and know in the meantime*).[5] As I understand them, how the study unfolded between me and the black women who chose to participate is part of an even larger, interconnected story with many chapters crisscrossing and carrying us off in different directions.

To tell the story of this book's epistemology-methods, then, I must start with another story. This story is of the porch and the tree and her. These three are how I learned many ways of knowing (*before I was taught to unknow and partially know by the academy*). These three shape what I consider to be knowledge or wisdom, and where it lives, how it moves, and the many ways it makes itself known. These three are a way I return to knowing what becomes "missing" in our social worlds. Thus, these three are my most important citation. Of course, I will keep much of this story to myself as tucking details and chapters of it away is in and of itself a very important part of my epistemology-methods—or shared collective lineage of knowing rooted in/from the deep US South where storytelling is equal parts survival, secret, livingness, and (---).

———

a southern black feminist story-epistemology-method on silence

Grand-(---) was a former Mississippi sharecropper. Most everybody knows that. She's also many, many other things. Everybody knows that, too. Whenever she decided, she would come barefoot out from the house or back from walking the land. On the porch and under the tree, she would gather her dress and sit in her chair. Sometimes, she would close her eyes and slump forward with her face hanging between her clasped hands toward the earth. Sometimes, she would lean back, stretched out with her face toward the sun. Sometimes, she would sway back and forth with the wind. Many times, she would pat her feet to a melody and beat unheard by me. Under the tree and on the porch, we would sit in silence for long stretches of time and times. Everybody knows why.

Still. Sometimes, I would ask her what she was doing. Without opening her eyes, she would turn her lips upward into a slight smile and humor (*gift*) me with a response. Spoken in a faint voice, low enough for me to know that she was not all the way here with me in the present, soft enough to not disturb her selves in all the places she was visiting, and loud enough for me to still make out, she would say: "I'm just resting my soul." (*sometimes when i'd ask her, and i would many, many times, she'd say "bones," but in this day's story she said "soul"*). In response, I'd nod and keep her silence with her—not quite sure exactly what a soul was but understanding full well already at a young age that it needed respect and resting.

Sometimes, others would arrive under the tree and on the porch. They would sit with her without words, too, rocking back and forth and harmonizing the silence. They would also sit and stand (*i will not tell you whether or not they laid or what else they did*) under the tree and on the porch. Sometimes, people would bring their other people and their problems and their selves to her, wanting a sense (*and other things i may or may not share later*). Everybody already knows I don't share. They know why, too.

Sometimes, under the tree and on the porch, there would be many voices speaking with each other (*you might be listening in on a conversation not meant for you and misunderstand it as over each other instead of with each other*). Everybody already knows that. Sometimes, voices were loud and fiery. Sometimes, voices were low and simmering. Sometimes, voices were bubbling and boisterous whispers. Watching and feeling, I learned how to listen to the ways different whispers were spoken under the tree and on the porch (*and in the kitchen . . . [especially late at night in the kitchen] . . .*). I learned how whispers shift and shiver as they roll over the body, with some revealing the (*un*)readiness of the story-teller to hear their own voice and narrative, some revealing the presence of unwanted listeners, and still, some revealing what the storyteller wants the other person to know and pay attention to (*see—some whispers scream*). There are other types of whispers, too. (*like the one's between---.*) I will not share these with you as you cannot have everything. Everybody really already knows that. Maybe one day you will, too (*everybody already knows that one day you will, too*).

I'd watch as burdened people would shift, sudden and slight, under that tree and on that porch, revealing (*un*)recognizable parts of themselves (*to themselves and others*). See—I'd meet people I'd already met many, many times for the very first time under the tree and on the porch (*and sometimes i'd never see them again*) (*at least not until---*). But no matter how people spoke with one another, whether in silence—*or in loud southern words strung together in melodic phrases often only understood on first listen by those meant to hear*—she would listen, see, and --- (*know*) what needed to be seen and --- (*known*). See—she would know it, too. We all really understood that (*so there was no need to hide*) (*or no point in it anyway*). Now, what she did with what she saw is a whole other story (*or stories*). And these stories will not be told here. Only passed down under the tree and on the porch (*from generation to generation, 'cause despite it all . . . we,* and our stories-epistemologies-methods, live on.

A Sociological Story-Epistemology-Method on Silence

Yet, sociologists often need a different type of story. So, from 2017 to 2021, I conducted fieldwork on police violence against black women and girls in two urban cities in the Southern region of the United States. Fieldwork included in-depth and life-history interviews, field observations, and surveys over three overlapping phases. While I describe the various methods and phases of the larger project, the book primarily draws from the second phase's life-history interviews and black women's reactions to the pre-interview survey. Research on policing documents the importance of neighborhood contexts, and initially, I planned to disclose the locations and discuss these specificities as they related to my project.[6] However, as interviews engaged in a life-history approach, the specificities of the city contexts where they were recruited were not important, as their encounters took place at different stages of their lives and varying locations. Further, from black women's interviews, I observed patterns in policing practices that cut across contexts. As such, the focus of this book became the similarities in practices of social control from police and others in black women's lives.

Phase 1

In the first phase of the project, I conducted thirty in-depth interviews in 2017 in a predominantly black city in a Southern region of the United States. This phase focused on how black working-class and middle-class mothers discussed or planned to talk about police violence with their children. Initially, I planned to conduct interviews in person. However, black women kept canceling and requesting to speak over the phone, and as feminist methods describe, offering a remote option is a practice of care when conducting qualitative interviews.[7] Once I started offering telephone interviews as an option, black mothers were less likely to cancel and opted for interview times that worked for them, such as during their job breaks, in transit to and from work or other care responsibilities, on the sidelines of their kids' activities, or at night when they were alone. Within these conversations, mothers reflected on talks they had with their caregivers, their police experiences, and the talks they had or planned to have with their kids. When I asked about themselves, some mothers shared their experiences of police violence only to then turn around and say their daughters did not need a talk or changed the subject back to their sons or to some other topic. Others spoke directly about what strategies they would give their daughters to ensure they were psychically and physically prepared. While their experiences were not presented in this book, I mention this fieldwork phase because these interviews greatly informed my thinking and ensuing methodological decisions. Specifically, I took a more explicit life-history approach, used a pre-interview survey in the second phase, and shifted to focus on heterogeneity among black women.

Phase 2

In the second phase, I conducted thirty-two in-depth, life-history interviews with black women in a predominantly white city in a Southern region of the United States. Participants were eligible for the study if they identified as black women, were over the age of eighteen, and resided or worked in the city or surrounding areas. Using snowball sampling, black women were recruited for this study through (1) formal organizations, such as social clubs, nonprofits, and educational institutions; (2) events focused on black communities, black women and girls, and criminalization and policing; (3) organizational and residents' social media accounts; (4) black women's personal and professional networks; and (5) direct contact with black women in my field site. To recruit from formal organizations, I made initial contact with leaders, members, and representatives of these groups. These gatekeepers made contact with potential participants via email, formal announcements at events and meetings, and organizational social media. While some organizations posted information about the study, I also asked long-term residents in the field or those active in their communities to post information about the study and share it with their networks. At community events, I passed out flyers containing information about the study and had conversations with black women about the project.

Feminist methodology discusses the importance of providing women with a safe environment to discuss their experiences of violence with researchers.[8] Thus, all interviews were voluntary and conducted at the time or place of each black woman's choosing. Five black women opted for telephone interviews, and twenty-seven black women participated in in-person interviews. The in-person interviews took place at coffee shops, parks, restaurants, homes, work breakrooms, and in parking lots and cars after community meetings. The interviews utilized a life-history approach around key topics on police and violence in black women's lives, such as their views on the police, childhood and adult conversations about policing, childhood and adult experiences with officers, police violence in the news and on social media, and their activism and community involvement.

I chose to transition to life-history interviews for several reasons. First, these interviews allow black women to tell their stories about different incidents of violence and reflect on the meaning of these encounters over time.[9] This was especially important given that the silence matrix made it difficult or dangerous for them to speak about these incidents when they initially happened, especially if they were children or adolescents at the time. Hence, life-history interviews reveal the shifting meaning black women made around these incidents nested within the context of multiple relationships and social environments. Accordingly, when writing about why she chose to use life-history interviews in her groundbreaking study on domestic violence in black women's lives, Beth E. Richie writes:

> Compared to other, more structured qualitative methods, conducting life-history interviews offered a more intense opportunity to learn about subjects' background, opinions, feelings, and the meanings they give to the mundane events and the exceptional experiences in their lives.[10]

A common positivist critique of these forms of interviews is the validity of memory, an argument centered around the accuracy of the accounts and specific details. Yet, life-history interviews and memory analysis is often used in sociological research on violence to investigate personal biographies, particularly those within marginalized communities, whose stories may not show up in dominant discourses, frames, categories, or other methods.[11] In this way, Saida Grundy writes that memories "are essentially a dialogical relationship we have with our former selves through the social world as we see it now (in which our backgrounds inform what we can see and of what we can make sense in our recollections)."[12] Drawing from this approach, I examined black women's accounts of events, the stories they told about their experiences, and how they chose to tell their stories. If black women shared details about their experiences of police violence or other types of violence but explicitly expressed that they did not want them shared in the write-up of their narratives, I respected their privacy and omitted them.[13] I ultimately put black women's stories in conversation with one another to understand the interrelated politics, norms, and sanctions that made it difficult and dangerous for them to speak about violence at different stages of their lives, varying contexts, and across their many differences.

Most interviews lasted between one and two hours, with some going much longer. In addition to black women choosing the location and time of their interviews, I also engaged in the feminist interviewing practice around violence that allowed time at the beginning of the interview for participants to ask questions.[14] During this time, black women asked questions about the project's background, my interest in the topic, my experience as a researcher, my plans for the data, my personal experiences with the police and others, and my political commitments. This process, along with the institutional and network trust from recruitment, facilitated rapport. Over the course of conducting the interviews, two of the first questions I came to ask black women were (1) How do you feel knowing that we are going to be discussing police violence today?; and (2) How did you feel taking the local survey? When questions focused on their experiences of police violence, I reminded black women that they could take breaks and could decline to answer any question they wanted. As the interviews progressed, I adapted, added, and removed questions based on analysis of previous interview responses. The final interview sample at this phase included thirty-two black women from diverse backgrounds, and appendix B includes detailed demographic information of all interview participants.

I audio-recorded all interviews except Simone's because she was uncomfortable with using a recording device. Additionally, a few black women did not allow me to record the beginning of our interviews, and it was only once they felt more comfortable that they allowed me to turn on the recording device. Last, a few black women asked during the interview if I could turn off the recorder when discussing details about police sexual violence or domestic violence. This especially happened with black women who had ongoing proximity to police officers, such as (1) black women who had family members who were officers, (2) black women activists working closely with officers in their community, and (3) black women who had repeated interactions with community liaison police officers. In these cases, black women expressed fears about retaliation. Those working with officers on police reform especially worried about having their access cut off or revoked from police departments. When the recorder was turned off, I asked permission to take notes, and all consented. I also took written or voice memo field notes after each interview. In these memos, I would comment on the context/environment in which the interviews took place, black women's demeanor throughout the interview, rapport, and my pre-, during-, and post-interview reflections. After the interviews, all participants were given pseudonyms to maintain confidentiality. Some black women chose pseudonyms they would like me to use in written projects. In some cases where black women had repeated and ongoing contact with the police, I changed a few details to further protect their anonymity.

Along with these interviews, the second phase included field observations where I attended community events on policing, community-police partnership convenings managed by departments and local municipalities, grassroots and initiative-driven coalition meetings to address policing in schools and other places, city-wide events serving black families and communities, healing and well-being programs focused exclusively on black women, and anti-police-violence protests and vigils. Throughout the project, I used ethnographic field methods to observe black women's activism and the broader cultural contexts that shaped their frames for understanding and resistance to policing. I took handwritten and typed notes on my computer during the first few field observations. Afterward, I typed up notes about the event on the same or following day. Most of the events occurred at night and during the weekends. As a graduate student parent at the time, I often had to hire a babysitter after daycare hours to attend events. This impacted the events I chose to attend, how many I attended, how long I could stay, and the time dedicated to writing notes afterward. Further, I quickly discovered that leaving the event and typing field notes was not a practice I could sustain for the duration of the project. Therefore, early in the project, I switched to voice memos during and after events so that I could transcribe and listen to them for analysis. In these memos, I described the context and purpose of the event and focused on one to three ethnographic moments or stories. Last, I recorded my reflections on attending and participating in these events. Importantly, my ethnographic strategy evolved throughout the project as I learned to take consistent field notes with limited time and availability. At events, I also saw several black women who had previously participated in interviews and conducted a small sample of mini follow-up interviews or conversations with them after the event. These black women gave me verbal permission to record our conversations and take notes afterward. Collectively, I used these field observations to ground and triangulate my analysis of the broader intra-communal and societal contexts in which black women navigated policing.

Phases 2 and 3

The second and third phases also included a local or pre-interview and national survey. The local/pre-interview survey was used to gather information on black women's personal and familial demographics, prior contact with the carceral system, experiences with officers, and police violence in their networks. This survey was conducted in my field site and administered online via Qualtrics. A link to the survey accompanied information circulated about the study. If I connected with black women through other people or in person, I would email or text them a link to the local survey. At first, this survey was developed based on black women's responses from the first phase of the project, as well as research from previous work on police violence against black women.[15] I also actively revised the local/pre-interview survey based on ongoing interviews with black women, which resulted in several versions. In total, eighty-two black women took a version of the local/pre-interview survey. Of the thirty-two black women interviewed in the second phase, thirty completed the survey before our interview. One black woman chose not to complete the survey, preferring to only participate in an interview. A second black woman completed the survey after our interview. When the survey was completed prior to the interview, I used the responses to guide the interview process and to ask follow-up questions. This included probing black women about their feelings and reactions to the survey questions, tailoring specific interview questions based on survey responses, and utilizing the survey as a guide for follow-up questions.

In addition to assisting with the interview process, distributing the local/pre-interview survey prior to interviews allowed me to methodologically observe black women's underreporting and minimizing of certain interactions with officers. Thus, I analyzed black women's reflections on the pre-interview survey and how it captured their police experiences. Black women also shared that the survey brought up memories of their prior encounters and made them reflect on these experiences before our interviews. Many shared how seeing their interactions reflected in the survey validated that their encounters counted and mattered. Finally, black women shared their critiques of the survey and made comments on how they would change it. Their feedback was used to edit the survey measures on violence. The book primarily focused on black women's stories, with some chapters highlighting their reactions to the survey.

(phases 1–3)

Now, to the story behind the sociological story that I many times hesitated to write. Not wanting it to be a distraction, the decision to share my journey through what Collins refers to as "requirements [that] typify positivist methodological approaches"[16] came about through extensive conversations with graduate student researchers of color confronting similar challenges in their projects, especially if their studies concerned social issues impacting communities they were a part of, social groups with whom they identified, or study designs that in any way decentered whiteness, masculinity, and heterosexuality. And so, I write this section of the appendix with them in mind as we journey through the academy, working to not become or succumb to it. Specifically, Collins states:

> First, research methods generally require a distancing of the researcher from her/his "object" of study by defining the researcher as a "subject" with full human subjectivity and objectifying the "object" of study. A second requirement is the absence of emotions from the research process. Third, ethics and values are deemed inappropriate in the research process, either as the reason for scientific inquiry or as part of the research process itself. Finally, adversarial debates, whether written or oral, become the preferred method of ascertaining truth: the arguments that can withstand the greatest assault and survive intact become the strongest truths.[17]

Throughout this study, each and every phase of this project confronted each and every one of these requirements.

In the early stages, the emphasis on variation was often used to delegitimatize the project altogether and center whiteness, masculinity, and heterosexuality. This often took the form of making assumptions regarding the absence of black women's experiences of violence, particularly in the middle-class, and pushing for me to also interview white families, white women, and black men. When I resisted, accusations aligned with Collins's first two requirements: "I was too close." "And I was too emotional." Pushed to think "objectively" by many non-black researchers, they argued that the inclusion of others, especially black men, would allow me to make claims about black women's experiences. That there could be variation among black women themselves was often dismissed. That there could be experiences of violence among black middle-class women did not fit their notions of middle-class. However, in speaking to black women in my life and black women mentors outside the academy about the project, even the *potential* for a study that centers black women and girls' everyday experiences of police violence and other forms of violence evoked many deeply held emotions. This *potential* of something existing that legitimated our experiences and countered the "missing-ness" created *real* space for them to share their untold stories. At the same time that I was listening to these stories outside (*and inside*) the academy, I was confronting the third and fourth requirements in trying to turn the project from a potential to a reality. Thus, in advocating for the importance of black women's stories, I was met with responses that "it was inappropriate at best and unscientific at least to argue for their importance." From there, I had to listen to others alternatively argue why our stories were not needed, how what I was trying to study was not a *real* social problem, and moreover, how our experiences only mattered in relation to the previously mentioned groups. These requirements, or delegitimizing arguments, persisted throughout all phases of the project.

So, it would be disingenuous to say that it was not a harrowing experience to navigate the sociological space between the lived experiences of black women I knew existed and mattered and support and recognition of a project focused on this important social issue. To navigate this space between as a graduate researcher, I turned to my communities both inside and outside the academy. Sustaining ongoing conversations with a diverse group of feminists who engage in intersectional approaches to their research and activism was critical in validating the study, especially in the beginning stages where it seemed like no one within sociology wanted the project to exist. These conversations were particularly helpful in facing the requirements during and after classroom presentations, workshops, anonymous reviews, and course feedback that persistently pushed me to center black men. Thank you, Shantel Buggs, Anima Adjepong, Carmen Gutierrez, Vrinda Marwah, Katie Rogers, Rui Jie Peng, Beth Prosnitz, Latoya Teagues, Jamie O'Quinn, and Erika Slaymaker for the daily, and often unseen, work of creating feminist spaces in hostile academic waters. Second, finding senior mentors and committee members who supported the work was pivotal in the early stages of the project when I was on the brink of quitting my graduate program. Throughout the different stages, they helped me learn how to navigate adversarial debates and these requirements as they understood the importance of centering black women and other marginalized groups' experiences in research. Thank you, Christine Williams, Yasmiyn Irizarry, Christen Smith, Gloria González-López, Sarah Brayne, and Nicole Burrowes. Collectively, these scholars guided me through the academic space between by sharing feminist and critical race research that also faced these obstacles and their experiences encountering these challenges in their own work as well as providing invaluable professional and personal support.

Analysis

In my analysis of black women's stories, I primarily utilized a combination of grounded theory and S. R. Toliver's endarkened storywork. Grounded theory uses comparative and iterative coding processes to develop themes.[18] As such, this coding process was uniquely suited for theoretical development based on the lived experiences of black women in the spaces between—or outside broader societal and dominant intracommunal knowing about policing. Throughout the coding process, I also drew from endarkened storywork, which engages historical black storytelling traditions to weave together collective meaning through connections between people's standpoints and experiences.[19] Toliver explains how the emphasis is less on distinguishing and reifying variation in analysis and more on how differences contribute to an interconnected narrative, to life-affirming world-making.

Drawing on grounded theory and endarkened storywork, I considered how stories ground us, provide a way for us to locate ourselves in historical experiences, create a space for validating lived experiences, and are a way of forming bonds and connections among social groups across time and space. From here, I centered my analysis on black women's stories in the space between—where, on one side, others create language, frames, definitions, systems, meanings, and ultimately worlds that exclude them, and on the other side are their lived experiences that they must make sense of and contend with. *Here*—I analyzed their emotions as an epistemology-method for understanding the margins and the expansive impact of policing. In doing so, I examined both the creation of a margin and how it shaped the risks of police violence and other types of violence along with their processes of meaning-making, moving through, and resisting "missing-ness."

(*analysis*)

Gathering is an alternative process to *everyday policing*—an epistemological and literal site black women create through their intimate and everyday searches for safety and solidarity. In these sites, black women reflect on and reconfigure their relationships between themselves and others. Gathering, in many ways, was an epistemology-method I shared with the black women I interviewed. Thus, throughout the project's development, fieldwork, analysis, and writing, I gathered. In conceptualizing the first phase of the project on black mothers' socialization practices around police violence, I had in-depth conversations with my mentors as well as black women in my family and networks. In these talks, many shared stories about police violence and other types of violence in their lives for the first time. As I conducted interviews with black mothers, I continued to talk with people in my family and communities outside the academy about what I was finding. We talked about the police talks and other conversations about violence. We talked about what it meant for many of us to enter and exit discussions on safety within our families and communities. We talked about double and multiple consciousness and how they manifest in our daily lives. We talked about respectability politics and policing as an institution and everyday forms of social control we experience from others. These ongoing conversations were critical in theorizing the police talks and my decision to shift and focus more on black women's police encounters and stories.

Moving forward, I was more intentional about gathering as I moved through the other phases, analysis, and writing. This included conversations with sisters, siblings, and elders, as well as learning some of their untold stories of police violence. I also talked with my brothers and black men friends in my life. I continued to talk with several black women who had been interviewed. Some of them received coded memos on the project. Sometimes, we had late-night calls and follow-ups. For a few, I heard more of their stories after the interviews and how the interview process shifted their narratives around their experiences. While this book presented some of their stories in the past—their lives and stories continue on. And throughout all of these many, many conversations with others about the project: *We listened. We reflected. We shared secrets. We argued. We found each other. We fell out. We repaired and found each other again. We remembered. And we did our best to care and listen while we moved through the messiness of "missing-ness."'*

Finally, in addition to the traditional publication review processes undertaken by presses, I gathered with black and Latina feminist scholars and organizers to review the manuscript. In this gathering, we spent a day together discussing black women's stories presented in this book and the implications for how we understand policing and abolition feminism. Grounded in black feminist praxis, this gathering provided invaluable support and gave me the courage to write about experiences and stories I, too, was taught to keep silent.

For this, I am forever grateful to Erica Banks, Brittany Battle, Monica Bell, Nicole Burrowes, Kellee Coleman, Faith Deckard, Carmen Gutierrez, LaShawn Harris, Yasmiyn Irizarry, Treva Lindsey, Tressie McMillan Cottom, Whitney Pirtle, A. W. Shields, and Latoya Teague. Thank you for gathering me.

Reflexivity

Within the tradition of black feminist thought and sociology, black women use their lived experiences as a resource in the research process.[20] Additionally, Anima Adjepong conceptualizes invading ethnography as a queer of color reflexive practice that introduces the researcher's history and body into the analysis with participants.[21] In this way, invading ethnography creates a conversation between readers with methodology as well as participants, inviting readers to interrogate how positionality shapes the narrative and interpretation of respondent's biographies. Throughout the book, I engaged in this tradition of black feminist thought and invading ethnographic practice to analyze how my positionality and lived experiences shaped the interviews, analysis, and writing of the book as a black, queer, middle-class woman from the US South.

In interviews, I was often considered an insider based on my race and gender. But, as shown throughout this book, this oftentimes was not enough as black women also asked several questions about my background and experiences with the police. Gloria González-López discusses how participants can see the researcher as an authority figure with whom they can share their unnamed and unrecognized experiences of violence.[22] She describes how this "silenced violence" finds a listener to their pain that they may not have had access to in their past.[23] Thus, for black women, a critical aspect of me being deemed a suitable witness to their stories was not sharing some static identity of "black" or "woman"—but sharing certain experiences. This *storytelling vetting process* was critical for building trust, facilitating rapport, and legitimizing my role as a witness. From *here*, they would thin the veil of dissemblance and share their stories, saying that I "knew how it was" or why they were silent. Collectively, I drew from my experiences and invading ethnography practice to develop questions, conduct interviews, analyze findings, and ultimately, include some of our interactions into the stories shared in this book. This also meant that while I interviewed sixty-two black women and informally talked with countless others, I was personally interviewed and told parts of my story *innumerable* times. This fact was not lost on many of the black women who asked their questions. Most assumed it was a necessary requirement for listening to their stories and that others before had asked and others in the future would continue to do so. We shared a deep recognition of what it meant for me to do this, to keep sharing my story and to carry theirs. I still remain in gratitude for the expressions of concern and care they extended to me. Many times, in our interviews, we gathered one another.

(reflexivity)

I do not remember the precise moment I began to recognize police violence against black women and girls as a legitimate and systemic social problem. Growing up, no one took me aside to warn me about the potential dangers of interacting with officers. I do not remember police violence against black women and girls being talked about openly (*or behind closed doors*). I do not remember hearing or seeing black women and girl victims of police violence in the media. However, in 2016, I participated in communal conversations on racial equity in Mississippi. During a convening, we discussed the recent police shooting of Terence Crutcher, an unarmed black man who was shot and killed by the police in Oklahoma.[24] Importantly, the conversations focused on the experiences of black men and boys with officers, and I remember listening to leaders in my community speak passionately about the challenges of raising and protecting black sons from becoming victims of police violence. I remember feeling a deep sorrow at the realities black men and boys faced every day. And I remember being grateful to have a daughter, believing I was pardoned somehow from the constant terror of worrying about how to protect a black son from police violence.

This feeling did not last long. Lingering in the back of my consciousness were my own lived experiences with the police and others. So, I began to ask myself: What would I tell my daughter? Yet, I remained silent and did not bring these thoughts, feelings, experiences, and concerns into the conversation. Like in the past, I considered these private and personal matters. Isolated and processing these and other incidents by myself, I would ruminate over questions like: *Did I cause this? Could I have prevented what happened? If people knew, would they blame me?* If the answers to any of these questions could possibly be yes, it did not feel worth it for me or my experiences to be seen by others. From where I stood—firmly in my place—I fully believed that my fears of the police were not valid enough, my encounters with officers not significant enough, and my trauma from police violence not important enough to warrant entrée into discussions on policing, let alone designation to what sociologists commonly refer to as a "social problem."

a poem about Abena's pauses written in loud silence

sometimes silence is loud

      a dry and raspy laugh
                    a pause
                            followed by a long

and exasperated exhale

can you still even call it a pause . . .

           . . . if she hesitates?
        . . . sardonically laughs?
              . . . waits?
          . . . and sighs?

           all before trying once more to explain her point

her voice

     is
     low

                             and distant

but her laugh?

it's loud

wry   and broken up   by long sighs

as she repeatedly pauses   before trying

                                                                          once more

          to explain to me

that there is absolutely no point in black women and girls speaking about violence . . .

                                                            . . . police or otherwise
                              because?

nothing is going to happen anyway

                              because?

she's shared her story before

                              because?

she's learned her lessons

[and from *here*]

she's sharing her stories and lessons with me

pausing

before detailing
exactly how she learned the hard way
just what types of consequences

lay on the other sides of violence disclosures

folks aren't willing
or ready
to hear

from black girls

Demographic Tables

TABLE B.1. Phase 1 Participant Demographics

Pseudonym	Age	Number of kids	Marital status	Education	Income
Alice	35	2	Single	Bachelor's	$120,000
Alicia	39	2	Single	High school	Declined
Angela	41	2	Married	Bachelor's	$400,000
Amanda	35	2	Married	Professional Doctorate/PhD	$175,000
Ava	31	1	Single	Bachelor's	$30,000
Claire	47	2	Married	Professional Doctorate/PhD	$200,000
Debbie	38	5	Married	Bachelor's	$25,000
Frances	38	3	Divorced	Master's	$43,000
Gwen	43	1	Married	Professional Doctorate/PhD	$290,000
Issa	39	3	Married	Master's	$100,000
Jada	34	1	Single	Master's	$50,000
Josie	36	2	Married	Master's	$90,000
Lisa	40	4	Married	Master's	$250,000
Lena	38	3	Married	Professional Doctorate/PhD	$110,000
Maya	37	1	Single	Professional Doctorate/PhD	$55,000
Nikki	44	3	Married	Associate's	$55,000
Nina	35	3	Single	High school	$28,000
Octavia	35	2	Married	Master's	$140,000
Patricia	37	1	Married	Professional Doctorate/PhD	$400,000
Phillis	36	3	Married	Professional Doctorate/PhD	$230,000
Phylicia	38	3	Single	High school	$30,000
Rita	46	6	Married	Bachelor's	$120,00
Ruby	29	2	Single	High school	$32,000
Sonia	32	1	Engaged	High school	$30,000
Terri	38	1	Married	Master's	$90,000
Toni	39	3	Married	Professional Doctorate/PhD	$200,000
Vanessa	33	2	Married	Professional Doctorate or PhD	$150,000
Vivica	27	2	Single	High school	$17,000
Whitney	43	2	Single	Bachelor's	$50,000
Zora	54	2	Married	Professional Doctorate/PhD	$170,000

TABLE B.2. Phase 2 Participant Demographics

Pseudonym	Age	Ethnicity	Gender	Sexuality	Education	Income
Abena	32	African	Cisgender	Heterosexual	High School	$20,000–29,000
Alexis	27	African American	Cisgender	Bisexual	Bachelor's	$30,000–39,000
Ashley	31	African and African American	Cisgender	Heterosexual	High school	$30,000–39,000
Audrey	35	African and Afro-Caribbean	Cisgender	Bisexual	Master's	$30,000–39,000
Candace	37	African American	Cisgender	Heterosexual	Master's	$40,000–49,000
Dana	27	African and African American	Cisgender	Heterosexual	Bachelor's	$20,000–29,000
Danielle	25	African	Cisgender	Bisexual	Master's	$20,000–29,000
Devin	37	Biracial or Multiracial	Cisgender	Queer	Bachelor's	$80,000–89,000
Ella	26	African American	Cisgender	Heterosexual	Bachelor's	$40,000–49,000
Gina	30	Latinx	Cisgender	Bisexual	Bachelor's	$40,000–49,000
Jade	38	–––	–––	–––	Bachelor's	–––
Joy	31	African American	Cisgender	Heterosexual	Master's	$40,000–49,000
Karen	26	African American	Cisgender	Bisexual	High school	$40,000–49,000
Keisha	24	African American	Cisgender	Heterosexual	Bachelor's	$40,000–49,000
Kerry	27	African American	Cisgender	Heterosexual, Queer	Bachelor's	$50,000–59,000
Kristen	23	African American	Cisgender	Bisexual	Bachelor's	$20,000–29,000
Krystal	32	African American and Biracial or Multiracial	Cisgender	Queer	Bachelor's	$20,000–29,000

Name	Age	Race/Ethnicity	Gender	Sexual Orientation	Education	Income
Laura	26	African American	Cisgender	Heterosexual	Bachelor's	$20,000–29,000
Layla	28	African American	Cisgender	Heterosexual	Bachelor's	$20,000–29,000
Lois	36	African American	Cisgender	Bisexual	Master's	$50,000–59,000
Michelle	35	Biracial or Multiracial	Cisgender	Lesbian	Master's	$90,000–99,000
Nema	18	African	Cisgender	Heterosexual	High school	$60,000–69,000
Quita	27	African American	Cisgender	Heterosexual	Bachelor's	$60,000–69,000
Robin	35	Biracial or Multiracial	Cisgender	Heterosexual	Master's	$30,000–39,000
Sadia	31	African American	Fluid: "Does not subscribe to societal norms."	Other: "Loves women."	Professional Doctorate or PhD	Less than $10,000
Shelia	25	African	Cisgender	Heterosexual	Bachelor's	$40,000–49,000
Simone	33	African American	Cisgender	Heterosexual	Professional Doctorate or PhD	$60,000–69,000
Tina	47	African American	Cisgender	Heterosexual	Bachelor's	$140,000–149,000
Teyana	33	African American	Cisgender	Bisexual	Bachelor's	$30,000–39,000
Toya	23	African American	Self-describes gender as not conforming to a gender binary	Other: "Why must we conform to these categories?"	Bachelor's	$20,000–29,000
Veronica	25	Latinx	Nonbinary and Transgender	Bisexual, Heterosexual, Lesbian, Queer	Technical or trade degree	Less than $10,000
Violet	41	African American	Cisgender	Heterosexual	Bachelor's	$90,000–99,000

Phase 2 Interview Guide

Establishing Rapport and General Views on Police

1. How do you feel knowing that you are going to be talking with me about police violence?
2. How was the survey for you? What did it bring up? What would you change?
3. What are your general thoughts about police? How do you feel about them?
4. Does the race/gender of the police officer matter to you?

Childhood Police Experiences and Conversations

5. Did anyone talk with you about police violence when you grew up? What was that conversation like? How did you feel?
6. How did you learn to interact with police? What makes you feel prepared?
7. Did you see anyone interact with police when you grew up? How did that feel for you? How did you cope with that?
8. What can you tell me about your first interaction with police?
9. Do you have any other childhood experiences with police? How did you cope with that? Did you talk with anyone?

Adult Police Experiences and Conversations

10. In your day to day, do you notice police? Where do you notice them? (PROBE: List specific locations.) How do you feel when you see them?

11. Are there places where you feel more vulnerable to the police? How do you feel when you are in those places?

12. Do you have any adult interactions with police you would like to share? How did you cope with this experience?

13. Are there specific things about yourself that make you vulnerable to police? How does that feel?

14. Do you have a plan/strategy for interacting with police?

15. Would you feel comfortable calling the police in an emergency?

16. What advice would you have for other black women or girls about police?

17. Are there places where you feel comfortable/uncomfortable talking about police violence? Police violence against black women?

Social Media and Police Reform

18. How do you feel when you see police violence on social media? Police violence against black women on social media? How do you cope with that?

19. Have you helped anyone with their experiences with police? How did that feel for you?

20. What recommendations would you have to address police violence?

Interview Wrap-Up

21. Is there anything I haven't asked that you think is important for understanding your views on police?

22. Of all the questions that I asked you, what was the most challenging question and/or topic for you? Please explain why.

23. My hope is that this project will produce a book at some point, what would you like to see included?

24. Is there anything you would want black women to know or any advice you have?

25. Is there anything you would like to ask me about the project or my own experiences?

Final Survey Measures for Types of Police Violence

APPENDIX D: Final Survey Measures for Types of Police Violence

Type of force	Survey question
Neglect	
Dismissed or ignored (report involving self)	Had an officer ever dismissed or ignored you when reporting an incident involving yourself?
Dismissed or ignored (report for someone else)	Had an officer ever dismissed or ignored you when reporting an incident involving someone else?
Verbal and psychological abuse	
Cursed or shouted at	Had an officer ever cursed or shouted at you?
Belittled or called names	Had an officer ever belittled or called you derogatory names?
Threatened with arrest	Had an officer ever threatened you with being arrested?
Sexual harassment	
Complimented on appearance	Had an officer ever complimented you on your physical appearance?
Stared at (leered)	Had an officer ever stared or looked at you in a sexual manner?
Asked for personal info	Had an officer ever asked you for personal information for a date or off-duty encounter?
Repeated visits (stalked)	Had an officer ever made repeated uninvited or unwanted visits to you?

(*Continued*)

APPENDIX D (*continued*)

Type of force	Survey question
Physical threats and assault	
Threatened with a weapon	Had an officer ever threatened you with a baton, taser, gun, or other type of weapon?
Roughed up	Had an officer ever pushed, hit, grabbed, or kicked you?
Assaulted with a weapon	Had an officer ever assaulted you with a baton, taser, gun, or other type of weapon?
Put in a chokehold	Had an officer ever put you in a chokehold?
Sexual coercion and assault	
Requested sexual favor	Had an officer ever told you that you would not receive a ticket or citation if you complied to an unwanted sexual act?
Sexual touching (groped)	Had an officer ever attempted or engaged in sexually touching or groping you?
Unwanted sexual acts	Had an officer ever asked you to engage in unwanted sexual acts?
Exposed genitals (flashed)	Had an officer ever intentionally exposed their genitals to you?
Raped by officer	Had an officer ever raped you?

ACKNOWLEDGMENTS

WHILE CLOSING OUT the writing of this book, I found myself at a coffee shop one day far away from home. Standing in line ahead of me was a white woman who appeared to be in her late forties with her father who seemed to be in his late eighties. They were joking about who would pay for the coffee this time. She laughed as she teased him about retiring and told him it was her turn to pay for it, but he could get the next one. I smiled at their banter and looked around the coffee shop at all the intergenerational white families: Grandparents chasing a young child around the table; another couple who appeared to be in their seventies having a midday coffee while chatting about what they were going to do on their next vacation; a young couple in their early twenties holding hands. As I took my coffee, I went for a walk to admire this little town—the green space, the trees and warmed park benches, the little shops with doors open to the public inviting them in, more kids running up and down the brick-paved street. I took in the life there, the young and old sharing this beautiful, present moment together. And for the briefest of moments, I let myself dream of what it could be like if my community got to age like this, to be in green and clean open spaces, to retire and be taken care of by those around them, and for elders to chase their grandkids around coffee shops in the middle of endless afternoons. As a praxis, I let myself lean into this moment, to imagine this life, to feel it and all that came along with it: the yearning, the joy, the hope. Yet, even as I write this, I can still feel the overwhelming grief bubbling up inside me at the reality that so many in my community didn't and won't get a chance to experience this because we lose so many people we love to quick and slow violence.

These people—my people—matter. And so, too, do our stories.

Thus, the experiences of violence we have, of losing each other in quick and slow ways, make the testimonies inevitable. The desires, hopes, and plans we have for something better make the testimonies inevitable. The strength, courage, and will we have to make the world we dream and deserve a reality make the testimonies inevitable.

Thus, it was inevitable that this book, filled with black women's testimonies that are often "missing" from understandings of policing and violence, would be a communal effort.

First and foremost, to the black women who shared some of their most intimate experiences of violence with me: *Thank you.* I am in deep gratitude for the chance to bear witness to your stories and learn from them in hopes that we could build something better.

To my ancestors, and first, to my grandmother, Amanda Ella: You were with us in 2016 when I started envisioning this project. While you are no longer here, I would like to say thank you. Many of our people's stories live on in us because of you, and our early conversations about the project and your blessing has meant so much to me throughout this process. To our ancestral lineage, thank you for guiding me, holding me, and carrying me through all the midnight hours in completing this book. Thank you for continuing to co-conspire with us to build something better.

To my Mississippi community, family, and chosen family spread throughout the many chapters of my life: You saw purpose in me when I was headed down some shaky paths, and I am forever grateful to my fleet of othermothers: Ms. Paulette, Ms. Mason, Ms. Deborah, Ms. Carla, Auntie Michelle, Auntie Tina, Auntie Shelia, and Auntie DeLois. To the folks at Tougaloo who stepped in and pushed me forward, thank you: Kristen, Kevya (and your momma), Markeshia, Candace, Dr. Love Jackson, Dr. Anderson, Dr. Morse-Gagne, Dr. Ray, Dr. Gagne, and many others. Thanks also to those who saw purpose in the work when it was just a possibility. I am thankful for your encouragement and support in transitioning the project from a potentiality to a reality, thank you: Aisha, Shelia, Kenisha, Margaret, Cassandra, BJ, Roland, Angelica, Kellee, Michelle, Jermeika, Caty (Big Al), Shallini, Tara, Retha, Evelia, Shona, Cade, Prasi, and Kate. I am grateful to be in community with you.

To Albert: *There is no book without you.* You were standing right there with me each and every step of the way. You are my biggest supporter and thank you for always having my back.

To my academic community: I am especially thankful to Christine Williams for her mentorship. When faced with pressure in the early stages of the project to include other social groups as a requirement for telling black women's stories, I am grateful that I could turn to an advisor who recognized that our stories could stand on their own. Thank you also to Yasmiyn Irizarry for gathering me in all of the academic spaces between. Your support of me and this work has meant so much (*i have no words for the type of support you gave*), and I am grateful to have you as a mentor-sister-advocate. I am also thankful to have had the chance to learn from feminist scholars with commitments to building something better, thank you: Christen Smith, Nicole Burrowes, Gloria González-López, Sarah Brayne, and Sharmila Rudrappa. Throughout this journey, I have also been inspired by the brilliant community of feminist collaborators and co-conspirators I met at UT Austin. You all mean so much to me, and I am deeply grateful for the support you gave me and my girls, and the innumerable times you helped me get back up when knocked down. I am now a true believer in the feminist bat signal, so thank you: Anima Adjepong, Shantel Buggs, Carmen Gutierrez, Eric Borja, Katie Rogers, Vrinda Marwah, Beth Prosnitz, Rui Jie Peng, Jamie O'Quinn, Erika Slaymaker, Latoya Teague, Faith Deckard, and Samantha Simon. As time has gone on, I also want to thank each and every scholar that has pushed me, given feedback, and supported me in this work along the way at other institutions and at UNC, thank you: Uriel Serrano, Edlin Veras, Whitney Pirtle, Saida Grundy, Hillary Potter, Zawadi Rucks Ahidiana, Prisca Gayles, Amaka Okechukwu, Piper Sledge, Nadirah Foley, Candice Miller, Taylor Hargrove, Chantel Martin, Daniel Kreiss, Alice Marwick, Shannon McGregor, Tressie McMillan Cottom, Francesca Tripodi, Scott Duxbury, Kate Weisshaar, Charles Kurzman, Lisa Pearce, and Mia Brantley. And specifically, to my black feminist criminology working group: Brittany Battle, Amber Joy Powell, Maretta McDonald, and Faith Deckard—thank you for supporting me and this research. Thank you for steadily bringing an abolition feminism perspective to the work. I am grateful to be surrounded by caring and fierce truth-tellers.

To the scholars and activists who gathered with me for the book workshop: It remains one of the most special moments I have ever had on this academic journey. You provided such critical and insightful feedback with equal amounts of care and thoughtfulness. I am still in awe of the magic of that space and the generosity you showed me as a junior scholar. It truly was a day of black feminist praxis with focus on building something better for us. Some of you will be listed again, but I want to make sure I name and thank each and every one of you: Nicole Burrowes, Treva B. Lindsey, LaShawn Harris, Tressie McMillan Cottom, Monica Bell, Whitney Pirtle, A. W. Shields, Kellee Coleman, Brittany Battle, Carmen Gutierrez, Yasmiyn Irizarry, Faith Deckard, Latoya Teague, and Erica Banks.

To the graduate students who provided support at the workshop and during the writing of this manuscript: Thank you Jarvis Benson and Kayla Corbin. You all have been a joy to work with over the past several years. Things happened, happened on time, and happened with ease because of you.

To the Root Cause Collective: Thank you for being in relation with me, the work, and for envisioning ways to translate the research into praxis.

Finally, I would like to thank Tamara K. Nopper for her editorial guidance throughout this process. Thank you for your insightful feedback, for pushing me as a writer, and for helping me center the voices of the black women in this study. I also want to thank the anonymous reviewers for not only engaging with the stories in these pages, but for also providing thoughtful suggestions that helped improve the manuscript. Last, this work received generous support from the UNC Center for Information, Technology, and Public Life (CITAP), Ford Foundation, National Science Foundation, and the Horowitz Foundation for Social Policy.

NOTES

Introduction

1. All names are pseudonyms.

2. For many, capitalizing the *b* in "Black" connotes a shared ethnic and cultural identity across the African diaspora (for example, see Appiah, "The Case for Capitalizing the *B* in Black"). I choose not to capitalize the *b* in recognition that in addition to racial identification, gender and sexuality identification also carry shared (*and distinct*) histories and cultures, and yet, are not presently capitalized. Also see T. Anansi Wilson's work on BlaQueer, which connects "Black" and "Queer" while also capitalizing the *b* and *q* in recognition of their inseparability and significance in shaping the lives of black queer people. T. Anansi Wilson, "What is BlaQueer?" https://blaqueerflow.wordpress.com/about/what-is-blaqueer-2014/.

3. Crenshaw et al., "Say Her Name: Resisting Police Brutality Against Black Women."

4. Neely, *You're Dead—So What?: Media, Police, and the Invisibility of Black Women as Victims of Homicide*; Williams, "Digital Defense: Black Feminists Resist Violence with Hashtag Activism."

5. Malone Gonzalez, "Making It Home: An Intersectional Analysis of the Police Talk."

6. See Crenshaw and African American Policy Forum, *#SayHerName: Black Women's Stories of Police Violence and Public Silence*; and Ritchie, *Invisible No More: Police Violence Against Black Women and Women of Color.*

7. Throughout the text, I fluctuate between using "we/us/our" and "they/them/their" when referring to black women. I use "we/us/our" when writing about shared, collective experiences of black women as a social group. I use "they/them/their" when specifically referring to the black women who participated in the study and black women's historical experiences.

8. Crenshaw et al., "Say Her Name."

9. Ritchie, *Invisible No More.*

10. Crenshaw et al., "Say Her Name," 4; Crenshaw and African American Policy Forum, *#SayHerName.*

11. For notable exceptions, see Brunson and Miller, "Gender, Race, and Urban Policing: The Experience of African American Youth"; Remster et al., "Race, Gender, and Police Violence in the Shadow of Controlling Images"; Travers and Risman (eds.), "Symposium: Say Her Name."

12. Luna and Pirtle, "Black Feminist Sociology Is the Past, Present and Future of Sociology. Period.," 6.

13. Luna and Pirtle, "Black Feminist Sociology Is the Past, Present and Future," 6.

14. Ritchie, *Arrested Justice: Black Women, Violence, and America's Prison Nation.*

15. Collins, "Black Feminist Epistemology." Collins theorizes the matrix of domination as a way to make visible how intersectional and hierarchal relations are formed and reproduced through four domains of power. One domain focuses on social structures, or the systems and interconnected institutions that impact our lives. Another domain centers bureaucracies and surveillance, or the rules we must follow and the ways we are watched to ensure that we do. Yet another domain involves our cultures and how the narratives and images we see and receive shape our ideas about ourselves and others. The fourth domain highlights the intimate and interpersonal aspects of our lives, or day-to-day experiences and how we interact with each other and treat one another.

16. Threadcraft, "Making Black Femicide Visible: Intersectional, Abolitionist People-Building Against Epistemic Oppression."

17. Crenshaw, "Mapping the Margins: Intersectionality, Identity Politics, and Violence Against Women of Color."

18. Collins, "Black Feminist Epistemology"; Dotson, "Conceptualizing Epistemic Oppression."

19. hooks, *Yearning: Race, Gender, and Cultural Politics*, 150.

20. Clair, "Criminalized Subjectivity: Du Boisian Sociology and Visions for Legal Change."

21. Clair, "Criminalized Subjectivity," 290.

22. Foucault, *Discipline and Punish: The Birth of the Prison*. Foucault and others describe surveillance as the various ways people are watched to guarantee conformance to their place, disciplining subjects' behavior, thoughts, and activities in daily life. Punishments are the ensuing physical and psychic consequences that follow when someone deviates or breaks the norms, rules, and laws that uphold the social order. See also Brayne, *Predict and Surveil: Data, Discretion, and the Future of Policing*; and Browne, *Dark Matters: On the Surveillance of Blackness*.

23. Rios, *Punished: Policing the Lives of Black and Latino Boys*.

24. Jones, *Between Good and Ghetto: African American Girls and Inner-City Violence*.

25. Serrano, "Feeling Carcerality: How Carceral Seepage Shapes Racialized Emotions." Serrano provides carceral seepage as a way to understand "the scale and pace" of policing as it moves across contexts and shapes the emotions and interior worlds of black and non-black Latinx youth, 6. I similarly understand policing as something that moves, demarcates, and carves out people's place to understand black women's experiences of policing in different contexts.

26. Anzaldúa, *Borderlands / La Frontera: The New Mestiza*; and Alexander, *Pedagogies of Crossing: Meditations on Feminism, Sexual Politics, Memory, and the Sacred*. Many feminists discuss liminality and spaces between in their writings. For example, in *Borderlands / La Frontera*, Gloria Anzaldúa theorizes *Nepantla* as a space between, writing "*Nepantla*, which is a Nahuatl word for the space between two bodies of water, the space between two worlds. It is a limited space, a space where you are not this or that but where you are changing. You haven't got into the new identity yet and haven't left the old identity behind either—you are in a kind of transition. And that is what *Nepantla* stands for. It is very awkward, uncomfortable and frustrating to be that *Nepantla* because you are in the midst of transformation," 276. M. Jacqui Alexander also speaks to the relationship between liminality and knowledge in *Pedagogies of Crossing*, writing:

Thus, I came to understand pedagogies in multiple ways: as something given, as in handed, revealed; as in breaking through, transgressing, disrupting, displacing, inverting inherited concepts and practices, those psychic, analytic and organizational methodologies we deploy to know what we believe we know so as to make different conversations and solidarities possible; as both epistemic and ontological project bound to our beingness and, therefore, akin to Freire's formulation of pedagogy as indispensable methodology. In this respect, *Pedagogies* summons subordinated knowledges that are produced in the context of the practices of marginalization in order that we might destabilize existing practices of knowing and thus cross the fictive boundaries of exclusion and marginalization. This, then, is the existential message of the Crossing—to apprehend how it might instruct us in the urgent task of configuring new ways of being and knowing and to plot the different metaphysics that are needed to move away from living alterity premised in difference to living intersubjectivity premised in relationality and solidarity. (7–8)

I draw from feminist understandings of liminality, like Anzaldúa and Alexander, to conceptualize the space between as a space where black women are transformed by violence and have to figure out, often alone, an epistemology, methodology, and way of developing a lexicon that allows them to name an experience that remains unnamed by others in their social worlds.

27. Bonilla-Silva, "Feeling Race: Theorizing the Racial Economy of Emotions"; Also see Harris-Perry, "Crooked Room," 28–50; and Friedman and Hitchens, "Theorizing Embodied Carcerality," 267–76.

28. Norwood, "Black Feminist Sociology and the Politics of Space and Place," 139–50; Carolette Norwood argues that space is intersectional, literal, and embodied. It connects lived experiences to geographies. As such, she writes, "The spaces that we construct and that construct us (terrains of transgression and resistance) shape who we are and determine if and how we access resources and what knowledge is available to us" (147). I draw from this understanding of literal spaces to examine how violence constructs and connects terrains that people commonly see as separate in their day-to-day lives.

29. Lorde, "The Master's Tools Will Never Dismantle the Master's House," 110–13.

30. Spivak, "Can the Subaltern Speak?"

31. Roy, "Peace and the New Corporate Liberation Theology."

32. Dotson, "Tracking Epistemic Violence, Tracking Practices of Silencing."

33. Carlson, "The Equalizer? Crime, Vulnerability, and Gender in Progun Discourse"; and Gross, "African American Women, Mass Incarceration, and the Politics of Protection."

34. Christine Horne and Stefanie Mollborn, "Norms: An Integrated Framework."

35. See Omi and Winant, *Racial Formation in the United States*.

36. Merritt, "Lest We Forget Black Patriarchy; or, Why I'm Over Calling Out White Women."

37. Lindsey, *America Goddam: Violence, Black Women, and the Struggle for Justice*, 12.

38. Dotson, "Tracking Epistemic Violence."

39. Dotson, "Tracking Epistemic Violence."

40. Dotson makes clear that the ignorance she is referring to is not simply "unknowing," but rather a reliable and harmful ignorance sustained in the face of testimonies that would challenge it. She refers to this as pernicious ignorance.

41. Dotson, "Conceptualizing Epistemic Oppression"; Threadcraft, "Making Black Femicide Visible."

42. Mills, "White Ignorance," 13–38; Mueller, "Racial Ideology or Racial Ignorance? An Alternative Theory of Racial Cognition."

43. See Collins, "The Social Construction of Black Feminist Thought"; and Zuberi and Bonilla-Silva, *White Logic, White Methods: Racism and Methodology.*

44. Mueller, "Racial Ideology," 155.

45. Du Bois, *The Souls of Black Folk*, 12.

46. Du Bois, *Souls of Black Folk*, 130.

47. See Phelps, *The Minneapolis Reckoning: Race, Violence, and the Politics of Policing in America.*

48. Graham, "Compounding Anti-Black Racial Disparities in Police Stops." In analyzing research on police stops, they found that the median stop rate disparity was 2.6 times more for black people than their white counterparts, and up to 19 times more likely in certain jurisdictions.

49. Boyd, "Police Violence and the Built Harm of Structural Racism"; Edwards et al., "Risk of Being Killed by Police Use of Force in the United States by Age, Race–Ethnicity, and Sex"; Gaston, "Producing Race Disparities: A Study of Drug Arrests Across Place and Race"; Pierson et al., "A Large-Scale Analysis of Racial Disparities in Police Stops Across the United States"; Remster, Smith, and Kramer, "Race, Gender, and Police Violence"; Rojek et al., "Policing Race: The Racial Stratification of Searches in Police Traffic Stops."

50. Edwards et al., "Risk of Being Killed."

51. Deckard, "Surveilling Sureties: How Privately Mediated Monetary Sanctions Enroll and Responsibilize Families"; Jones, "Racism, Fines and Fees and the US Carceral State."

52. Clair, *Privilege and Punishment: How Race and Class Matter in Criminal Court.*

53. Crutchfield et al., "Racial and Ethnic Disparity and Criminal Justice: How Much Is Too Much?"; and Pettit and Gutierrez, "Mass Incarceration and Racial Inequality."

54. Roehrkasse and Wildeman, "Lifetime Risk of Imprisonment in the United States Remains High and Starkly Unequal." Roehrkasse and Wildeman find that black people have an 8.97 percent risk of imprisonment in their lifetime.

55. Omi and Winant, *Racial Formation*, 109–12.

56. See Epp et al., *Pulled Over: How Police Stops Define Race and Citizenship*; McHarris, *Beyond Policing: What Better Way to Make the Case for a Police-Free World Than to Show a World Where It's Possible*; and Vitale, *The End of Policing.*

57. Mays, *An Afro-Indigenous History of the United States*; Steinmetz et al., "Wicked Overseers: American Policing and Colonialism."

58. Mays, *Afro-Indigenous History*; Spillers, "Mama's Baby, Papa's Maybe: An American Grammar Book."

59. Hadden, *Slave Patrols: Law and Violence in Virginia and the Carolinas.*

60. Hadden, *Slave Patrols*; Steinmetz et al., "Wicked Overseers."

61. Hadden, *Slave Patrols*; Reichel, "Southern Slave Patrols as a Transitional Police Type."

62. Potter, "The History of Policing in the United States"; Vitale, *End of Policing.*

63. Muhammad, *The Condemnation of Blackness: Race, Crime, and the Making of Modern Urban America.*

64. Muhammad, *Condemnation of Blackness.*

65. See Hadden, *Slave Patrols*; and Go, "The Imperial Origins of American Policing: Militarization and Imperial Feedback in the Early 20th Century."

66. Lindsey, *America Goddam*; Spillers, "Mama's Baby, Papa's Maybe."

67. Davis, *Women, Race and Class.*

68. Haley, *No Mercy Here: Gender, Punishment, and the Making of Jim Crow Modernity.*

69. Haley, *No Mercy Here*; See also: LeFlouria, *Chained in Silence: Black Women and Convict Labor in the New South*.

70. See Ferguson, *Aberrations in Black: Toward a Queer of Color Critique*; and Harris, *Sex Workers, Psychics, and Numbers Runners: Black Women in New York City's Underground Economy*. For more on these laws and the targeting of black LGBTQ+ women, see Ritchie, "Law Enforcement Violence Against Women of Color"; and Piser, "The Walking While Trans Bill Is 'Stop and Frisk 2.0.'"

71. Lindsey, *America Goddam*, 18.

72. Lindsey, *America Goddam*. 18.

73. Kramer and Remster, "The Slow Violence of Contemporary Policing," 45.

74. Smith, "Facing the Dragon: Black Mothering, Sequelae, and Gendered Necropolitics in the Americas." For examples about the impact of the slow violence of policing on black lives, see Bor et al., "Police Killings and Their Spillover Effects on the Mental Health of Black Americans: A Population-Based, Quasi-Experimental Study"; Sewell et al., "Illness Spillovers of Lethal Police Violence: The Significance of Gendered Marginalization"; Turney, "Depressive Symptoms Among Adolescents Exposed to Personal and Vicarious Police Contact."

75. Tillman, "Carceral Liberalism: The Coloniality and Antiblackness of Coercive Benevolence, 637."

76. Lindsey, *America Goddam*; Rios et al., "*Mano Suave–Mano Dura*: Legitimacy Policing and Latino Stop-and-Frisk."

77. Du Bois, *Souls of Black Folk*, 15; For more on Du Bois and the relationship between his personal life and theoretical contributions, see Morris, *The Scholar Denied: W. E. B. Du Bois and the Birth of Modern Sociology*.

78. Itzigsohn and L. Brown, *The Sociology of W. E. B. Du Bois: Racialized Modernity and the Global Color Line*, 17.

79. Du Bois, *Souls of Black Folk*, 16.

80. Lorde, *Sister Outsider: Essays and Speeches*, 114.

81. Cohen, *Boundaries of Blackness: AIDS and the Breakdown of Black Politics*, 15.

82. Cohen, *Boundaries of Blackness*, 27.

83. Grundy, *Respectable: Politics and Paradox in Making the Morehouse Man*.

84. Grundy, *Respectable*, 135–85; See also Adichie, "The Danger of a Single Story." Adichie describes the single story as a restrictive narrative that harnesses the power to conclusively tell the story about people and social problems in ways that obstruct recognition of personhood and experiences. She states that "the consequence of the single story is this: It robs people of dignity. It makes our recognition of our equal humanity difficult. It emphasizes how we are different rather than how we are similar." The maintenance of a single story is as much about elevating a particular narrative as it is about suppressing other narratives that expand, contradict, or challenge it.

85. Carlson, "The Equalizer?," 61.

86. Higginbotham, *Righteous Discontent: The Women's Movement in the Black Baptist Church, 1880–1920*.

87. Carlson, "Police Warriors and Police Guardians: Race, Masculinity, and the Construction of Gun Violence." See also Simon, *Before the Badge: How Academy Training Shapes Police Violence*.

88. Madriz, "Images of Criminals and Victims: A Study on Women's Fear and Social Control." Madriz discusses how "ideal victims" are racialized and gendered, wherein white women

are seen as "ideal victims" in relation to black men who are alternatively seen as "ideal criminals." For more on police and racialized threat, see Ray et al., "The Sociology of Police Behavior"; and Flowe, *Uncontrollable Blackness: African American Men and Criminality in Jim Crow New York*.

89. Collins, *Black Feminist Thought: Knowledge, Consciousness, and the Politics of Empowerment*, 69–70.

90. Stuart and Benezra, "Criminalized Masculinities: How Policing Shapes the Construction of Gender and Sexuality in Poor Black Communities."

91. Bailey, *Misogynoir Transformed: Black Women's Digital Resistance*. Bailey describes how images and narratives shape the way black women and girls are constructed as deviant and defines misogynoir as "the uniquely co-constitutive racialized and sexist violence that befalls Black women as a result of their simultaneous and interlocking oppression at the intersection of racial and gender marginalization" (1).

92. Kendall, *Hood Feminism: Notes from the Women That a Movement Forgot*, 51.

93. Horne and Mollborn, "Norms."

94. Richie, *Arrested Justice*, 132.

95. Ditcher and Osthoff, "Women's Experiences of Abuse as a Risk Factor for Incarceration: A Research Update."

96. Saar et al., "The Sexual Abuse to Prison Pipeline: The Girls' Story." See also Morris, *Pushout: The Criminalization of Black Girls in Schools*.

97. Menjívar, "State Categories, Bureaucracies of Displacement, and Possibilities from the Margins."

98. Collins, "Social Construction"; Harding, "Rethinking Standpoint Epistemology: What Is 'Strong Objectivity?'"; Smith, *The Everyday World as Problematic: A Feminist Sociology*.

99. Threadcraft, "Making Black Femicide Visible," 39.

100. Collins, *On Intellectual Activism*. See also Polletta et al., "The Sociology of Storytelling" for more on how sociologists have traditionally analyzed storytelling by political actors and institutions.

101. González-López, *Family Secrets: Stories of Incest and Sexual Violence in Mexico*.

102. Toliver, *Recovering Black Storytelling in Qualitative Research: Endarkened Storywork*.

103. Adjepong, "Invading Ethnography: A Queer of Color Reflexive Practice."

104. Hine, "Rape and the Inner Lives of Black Women in the Middle West."

105. Hine, "Rape and the Inner Lives"; and Sweet, *The Politics of Surviving: How Women Navigate Domestic Violence and Its Aftermath*.

106. Hine, "Rape and the Inner Lives." See also Collins, *Black Sexual Politics*.

107. Hine, "Rape and the Inner Lives," 915.

108. Hine, "Rape and the Inner Lives"; See also Nash, "Black Feminine Enigmas, or Notes on the Politics of Black Feminist Theory."

109. Harris-Perry, *Sister Citizen: Shame, Stereotypes, and Black Women in America*.

110. Harris-Perry, "Crooked Room," 28–50.

111. King, "Multiple Jeopardy, Multiple Consciousness: The Context of a Black Feminist Ideology."

112. Harris-Perry, *Sister Citizen*, 4.

113. Ahmed, *The Cultural Politics of Emotion*; hooks, *All About Love: New Visions*; hooks, *Killing Rage: Ending Racism*; Lorde, *Sister Outsider*.

114. See Collins, "Social Construction"; Compton et al., *Other, Please Specify: Queer Methods in Sociology*; Zuberi and Bonilla-Silva, *White Logic, White Methods*.

115. Boyles, *Race, Place, and Suburban Policing: Too Close for Comfort*. For more on how the black middle-class experiences and navigates racism and violence, see Karyn R. Lacy, *Blue-Chip Black: Race, Class, and Status in the New Black Middle Class*; and Pattillo, *Black Picket Fences: Privilege and Peril Among the Black Middle Class*.

116. For more on intersectionality, methods, and the examination of intracategorical differences, see Leslie McCall, "The Complexity of Intersectionality"; and Jennifer C. Nash, "Re-Thinking Intersectionality."

117. Othermothering is the communal practice of mothering, wherein nonbiological mothers share caregiving responsibilities for black children. See Collins, *Black Feminist Thought*, 178–83.

1. "I Wish I Was Taught to Be Okay in Me": The Space Between the Talks and Vulnerabilities to Violence

1. For more on policing and Islamophobia, see Selod, *Forever Suspect: Racialized Surveillance of Muslim Americans in the War on Terror*; and Yazdiha, "The Relational Dynamics of Racialised Policing: Community Policing for Counterterrorism, Suspect Communities, and Muslim Americans' Provisional Belonging."

2. Adultification is a social process of seeing children as more emotionally mature and physically developed compared to their age. Research documents how black children are more likely to experience adultification from police and other authority figures in comparison to white children. See Gilmore and Bettis, "Antiblackness and the Adultification of Black Children in a U.S. Prison Nation"; and Goff et al., "The Essence of Innocence: Consequences of Dehumanizing Black Children."

3. For adultification and black girls, see Nuamah and Mulroy, "'I am a Child!': Public Perceptions of Black Girls and Their Punitive Consequences"; and Perillo et al., "Examining the Consequences of Dehumanization and Adultification in Justification of Police Use of Force Against Black Girls and Boys."

4. April et al., "Let's 'Talk' About the Police: The Role of Race and Police Legitimacy Attitudes in the Legal Socialization of Youth"; Evans and Feagin, "The Costs of Policing Violence: Foregrounding Cognitive and Emotional Labor."

5. For examples on parental socialization, policing, and racism, see Brantley, "Can't Just Send Our Children Out: Intensive Motherwork and Experiences of Black Motherhood"; and Harris and Amutah-Onukagha, "Under the Radar: Strategies Used by Black Mothers to Prepare Their Sons for Potential Police Interactions."

6. For news articles, see McDonald, "The Talk: It's Time for White Parents to Take Over a Grim Ritual That Black Families Have Performed for Decades"; and Mahbubani, "As Police Violence Comes Under More Scrutiny, Black Parents Say They're Still Giving Their Kids 'The Talk' about Dealing with Cops." For television, see Rhimes et al., *Grey's Anatomy*.

7. The White House. "Remarks of President Joe Biden—State of the Union Address as Prepared for Delivery."

8. Anderson et al., "'The Talk' and Parenting While Black in America: Centering Race, Resistance, and Refuge"; Malone Gonzalez, "Black Girls and the Talk? Policing, Parenting, and the Politics of Protection."

9. See Felker-Kantor, *DARE to Say No: Policing and the War on Drugs in Schools.*

10. "#AssaultAtSpringValley: An Analysis of Police Violence." Using media reports of police assaults in schools, they find that black boys account for 56.9 percent of the assault victims and black girls account for 30.7 percent. Police sexual assault was the fourth-most-frequent type of officer assault and accounted for 8.4 percent of cases.

11. See Saar et al., "Sexual Abuse to Prison Pipeline"; and Wun,"Unaccounted Foundations: Black Girls, Anti-Black Racism, and Punishment in Schools."

12. Davis, *Women, Race and Class.*

13. Gross, "African American Women," 25.

14. Foster, "The Sexual Abuse of Black Men Under American Slavery"; Ritchie *Invisible No More*; Roberts, *Killing the Black Body: Race, Reproduction, and the Meaning of Liberty.*

15. Ritchie, *Invisible No More*, 25–37; Berry and Gross, *A Black Women's History of the United States.*

16. Collins, "The Tie That Binds: Race, Gender and US Violence."

17. Collins, "Tie That Binds," 919.

18. Collins, *Black Feminist Thought*, 77–84.

19. See Alexander, *New Jim Crow: Mass Incarceration in the Age of Colorblindness*; and Hinton, *From the War on Poverty to the War on Crime: The Making of Mass Incarceration in America.*

20. Collins, *Black Feminist Thought*, 73–75.

21. Haley, *No Mercy Here*, 160–62.

22. Collins, *Black Feminist Thought*, 81–84.

23. Jacobs, "The Violent State: Black Women's Invisible Struggle Against Police Violence," 50.

24. LeFlouria, *Chained in Silence.*

25. Thompson-Miller and Picca, " 'There Were Rapes!': Sexual Assaults of African American Women and Children in Jim Crow."

26. Wells-Barnett, *The Red Record: Tabulated Statistics and Alleged Causes of Lynchings in the United States 1892–1893–1894.* In Wells-Barnett's systemic cataloguing of lynchings and white vigilante violence, she provides details on the murders and assaults of black women.

27. Dotson, "Tracking Epistemic Violence."

28. Higginbotham, *Righteous Discontent*, 14.

29. Gaines, *Uplifting the Race: Black Leadership, Politics, and Culture in the Twentieth Century,* 5–6. Gaines offers the term "racial uplift" to describe black communities' and families' political strivings toward respectability and legibility, which is often grounded in heteropatriarchal and elitist ideals.

30. hooks, *Killing Rage*, 72.

31. Hollander, "Vulnerability and Dangerousness: The Construction of Gender through Conversation about Violence." Hollander argues that discourses about vulnerability are integral to understanding the reproduction of gendered, racialized beliefs about violence in everyday life. Importantly, she demonstrates how people hold onto these beliefs about criminality and vulnerability despite empirical evidence on people's lived experiences that would challenge these beliefs. See also Presser, *Unsaid: Analyzing Harmful Silences.*

32. Ritterhouse, *Growing up Jim Crow: How Black and White Southern Children Learned Race*, 16.

33. See Daiquoi, "Symbols in the Strange Fruit Seeds: What 'the Talk' Black Parents Have with Their Sons Tells Us About Racism"; Dow, *Mothering While Black: Boundaries and Burdens of Middle-Class Parenthood*; Malone Gonzalez, "Making It Home."

34. Dow, "The Deadly Challenges of Raising African American Boys: Navigating the Controlling Image of the 'Thug'"; Malone Gonzalez, "Making It Home."

35. Brunson and Weitzer, "Negotiating Unwelcome Police Encounters: The Intergenerational Transmission of Conduct Norms"; Malone Gonzalez, "Black Girls and the Talk?"

36. Malone Gonzalez, "Black Girls and the Talk?"

37. hooks, *Teaching to Transgress*, 59–60.

38. See DeSilver et al., "10 Things We Know About Race and Policing in the U.S."; Parker et al., "Trust in America: Do Americans Trust the Police?"; Cochran and Warren, "Racial, Ethnic, and Gender Differences in Perceptions of the Police: The Salience of Officer Race within the Context of Racial Profiling"; Grasso et al., Policing Progress: *Findings from a National Survey of LGBTQ+ People's Experiences with Law Enforcement*; Henry and Franklin, "Police Legitimacy in the Context of Street Stops: The Effects of Race, Class, and Procedural Justice"; Meyer, "'So Much for Protect and Serve': Queer Male Survivors' Perceptions of Negative Police Experiences."

39. Du Bois, *Souls of Black Folk*, 16.

40. Underhill, "Parenting During Ferguson: Making Sense of White Parents' Silence"

41. Malone Gonzalez, "Making It Home."

42. See Whitaker and Snell, "Parenting While Powerless: Consequences of 'The Talk.'"

43. Edwards et al., "Risk of Being Killed."

44. Elliot et al., "Brothermothering: Gender, Power, and the Parenting Strategies of Low-Income Black Single Mothers of Teenagers." Elliot, Brenton, and Powell found that low-income, single black mothers materially and symbolically lean on their older sons to parent younger siblings and ensure their safety. In my interviews, I found that black women across social class who were older sisters also socialized their younger siblings to interact with officers—especially in the perceived absence of parental or guardian socialization around police violence.

45. Crenshaw and African American Policy Forum, *#SayHerName*; INCITE! Women of Color Against Violence, "Law Enforcement Violence."

46. Butler, *Chokehold: Policing Black Men.*; Ritchie, *Invisible No More*, 104–26, and 195–98; Robinson, "The Lavender Scare in Homonormative Times: Policing, Hyper-Incarceration, and LGBTQ Youth Homelessness"; Office of Public Affairs, "Six Former Mississippi Law Enforcement Officers Sentenced for Torturing and Abusing Two Black Men."

47. DuMonthier et al., *"The Status of Black Women in the United States."*

48. Jones, *Between Good and Ghetto*, 11.

49. Combahee River Collective, "The Combahee River Collective Statement," 16.

50. Richie, "Battered Black Women a Challenge for the Black Community."

51. Harris-Perry, *Sister Citizen*; Morris, "'Ladies' or 'Loudies'? Perceptions and Experiences of Black Girls in Classrooms."

52. For more on the relationship between whiteness and the weaponization of the police, see Armstrong, "From Lynching to Central Park Karen: How White Women Weaponize White Womanhood"; and Williams, "Black Memes Matter: #LivingWhileBlack with Becky and Karen."

2. "What Happens in Our House" / "You Don't Call the Police on Your Family": The Space Between Home and Police Contact

1. National Coalition Against Domestic Violence, "Domestic Violence and the Black Community."

2. See Bryant-Davis et al., "From the Margins to the Center: Ethnic Minority Women and the Mental Health Effects of Sexual Assault"; Coker et al., "Physical and Mental Health Effects of Intimate Partner Violence for Men and Women."

3. Potter, *Battle Cries: Black Women and Intimate Partner Abuse.*

4. In my post-interview memo, I note feeling ambivalent about interrupting a woman who was sharing an experience of domestic violence and police violence. However, I also regretted not stopping her and letting her know that she was intruding on a private conversation.

5. See Elizabeth Hinton, *From the War on Poverty to the War on Crime.*

6. Moynihan, *The Negro Family: The Case for National Action,* 27.

7. Battle, "The Carceral Logic of Parental Responsibility"; Roberts, *Torn Apart: How the Child Welfare System Destroys Black Families—and How Abolition Can Build a Safer World*; Garcia-Hallett, *Invisible Mothers: Unseen Yet Hypervisible After Incarceration.*

8. Garcia-Hallett, *Invisible Mothers.*

9. See The Pew Charitable Trusts, "Local Spending on Jails Tops $25 Billion in Latest Nationwide Data."

10. Braga et al., "Race, Place, and Effective Policing"; Hinton, *America on Fire: The Untold History of Police Violence and Black Rebellion Since the 1960s.*

11. See Harcourt, "Illusion of Order: The False Promise of Broken Windows Policing"; and Steinmetz et al., "Wicked Overseers."

12. Gurusami and Kurwa, "From Broken Windows to Broken Homes: Homebreaking as Racialized and Gendered Poverty Governance."

13. hooks, "Homeplace (a site of resistance)."

14. Gaines, *Uplifting the Race.*

15. Richie, *Compelled to Crime: The Gender Entrapment of Battered Black Women.*

16. Richie, *Compelled to Crime,* 5.

17. Gómez, *The Cultural Betrayal of Black Women and Girls: A Black Feminist Approach to Healing from Sexual Abuse.*

18. Gómez, *Cultural Betrayal*; Sweet, *Politics of Surviving.*

19. Richie, *Arrested Justice,* 131–36.

20. Richie, *Arrested Justice,* 131–36; Potter, *Battle Cries,* 3–7.

21. National Coalition Against Domestic Violence, "Domestic Violence and the Black Community."

22. Beckett and Clayton, "'An Unspoken Epidemic': Homicide Rate Increase for Black Women Rivals That of Black Men."

23. Richie, "A Black Feminist Reflection on the Antiviolence Movement"; Potter, "An Argument for Black Feminist Criminology: Understanding African American Women's Experiences with Intimate Partner Abuse Using an Integrated Approach."

24. See Goodmark, *Imperfect Victims: Criminalized Survivors and the Promise of Abolition Feminisms*; Kim, "The Carceral Creep: Gender-Based Violence, Race, and the Expansion of the Punitive State, 1973–1983."

25. Goodmark, *Imperfect Victims*; Kim, "Carceral Creep."

26. Ritchie, *Invisible No More*, 189.

27. Collins, *Black Feminist Thought*.

28. Powell and Phelps, "Gendered Racial Vulnerability: How Women Confront Crime and Criminalization."

29. Bell, "Situational Trust: How Disadvantaged Mothers Reconceive Legal Cynicism."

30. See Jennings-Fitz-Gerald et al., "A Scoping Review of Policing and Coercive Control in Lesbian, Gay, Bisexual, Transgender, and Queer Plus Intimate Relationships"; and LaMartine et al., "'Even the Officers Are in on It': Black Transgender Women's Experiences of Violence and Victimization in Los Angeles."

31. Potter, *Battle Cries*, 128.

32. See also Buchanan and Ikuku, "We Major."

33. Buchanan and Ikuku, "We Major." Buchanan and Ikuku call for a rejection of "realness," of being "uninterested in reinscribing claims of authenticity or passability" (293). They argue that "realness" becomes an ontological and material condition that works to legitimate the murder of trans people. Further, as illustrated by officers' responses in this book, the police use multiple exclusionary frames to deny protection based on race, gender identity, class, sexuality, and disability.

34. Jones, *Between Good and Ghetto*, 48–49.

35. Stacey Patton, *Spare the Kids: Why Whupping Children Won't Save Black America*, 13–14.

36. Patton, *Spare the Kids*.

37. Patton, *Spare the Kids*, 149.

3. "He's Just Gonna Be Right Back Out There": The Space Between Violence Definitions and Disclosure of Police Gender-Based and Sexual Violence

1. While Gina mentions her father's ethnicity as Latinx, she does not specify his race. For more on the relationship between race and ethnicity, see Irizarry et al., "Race-Shifting in the United States: Latinxs, Skin Tone, and Ethnoracial Alignments."

2. Collins, "Tie That Binds," 920.

3. Armstrong et al., "Silence, Power, and Inequality: An Intersectional Approach to Sexual Violence."

4. Stinson, *Criminology Explains Police Violence*, 21–37; Ritchie, "Shrouded in Silence—Police Sexual Violence: What We Know and What We Can Do About It."

5. For police departments, see Simon, *Before the Badge*; for research institutions, see Collins, *On Intellectual Activism*; for media and journalism, see Davies, "'Culture of Exclusion' Keeps Women of Colour from Top Media Jobs, Report Reveals."

6. See Bryant-Davis et al., "From the Margins to the Center"; Slatton and Richard, "Black Women's Experiences of Sexual Assault and Disclosure: Insights from the Margins."

7. Deadnaming is the usage of transgender and gender-nonconforming people's birth name instead of their chosen name that affirms their gender identity. Using the chosen name for transgender youth reduces mental health risks, including depression and suicidal ideation. See Russell et al., "Chosen Name Use Is Linked to Reduced Depressive Symptoms, Suicidal Ideation and Behavior Among Transgender Youth."

8. Berry, *The Price for Their Pound of Flesh: The Value of the Enslaved, from Womb to Grave, in the Building of a Nation*; Roberts, *Killing the Black Body*.

9. See Berry, *Price for Their Pound of Flesh*; and Davis, *Women, Race and Class*.

10. Stern, "Shadow Trials, or A History of Sexual Assault Trials in the Jim Crow South"; Thompson-Miller and Picca, "'There Were Rapes!': Sexual Assaults of African American Women and Children in Jim Crow."

11. Harris, "'Women and Girls in Jeopardy by His False Testimony': Charles Dancy, Urban Policing, and Black Women in New York City During the 1920s."

12. Bell, "Police Reform and the Dismantling of Legal Estrangement," 2083.

13. Lindsey, *America Goddam*, 18.

14. See Burghart, "Fatal Encounters"; Campaign Zero, "Mapping Police Violence"; *Washington Post*, "Police Shootings Database."

15. Davis and Whyde, *Contacts Between Police and the Public, 2015*; Tapp and Davis, *Contacts Between Police and the Public, 2020*. Previous measures included: pushing, grabbing, hitting or kicking, using chemical or pepper spray, using an electroshock weapon, pointing a gun, handcuffing, cursing, shouting, and threatening arrest or force. After 2020, sexual misconduct was defined as officers who "made a sexual comment to, touched in a sexual way, or had any physical contact with that was sexual in nature," 10.

16. Stinson, *Criminology Explains Police Violence*.

17. See Edwards et al., "Risk of Being Killed"; Remster et al., "Race, Gender, and Police Violence"; Smith and Holmes, "Police Use of Excessive Force in Minority Communities: A Test of the Minority Threat, Place, and Community Accountability Hypothesis."

18. Lindsey, *America Goddam*, 18.

19. INCITE! Women of Color Against Violence, "Law Enforcement Violence."

20. Ritchie, *Shrouded in Silence*, 4.

21. Hitchens et al., "The Context for Legal Cynicism: Urban Young Women's Experiences with Policing in Low-Income, High-Crime Neighborhoods," 38.

22. Ritchie, "Shrouded in Silence."

23. Alter, "Why Oklahoma Cop's Rape Conviction Is a Major Victory"; Ritchie, "Say Her Name: What It Means to Center Black Women's Experiences of Police Violence."

24. Alter, "Why Oklahoma Cop's Rape Conviction is a Major Victory"; Ritchie, "Say Her Name."

25. Stinson et al., "Police Sexual Misconduct: A National Scale Study of Arrested Officers."

26. Simon, *Before the Badge*, 12.

27. Kerner National Advisory Commission on Civil Disorders, *Report of the National Advisory Commission on Civil Disorders*; President's Task Force on 21st Century Policing, *Final Report of the President's Task Force on 21st Century Policing*. President Lyndon B. Johnson's 1967 *Report of the National Advisory Commission on Civil Disorders*, or *Kerner Report*, and President Barack Obama's 2015 *Task Force on 21st Century Policing* report share an advocacy for diversifying police departments—a push that is often made in times of social upheaval to address uprisings and police violence. See also Hinton, *America on Fire*.

28. Goodison, *Local Police Departments Personnel*.

29. Ba et al., "The Role of Officer Race and Gender in Police-Civilian Interactions in Chicago." Ba et al. find that black police officers in Chicago were less likely to engage in discretionary

stops and arrests as well as use of force against black residents. Nicholson-Crotty et al., "Will More Black Cops Matter? Officer Race and Police-Involved Homicides of Black Citizens." Nicholson-Crotty, Nicholson-Crotty, and Fernandez find that increasing the number of black police officers does not reduce fatal police violence, and in some cases increases lethal police violence against black populations. Smith, "The Impact of Police Officer Diversity on Police-Caused Homicides." Smith shows that police departments having increased racial representation in police departments did not influence police violence; however, departments with more women had increased police-caused homicides.

30. Crenshaw et al., "Say Her Name"; Garza, "A Herstory of the #BlackLivesMatter Movement," *Are All the Women Still White? Rethinking Race, Expanding Feminisms*; Gregory, "The Original 'Me Too.': Tarana Burke Discusses the Movement She Made."

31. Interrupting Criminalization, "Sexualization Not Safety: Black Girls, Trans and Gender Nonconforming Youth's Experiences of Police Presence in Schools"; INCITE! Women of Color Against Violence, "Law Enforcement Violence."

32. Epstein et al., "Girlhood Interrupted: The Erasure of Black Girls' Childhood."

33. See American Psychological Association, "Report of the APA Task Force on the Sexualization of Girls" and Grower et al., "Beyond Objectification: Understanding the Correlates and Consequences of Sexualization for Black and White Adolescent Girls."

34. Morris, *Pushout*, 175.

35. Ritchie, *Invisible No More*, 127–43.

36. Ritchie, *Invisible No More*, 127–43; Kolysh, *Everyday Violence: The Public Harassment of Women and LGBTQ People*.

37. Robinson, "Lavender Scare"; and Iwama et al. "Segregation, Securitization, and Bullying: Investigating the Connections Between Policing, Surveillance, Punishment, and Violence." Iwama et al. also show how the presence of police and other crime-control strategies does not significantly impact various types of bullying in minority schools.

38. Clayton et al., *Dating Violence, Sexual Violence, and Bullying Victimization Among High School Students—Youth Risk Behavior Survey, United States, 2021*.

39. Interrupting Criminalization, "Sexualization Not Safety"; Ritchie, "Shrouded in Silence."

40. Interrupting Criminalization, "Sexualization Not Safety"; Ritchie, "Shrouded in Silence."

41. Ritchie, "Shrouded in Silence."

42. Sweet, *Politics of Surviving*; Ritchie, "Shrouded in Silence."

43. Ritchie, *Invisible No More*.

44. Gross, "African American Women."

45. Bailey and Mobley, "Work in the Intersections: A Black Feminist Disability Framework."

46. Slatton and Richard, "Black Women's Experiences."

47. Hitchens et al., "Context for Legal Cynicism"; Ritchie, "Shrouded in Silence."

48. Ritchie, "Shrouded in Silence."

49. Hitchens et al., "Context for Legal Cynicism"; Ritchie, "Shrouded in Silence."

50. See also: McGuffey, "Rape and Racial Appraisals: Culture, Intersectionality, and Black Women's Accounts of Sexual Assault."

4. "I Was Kinda Scared to Report It": The Space Between Speaking and Intracommunal Backlash and Police Retaliation

1. Sierra-Arévalo, *The Danger Imperative: Violence, Death, and the Soul of Policing*; Simon, "Training for War: Academy Socialization and Warrior Policing."

2. Skolnick, "Corruption and the Blue Code of Silence."

3. Chin and Wells, "The Blue Wall of Silence as Evidence of Bias and Motive to Lie: A New Approach to Police Perjury"; Skolnick, "Corruption and the Blue Code of Silence."

4. Chin and Wells, "Blue Wall of Silence"; Westmarland, "Police Ethics and Integrity: Breaking the Blue Code of Silence."

5. Gonzalez Van Cleave, *Crook County: Racism and Injustice in America's Largest Criminal Court*; Schwartz, "The Case Against Qualified Immunity."

6. See Hickman, "Citizen Complaints About Police Use of Force"; Terrill and Ingram, "Citizen Complaints Against the Police: An Eight City Examination."

7. Simon, *Before the Badge*, 94–99.

8. Bell, "Police Reform"; For example, see Rocha Beardall, "Police Legitimacy Regimes and the Suppression of Citizen Oversite in Response to Police Violence."

9. Gascón and Roussell, *The Limits of Community Policing: Civilian Power and Police Accountability in Black and Brown Los Angeles*.

10. Cheng, "Input Without Influence: The Silence and Scripts of Police and Community Relations."

11. Rios et al., "*Mano Suave–Mano Dura*."

12. See also Gascón and Roussell, *Limits of Community Policing*.

13. See Anderson, *Code of the Street: Decency, Violence, and the Moral Life of the Inner City*. The code of the street is intertwined with police surveillance and the broader carceral system. Thus, Anderson states: "The code of the street is actually a cultural adaptation to a profound lack of faith in the police and the judicial system—and in others who would champion one's personal security. The police, for instance, are most often viewed as representing the dominant white society and not caring to protect inner-city residents" (34). While I am not directly analyzing the code of the street, I am examining how different politics, norms, and sanctions around speaking to outsiders are formed and used in black communities.

14. Brunson and Wade, "Oh Hell No, We Don't Talk to Police: Insights on the Lack of Cooperation in Police Investigations of Urban Gun Violence."

15. Gómez, *Cultural Betrayal*.

16. Ransby, *Making All Black Lives Matter: Reimagining Freedom in the Twenty-First Century*; Weitzer and Brunson, "Strategic Responses to Police Among Inner City Youth."

17. Goff et al., "Not Yet Human: Implicit Knowledge, Historical Dehumanization, and Contemporary Consequences."

18. Fleury et al., "When Ending the Relationship Does Not End the Violence: Women's Experiences of Violence by Former Partners."

19. Gómez, *Cultural Betrayal*; McGuffey, "Rape and Racial Appraisals."

20. Koslicki et al., "'Rhetoric Without Reality' or Effective Policing Strategy? An Analysis of the Relationship Between Community Policing and Police Fatal Force"; Prieto-Hodge and Tomaskovic-Devey, "A Tale of Force: Examining Policy Proposal to Address Police Violence"; Smith and Holmes, "Police Use of Excessive Force." Koslicki et al. find that community policing

models do not mitigate use of lethal force, and instead find that a department having a higher proportion of officers assigned to specific communities increases fatal force. Prieto-Hodge and Tomaskovic-Devey find that proactive community policing models increase use of force, while those that encouraged relationships in communities had a decrease in use of force. Smith and Holmes did not find evidence of decreased use of force by police departments with policies that promote accountability between residents and officers.

5. "When We Gather": The Space Between Lived Experiences and Self-Definition

1. For more on the lingering consequences of police violence on social media, see Malone Gonzalez et al., "Mourning for Strangers: Black Women, Sequelae, and the Digital Afterlife of Police Violence."

2. Collins, *Black Feminist Thought*, 118 and 300.

3. Collins, *Black Feminist Thought*.

4. Collins, "Social Construction."

5. hooks, *Feminist Theory: From Margin to Center*. In describing the margins, hooks writes: "To be in the margin is to be part of the whole but outside the main body" (xvi). As black women's stories about violence go unrecognized, I draw from hooks's understanding of the margin to trace when and how they (re)claim authority to tell their own stories.

6. For more on black women's witnessing as a form of advocacy, see Malone Gonzalez and Deckard, "'We Got Witnesses': Black Women's Counter-Surveillance for Navigating Police Violence and Legal Estrangement."

7. See Montgomery and Wines, "Dispute over Sandra Bland's Mental State Follows Death in a Texas Jail."

8. Lorde, *Sister Outsider*, 37.

9. Lorde, *Sister Outsider*, 37.

10. See Destine, "The Interior of the Movement for Black Lives: 'A New Political Generation.'"

11. Audrey's concerns about being surveilled and targeted by the police are legitimate, as activists have historically been targeted and retaliated against for resisting state violence. Farmer, "Tracking Activists: The FBI's Surveillance of Black Women Activists Then and Now."

12. hooks, *All About Love*, 132.

13. Collins, "Social Construction."

14. Pittman, *Grandmothering While Black: A Twenty-First-Century Story of Love, Coercion, and Survival*.

15. Battle and Powell, "'We Keep Us Safe!': Abolition Feminism as a Challenge to Carceral Feminist Responses to Gendered Violence."

16. Davis et al., *Abolition. Feminism. Now.*, 4.

17. Davis et al., *Abolition. Feminism. Now.*

18. Gilmore and Tippett, "Where Life Is Precious, Life Is Precious."

19. I am unaware of where Alexis heard the term "positive disruptor;" however, she used it throughout our interview to talk about disrupting everyday social processes of oppression to bring about long-term social change.

20. Collins, *Black Feminist Thought*, 114.

21. Burrowes, "Building the World We Want to See: A Herstory of Sista II Sista and the Struggle Against State and Interpersonal Violence," 376.

22. Burrowes, "Building the World We Want to See," 376.

23. Threadcraft, "Making Black Femicide Visible."

gathering poem

1. Collins, "Learning from the Outsider Within: The Sociological Significance of Black Feminist Thought." Collins writes about how black women can use their "outsider-within" status, or their position on the inside and outside of multiple social worlds, as a resource while conducting research. In this poem, I place black women's quotes in conversation with one another to replicate the experience of being an outsider-within, or what it was like to listen to and observe patterns among black women who would not get the chance to be in dialogue otherwise.

Conclusion

1. See McKittrick, *Dear Science and Other Stories*; Toliver, *Recovering Black Storytelling*.

2. Crenshaw et al., "Say Her Name."

3. Richie, *Arrested Justice*.

4. Stuart and Benezra, "Criminalized Masculinities."

5. Cohen, *Boundaries of Blackness*; Grundy, *Respectable*.

6. Carlson, "The Equalizer?"

7. President's Task Force on 21st Century Policing, *Final Report*.

8. Gómez, *Cultural Betrayal*.

9. Richie, *Compelled to Crime*.

10. Mueller, "Racial Ideology or Racial Ignorance? An Alternative Theory of Racial Cognition."

11. Garcia-Hallett, *Invisible Mothers*.

12. King, "Multiple Jeopardy."

13. Boyles, *Race, Place, and Suburban Policing*.

14. Bell, "Situational Trust."

15. Kolysh, *Everyday Violence*; Robinson, "Lavender Scare."

16. Bailey and Mobley, "Work in the Intersections"; Ritchie, *Invisible No More*, 88–103.

17. For more on age, see Allen et al., "Why DON'T We 'Say Her Name'? An Intersectional Model of the Invisibility of the Police Violence Against Black Women and Girls."

18. Combahee River Collective, "Combahee River Collective Statement," 16.

19. Collins, "Social Construction"; Compton et al., *Other, Please Specify*; Zuberi and Bonilla-Silva, *White Logic, White Methods*.

20. Lindsey, *America Goddam*, 18.

21. Menjívar, "State Categories."

22. Collins, "Tie That Binds."

23. See Ahmed, *Cultural Politics*; Friedman and Hitchens, "Theorizing Embodied Carcerality"; Harris-Perry, "Crooked Room"; hooks, *Killing Rage*.

24. Spira et al., "ACAB Means Abolishing the Cop in Our Heads, Hearts, and Homes: An Intergenerational Demand for Family Abolition."

25. Battle and Powell, "'We Keep Us Safe!'," 533.

26. Kaba and Ritchie, *No More Police: A Case for Abolition*, 23.

27. Threadcraft, "Making Black Femicide Visible."

28. Collins, *Black Feminist Thought*, 8–12; Kaba and Ritchie, *No More Police*; Sojoyner, *Against the Carceral Archive: The Art of Black Liberatory Practice*.

29. Gilmore and Tippett, "Where Life Is Precious, Life Is Precious."

30. See Lorde, "Epilogue." In reflecting on her own over exertion, Lorde notes how, for marginalized subjects, self-valuation and care is a political act of resistance within systems of disposability.

31. See Benjamin, *Viral Justice: How We Grow the World We Want*; Davis et al., *Abolition. Feminism. Now.*; Kaba and Ritchie, *No More Police*; McHarris, *Beyond Policing*.

32. Parker et al., "Amid Protests, Majorities Across Racial and Ethnic Groups Express Support for the Black Lives Matter Movement."

33. Dotson, "Conceptualizing Epistemic Oppression." While Dotson is referring to epistemological systems and resources, stories, in many ways, carry epistemological systems and are a way of sharing and co-creating epistemic resources. See also Toliver, *Recovering Black Storytelling*.

34. Dotson, "Conceptualizing Epistemic Oppression," 8.

35. Dotson, "Tracking Epistemic Violence." See also Polletta and Redman, "When Do Stories Change Our Minds? Narrative Persuasion About Social Problems."

36. Dotson, "Conceptualizing Epistemic Oppression." Dotson uses Plato's allegory of the cave as a way to parse through irreducible and reducible forms of epistemic exclusion grounded in social and political domination. While she argues that epistemological resilience is the backdrop for all epistemological systems, Dotson analyzes the different ways groups engage in epistemic exclusion and work to maintain and justify their ignorance in the face of new information. I draw from Dotson's description of the three orders of epistemic exclusion based on inefficient, insufficient, and inadequate shared epistemic resources to discuss the ways people justify their unlistening to black women and girls' stories about violence and alternatives to policing. See also Threadcraft, "Making Black Femicide Visible."

37. Dotson, "Conceptualizing Epistemic Oppression," 11.

38. Morris, *Pushout*.

39. Office for Civil Rights, *Student Discipline and School Climate in U.S. Public Schools, 2020–21 Civil Rights Data Collection*.

40. See Wun, "Against Captivity: Black Girls and School Discipline Policies in the Afterlife of Slavery"; Crenshaw et al., "Black Girls Matter: Pushed Out, Overpoliced and Underprotected."

41. French-Marcelin and Hinger, "Bullies in Blue: Origins and Consequences of School Policing."

42. Goodmark, *Imperfect Victims*; Kim, "Carceral Creep"; Ritchie, *Invisible No More*, 195–98.

43. Dotson, "Conceptualizing Epistemic Oppression."

44. Dotson, "Conceptualizing Epistemic Oppression," 14.

45. Thomas and Horowitz, "Support for Black Lives Matter Has Decreased Since June but Remains Strong Among Black Americans."

46. See also: Malone Gonzalez et al., "The Diversity Officer: Police Officers' and Black Women Civilians' Epistemologies on Race and Racism in Policing."

47. Phelps, *Minneapolis Reckoning*.

48. Dotson, "Conceptualizing Epistemic Oppression," 16.

A Brief Note on Methods, Continued

1. McKittrick, *Dear Science*, 7.

2. McKittrick, *Dear Science*; Toliver, *Recovering Black Storytelling*.

3. Alexander, *Pedagogies of Crossing*; Collins, "Social Construction."

4. Alexander, *Pedagogies of Crossing*; Dotson, "Conceptualizing Epistemic Oppression." For example, see Reyes, *Academic Outsider: Stories of Exclusion and Hope*.

5. Alexander, *Pedagogies of Crossing*; Collins, "Social Construction"; Toliver, *Recovering Black Storytelling*.

6. See Boyles, *Race, Place, and Suburban Policing*; Braga et al., "Race, Place, and Effective Policing"; Gordon, *Policing the Racial Divide: Urban Growth Politics and the Remaking of Segregation*.

7. O'Quinn et al., "Sociology from a Distance: Remote Interviews and Feminist Methods."

8. DeVault, "Talking and Listening from Women's Standpoint: Feminist Strategies for Interviewing and Analysis"; González-López, "Ethnographic Lessons: Researching Incest in Mexican Families."

9. Plummer *Documents of Life 2: An Invitation to a Critical Humanism*.

10. Richie, *Compelled to Crime*, 16–17.

11. Plummer, *Documents of Life 2*. See González-López, *Family Secrets*; Richie, *Compelled to Crime*.

12. Grundy, *Respectable*, 28.

13. For more on black women and privacy around policing, see Smith, "Impossible Privacy: Black Women and Police Terror."

14. DeVault, "Talking and Listening from Women's Standpoint"; González-López, "Ethnographic Lessons."

15. Davis and Whyde, *Contacts Between Police and the Public, 2015*; Crenshaw et al., "Say Her Name"; Ritchie, *Invisible No More*.

16. Collins, *Black Feminist Thought*, 255.

17. Collins, *Black Feminist Thought*, 255–56.

18. Charmaz, *Constructing Grounded Theory: A Practical Guide Through Qualitative Analysis*.

19. Toliver, *Recovering Black Storytelling*.

20. Collins, "Learning from the Outsider Within."

21. Adjepong, "Invading Ethnography."

22. González-López, "Ethnographic Lessons."

23. González-López, "Ethnographic Lessons," 576.

24. Stack, "Tulsa Police Officer Who Killed Unarmed Black Man Won't Face Civil Rights Charges."

BIBLIOGRAPHY

Adichie, Chimamanda Ngozi. "The Danger of a Single Story." TED Talk, July 2009, https://www
 .ted.com/talks/chimamanda_adichie_the_danger_of_a_single_story.
Adjepong, Anima. "Invading Ethnography: A Queer of Color Reflexive Practice." *Ethnography*
 20, no. 1 (2019): 27–46.
Ahmed, Sara. *The Cultural Politics of Emotion.* Routledge, 2013.
Alexander, M. Jacqui. *Pedagogies of Crossing: Meditations on Feminism, Sexual Politics, Memory,
 and the Sacred.* Durham, NC: Duke University Press, 2005.
Alexander, Michelle. *New Jim Crow: Mass Incarceration in the Age of Colorblindness.* New York:
 New Press, 2010.
Allen, Aerielle M. "Why DON'T We 'Say Her Name'? An Intersectional Model of the Invisibil-
 ity of the Police Violence Against Black Women and Girls." *Perspectives on Psychological
 Science* (2024): https://doi.org/10.1177/17456916241277554.
Alter, Charlotte. "Why Oklahoma Cop's Rape Conviction Is a Major Victory." *Time Magazine,*
 December 12, 2015. https://time.com/4145868/why-an-oklahoma-cops-rape-conviction-is
 -a-major-victory/.
American Psychological Association, Task Force on the Sexualization of Girls. "Report of the
 APA Task Force on the Sexualization of Girls." Washington, DC, 2007. www.apa.org/pi
 /wpo/sexualization.html.
Anderson, Elijah. *Code of the Street: Decency, Violence, and the Moral Life of the Inner City.* New
 York: W. W. Norton, 2000.
Anderson, Leslie A., Margaret O'Brien Caughy, and Margaret T. Owen. "'The Talk' and Parent-
 ing While Black in America: Centering Race, Resistance, and Refuge." *Journal of Black Psy-
 chology* 48, nos. 3–4 (2022): 475–506.
Anzaldúa, Gloria. *Borderlands / La Frontera: The New Mestiza.* San Francisco: Spinsters, Aunt
 Lute, 1987.
Appiah, Kwame Anthony. "The Case for Capitalizing the B in Black." *The Atlantic,* June 18, 2020.
 https://www.theatlantic.com/ideas/archive/2020/06/time-to-capitalize-blackand-white
 /613159/).
April, Keisha, Lindsey M. Cole, and Naomi E. S. Goldstein. "Let's 'Talk' About the Police: The
 Role of Race and Police Legitimacy Attitudes in the Legal Socialization of Youth." *Current
 Psychology* 42 (2023): 15422–37.
Armstrong, Elizabeth A., Mariam Gleckman-Krut, and Lanora Johnson. "Silence, Power, and
 Inequality: An Intersectional Approach to Sexual Violence." *Annual Review of Sociology* 44
 (2018): 99–122.

Armstrong, Megan. "From Lynching to Central Park Karen: How White Women Weaponize White Womanhood." *Hastings Women's Law Journal* 32, no. 1 (2021): 27–52.

"#AssaultAtSpringValley: An Analysis of Police Violence." #PoliceFreeSchools, December 12, 2022. https://policefreeschools.org/resources/assaultat-spring-valley-an-analysis-of-police-violence/.

Ba, Bocar, Dean Knox, Jonathan Mummolo, and Roman Rivera. "The Role of Officer Race and Gender in Police-Civilian Interactions in Chicago." *Science* 371, no. 6530 (2021): 696–702.

Bailey, Moya. *Misogynoir Transformed: Black Women's Digital Resistance.* New York: New York University Press, 2021.

Bailey, Moya, and Izetta Autumn Mobley. "Work in the Intersections: A Black Feminist Disability Framework." *Gender and Society* 33, no. 1 (2019): 19–40.

Battle, Brittany Pearl. "The Carceral Logic of Parental Responsibility." *Journal of Marriage and Family* 85, no. 3 (2023): 679–700.

Battle, Brittany Pearl, and Amber Joy Powell. "'We Keep Us Safe!': Abolition Feminism as a Challenge to Carceral Feminist Responses to Gendered Violence." *Gender and Society* 38, no. 4 (2024): 523–56.

Beckett, Lois, and Abené Clayton. "'An Unspoken Epidemic': Homicide Rate Increase for Black Women Rivals That of Black Men." *The Guardian*, June 25, 2022. https://www.theguardian.com/world/2022/jun/25/homicide-violence-against-black-women-us.

Bell, Monica C. "Police Reform and the Dismantling of Legal Estrangement." *Yale Law Journal* 126, no. 7 (2017): 2054–2151.

Bell, Monica C. "Situational Trust: How Disadvantaged Mothers Reconceive Legal Cynicism." *Law and Society Review* 50, no. 2 (2016): 314–47.

Benjamin, Ruha. *Viral Justice: How We Grow the World We Want.* Princeton, NJ: Princeton University Press, 2022.

Berry, Daina Ramey. *The Price for Their Pound of Flesh: The Value of the Enslaved, from Womb to Grave in the Building of a Nation.* Boston: Beacon Press, 2017.

Berry, Daina Ramey, and Kali Nicole Gross. *A Black Women's History of the United States.* Boston: Beacon Press, 2020.

Bonilla-Silva, Eduardo. "Feeling Race: Theorizing the Racial Economy of Emotions." *American Sociological Review* 84, no. 1 (2019): 1–25.

Bor, Jacob, Atheendar S. Venkataramani, David R. Williams, and Alexander C. Tsai. "Police Killings and Their Spillover Effects on the Mental Health of Black Americans: A Population-Based, Quasi-Experimental Study." *The Lancet* 392, no. 10144 (2018): 302–10.

Boyd, Rhea W. "Police Violence and the Built Harm of Structural Racism." *The Lancet* 392, no. 10144 (2018): 258–59.

Boyles, Andrea S. *Race, Place, and Suburban Policing: Too Close for Comfort.* Oakland: University of California Press, 2015.

Braga, Anthony A., Rod K. Brunson, and Kevin M. Drakulich. "Race, Place, and Effective Policing." *Annual Review of Sociology* 45 (2019): 535–55.

Brantley, Mia. "Can't Just Send Our Children Out: Intensive Motherwork and Experiences of Black Motherhood." *Social Problems*, 2023. https://doi.org/10.1093/socpro/spad047.

Brayne, Sarah. *Predict and Surveil: Data, Discretion, and the Future of Policing.* New York: Oxford University Press, 2021.

Browne, Simone. *Dark Matters: On the Surveillance of Blackness.* Durham, NC: Duke University Press, 2015.

Brunson, Rod K., and Jody Miller. "Gender, Race, and Urban Policing: The Experience of African American Youth." *Gender and Society* 20, no. 4 (2006): 531–52.

Brunson, Rod K., and Brian A. Wade. "'Oh Hell No, We Don't Talk to Police': Insights on the Lack of Cooperation in Police Investigations of Urban Gun Violence." *Criminology and Public Policy* 18, no. 3 (2019): 623–48.

Brunson, Rod K., and Ronald Weitzer. "Negotiating Unwelcome Police Encounters: The Intergenerational Transmission of Conduct Norms." *Journal of Contemporary Ethnography* 40, no. 4 (2011): 425–56.

Bryant-Davis, Thema, Heewoon Chung, Shaquita Tillman, and Annie Belcourt. "From the Margins to the Center: Ethnic Minority Women and the Mental Health Effects of Sexual Assault." *Trauma, Violence, and Abuse* 10, no. 4 (2009): 330–57.

Buchanan, Blu, and Ayotunde Khyree Ikuku. "We Major." In *Black Feminist Sociology: Perspectives and Praxis*, edited by Zakiya Luna and Whitney L. Laster Pirtle, 291–99. Routledge, 2022.

Burghart, Brian D. "Fatal encounters." Fatal Encounters, 2023. https://fatalencounters.org.

Burrowes, Nicole A. "Building the World We Want to See: A Herstory of Sista II Sista and the Struggle Against State and Interpersonal Violence." *Souls: A Critical Journal on Black Politics, Culture, and Society* 20, no. 4 (2018): 375–98.

Butler, Paul. *Chokehold: Policing Black Men.* New York: New Press, 2018.

Campaign Zero. "Mapping Police Violence." Campaign Zero, 2023. https://mappingpoliceviolence.us.

Carlson, Jennifer. "The Equalizer? Crime, Vulnerability, and Gender in Pro-Gun Discourse." *Feminist Criminology* 9, no. 1 (2014): 59–83.

Carlson, Jennifer. "Police Warriors and Police Guardians: Race, Masculinity, and the Construction of Gun Violence." *Social Problems* 67, no. 3 (2019): 399–417.

Charmaz, Kathy. *Constructing Grounded Theory: A Practical Guide Through Qualitative Analysis.* Thousand Oaks, CA: Sage, 2006.

Cheng, Tony. "Input Without Influence: The Silence and Scripts of Police and Community Relations." *Social Problems* 67, no. 1 (2020): 171–89.

Chin, Gabriel J., and Scott C. Wells. "The Blue Wall of Silence as Evidence of Bias and Motive to Lie: A New Approach to Police Perjury." *University of Pittsburg Law Review* 59 (1998): 233–99.

Clair, Matthew. "Criminalized Subjectivity: Du Boisian Sociology and Visions for Legal Change." *Du Bois Review: Social Science Research on Race* 18, no. 2 (2021): 289–319.

Clair, Matthew. *Privilege and Punishment: How Race and Class Matter in Criminal Court.* Princeton University Press, 2020.

Clayton, Heather B, Greta Kilmer, Sarah DeGue, Lianne F. Estefan, Vi D. Le, Nicolas A. Suarez, Bridget H. Lyons, Jemekia E. Thornton. *Dating Violence, Sexual Violence, and Bullying Victimization Among High School Students—Youth Risk Behavior Survey, United States, 2021.* Centers for Disease Control and Prevention, 2023. https://www.cdc.gov/mmwr/volumes/72/su/pdfs/su7201-H.pdf.

Cochran, Joshua C., and Patricia Y. Warren. "Racial, Ethnic, and Gender Differences in Perceptions of the Police: The Salience of Officer Race Within the Context of Racial Profiling." *Journal of Contemporary Criminal Justice* 28, no. 2 (2012): 206–27.

Coker, Ann L., Keith E. Davis, Ileana Arias, Sujata Desai, Maureen Sanderson, Heather M. Brandt, and Paige H. Smith. "Physical and Mental Health Effects of Intimate Partner Violence for Men and Women." *American Journal of Preventative Medicine* 23, no. 4 (2002): 260–68.

Cohen, Cathy J. *The Boundaries of Blackness: AIDS and the Breakdown of Black Politics.* Chicago: University of Chicago Press, 2009.

Collins, Patricia Hill. "Black Feminist Epistemology." In *Black Feminist Thought: Knowledge, Consciousness, and the Politics of Empowerment.* New York: Routledge, 2000.

Collins, Patricia Hill. *Black Feminist Thought: Knowledge, Consciousness, and the Politics of Empowerment.* New York: Routledge, 2000.

Collins, Patricia Hill. *Black Sexual Politics.* New York: Routledge, 2004.

Collins, Patricia Hill. "Learning from the Outsider Within: The Sociological Significance of Black Feminist Thought." *Social Problems* 33, no. 6 (1986): 14–32.

Collins, Patricia Hill. *On Intellectual Activism.* Philadelphia: Temple University Press, 2013.

Collins, Patricia Hill. "The Social Construction of Black Feminist Thought." *Signs: Journal of Women in Culture and Society* 14, no. 4 (1989): 745–77.

Collins, Patricia Hill. "The Tie That Binds: Race, Gender and US Violence." *Ethnic and Racial Studies* 21, no. 5 (1998): 917–38.

Combahee River Collective. "The Combahee River Collective Statement." In *How We Get Free: Black Feminism and the Combahee River Collective,* edited by Keeanga-Yamahtta Taylor, 15–22. Chicago: Haymarket Books, 2017.

Compton, D'Lane R., Tey Meadow, and Kristen Schilt. *Other, Please Specify: Queer Methods in Sociology.* Oakland: University of California Press, 2018.

Crenshaw, Kimberlé. "Mapping the Margins: Intersectionality, Identity Politics, and Violence Against Women of Color." *Stanford Law Review* 43, no. 6 (1991): 1241–99.

Crenshaw, Kimberlé, and African American Policy Forum. *#SayHerName: Black Women's Stories of Police Violence and Public Silence.* Chicago: Haymarket Books, 2023.

Crenshaw, Kimberlé, Priscilla Ocen, and Jyoti Nanda. "Black Girls Matter: Pushed Out, Over-policed and Underprotected." *Faculty Scholarship,* 2015. https://scholarship.law.columbia .edu/faculty_scholarship/3227.

Crenshaw, Kimberlé Williams, Andrea J. Ritchie, Rachel Anspach, Rachel Gilmer, and Luke Harris. "Say Her Name: Resisting Police Brutality Against Black Women," African American Policy Forum, 2015. https://www.aapf.org/_files/ugd/62e126_9223ee35c2694ac3bd3f21 71504ca3f7.pdf.

Crutchfield, Robert D., April Fernandes, and Jorge Martinez. "Racial and Ethnic Disparity and Criminal Justice: How Much Is Too Much?" *Journal of Criminal Law and Criminology (1973-)* 100, no. 3 (2010): 903–32.

Daiquoi, Raygine. "Symbols in the Strange Fruit Seeds: What 'the Talk' Black Parents Have with Their Sons Tells Us About Racism." *Harvard Educational Review* 87, no. 4 (2017): 512–37.

Davies, Lizzy. "'Culture of Exclusion' Keeps Women of Colour from Top Media Jobs, Report Reveals." *The Guardian,* November 30, 2022. https://www.theguardian.com/global -development/2022/nov/30/culture-of-exclusion-keeps-women-of-colour-from-top -media-jobs-report-reveals.

Davis, Angela Y. *Women, Race and Class.* Vintage, 2011.

Davis, Angela Y., Gina Dent, Erica R. Meiners, and Beth E. Richie. *Abolition. Feminism. Now.* Chicago: Haymarket Books, 2022.

Davis, Elizabeth, and Anthony Whyde. *Contacts Between Police and the Public, 2015.* Bureau of Justice Statistics. Washington, DC: Department of Justice, 2018. https://bjs.ojp.gov/redirect-legacy/content/pub/pdf/cpp15.pdf.

Deckard, Faith M. "Surveilling Sureties: How Privately Mediated Monetary Sanctions Enroll and Responsibilize Families." *Social Problems* (2024): spae041. https://doi.org/10.1093/socpro/spae041.

DeSilver, Drew, Michael Lipka, and Dalia Fahmy. "10 Things We Know About Race and Policing in the U.S." Pew Research Center, June 3, 2020. https://www.pewresearch.org/short-reads/2020/06/03/10-things-we-know-about-race-and-policing-in-the-u-s/.

Destine, Shaneda. "The Interior of the Movement for Black Lives: 'A New Political Generation.'" *Gender and Society* 37, no. 2 (2023): 292–320.

DeVault, Marjorie L. "Talking and Listening from Women's Standpoint: Feminist Strategies for Interviewing and Analysis." *Social Problems* 37, no. 1 (1990): 96–116.

Ditcher, Melissa E., and Sue Osthoff. "Women's Experiences of Abuse as a Risk Factor for Incarceration: A Research Update." VAWnet: The National Online Resource Center on Violence Against Women, July 2015. https://vawnet.org/material/womens-experiences-abuse-risk-factor-incarceration-research-update.

Dotson, Kristie. "Conceptualizing Epistemic Oppression." *Social Epistemology* 28, no. 2 (2014): 115–38.

Dotson, Kristie. "Tracking Epistemic Violence, Tracking Practices of Silencing." *Hypatia* 26, no. 2 (2011): 236–57.

Dow, Dawn Marie. "The Deadly Challenges of Raising African American Boys: Navigating the Controlling Image of the 'Thug.'" *Gender and Society* 30, no. 2 (2016): 161–88.

Dow, Dawn Marie. *Mothering While Black: Boundaries and Burdens of Middle-Class Parenthood.* Oakland: University of California Press, 2019.

Du Bois, W. E. B. *The Souls of Black Folk.* New York: Open Road Integrated Media, 1973.

DuMonthier, Asha, Chandra E. Childers, and Jessica Milli. *The Status of Black Women in the United States.* Washington, DC: Institute for Women's Policy Research, 2017. https://iwpr.org/wp-content/uploads/2020/08/The-Status-of-Black-Women-6.26.17.pdf.

Edwards, Frank, Hedwig Lee, and Michael Esposito. "Risk of Being Killed by Police Use of Force in the United States by Age, Race–Ethnicity, and Sex." *Proceedings of the National Academy of Sciences* 116, no. 34 (2019): 16793–98.

Elliot, Sinikka, Joslyn Brenton, and Rachel Powell. "Brothermothering: Gender, Power, and the Parenting Strategies of Low-Income Black Single Mothers of Teenagers." *Social Problems* 65, no. 4 (2018): 439–55.

Epp, Charles R., Steven Maynard-Moody, and Donald Haider-Markel. *Pulled Over: How Police Stops Define Race and Citizenship.* Chicago: University of Chicago Press, 2014.

Epstein, Rebecca, Jamilia J. Blake, and Thalia Gonzalez. "Girlhood Interrupted: The Erasure of Black Girls' Childhood." Center on Poverty and Inequality. Georgetown Law. *SSRN Electronic Journal* 17 (2017). https://doi.org/10.2139/ssrn.3000695.

Evans, Louwanda, and Joe R. Feagin. "The Costs of Policing Violence: Foregrounding Cognitive and Emotional Labor." *Critical Sociology* 41, no. 6 (2015): 887–95.

Farmer, Ashley. "Tracking Activists: The FBI's Surveillance of Black Women Activists Then and Now." *American Historian*, September 2020. https://www.oah.org/tah/history-for-black -lives/tracking-activists-the-fbis-surveillance-of-black-women-activists-then-and-now/.

Felker-Kantor, Max. *DARE to Say No: Policing and the War on Drugs in Schools.* Chapel Hill: University of North Carolina Press, 2024.

Ferguson, Roderick A. *Aberrations in Black: Toward a Queer of Color Critique.* University of Minnesota Press, 2004.

Fleury, Ruth E., Cris M. Sullivan, and Deborah I. Bybee. "When Ending the Relationship Does Not End the Violence: Women's Experiences of Violence by Former Partners." *Violence Against Women* 6, no. 2 (2000): 1363–83.

Flowe, Douglas. *Uncontrollable Blackness: African American Men and Criminality in Jim Crow New York.* Chapel Hill: University of North Carolina Press, 2020.

Foster, Thomas. "The Sexual Abuse of Black Men Under American Slavery." *Journal of the History of Sexuality* 20, no. 3 (2011): 445–64.

Foucault, Michel. *Discipline and Punish: The Birth of the Prison.* New York: Vintage Books, 1977.

French-Marcelin, Megan, and Sarah Hinger. "Bullies in Blue: Origins and Consequences of School Policing." American Civil Liberties Union. Accessed October 25, 2024. https://www .aclu.org/publications/bullies-blue-origins-and-consequences-school-policing.

Friedman, Brittany, and Brooklynn K. Hitchens. "Theorizing Embodied Carcerality." In *Black Feminist Sociology: Perspectives and Praxis*, edited by Zakiya Luna and Whitney L. Laster Pirtle, 267–76. Routledge Press, 2021.

Gaines, Kevin K. *Uplifting the Race: Black Leadership, Politics, and Culture in the Twentieth Century.* Chapel Hill University of North Carolina Press, 2012.

Garcia-Hallett, Janet. *Invisible Mothers: Unseen Yet Hypervisible After Incarceration.* Oakland: University of California Press, 2022.

Garza, Alicia. "A Herstory of the #BlackLivesMatter Movement." In *Are All the Women Still White? Rethinking Race, Expanding Feminisms*, edited by Janell Hobson, 23–28. Albany: State University of New York Press, 2017.

Gascón, Luis Daniel, and Aaron Roussell. *The Limits of Community Policing: Civilian Power and Police Accountability in Black and Brown Los Angeles.* New York: New York University Press, 2019.

Gaston, Shytierra. "Producing Race Disparities: A Study of Drug Arrests Across Place and Race." *Criminology* 57, no. 3 (2019): 424–51.

Gilmore, Amir A., and Pamela J. Bettis. "Antiblackness and the Adultification of Black Children in a U.S. Prison Nation." *Oxford Research Encyclopedia of Education*, 2012. https://doi.org/10 .1093/acrefore/9780190264093.013.1293.

Gilmore, Ruth Wilson, and Krista Tippett. "'Where Life Is Precious, Life Is Precious.': On Being with Krista Tippett, March 30, 2023. https://onbeing.org/programs/ruth-wilson-gilmore -where-life-is-precious-life-is-precious/.

Go, Julian. "The Imperial Origins of American Policing: Militarization and Imperial Feedback in the Early 20th Century." *American Journal of Sociology* 125, no. 5 (2020): 1193–1245.

Goff, Phillip Atiba. "Not Yet Human: Implicit Knowledge, Historical Dehumanization, and Contemporary Consequences." *Journal of Personality and Social Psychology* 94, no. 2 (2008): 292–306.

Goff, Phillip Atiba, Matthew Christian Jackson, Brooke Allison Lewis Leone, Carmen Marie Culotta, and Natalie Ann DiTomasso. "The Essence of Innocence: Consequences of Dehumanizing Black Children." *Journal of Personality and Social Psychology* 106, no. 4 (2014): 526–45.

Gómez, Jennifer M. *The Cultural Betrayal of Black Women and Girls: A Black Feminist Approach to Healing from Sexual Abuse.* Washington, DC: American Psychological Association, 2023.

González-López, Gloria. "Ethnographic Lessons: Researching Incest in Mexican Families." *Journal of Contemporary Ethnography* 39, no. 5 (2010): 569–81.

González-López, Gloria. *Family Secrets: Stories of Incest and Sexual Violence in Mexico.* New York: New York University Press, 2015.

Gonzalez Van Cleave, Nicole. *Crook County: Racism and Injustice in America's Largest Criminal Court.* Stanford, CA: Stanford University Press, 2016.

Goodison, Sean E. *Local Police Departments Personnel, 2020.* Bureau of Justice Statistics, 2022. https://bjs.ojp.gov/sites/g/files/xyckuh236/files/media/document/lpdp20.pdf.

Goodmark, Leigh. *Imperfect Victims: Criminalized Survivors and the Promise of Abolition Feminisms.* Berkeley: University of California Press, 2023.

Gordon, Daanika. *Policing the Racial Divide: Urban Growth Politics and the Remaking of Segregation.* New York: New York University Press, 2022.

Graham, Matthew A. "Compounding Anti-Black Racial Disparities in Police Stops." Center for Policing Equity, October 9, 2024. https://policingequity.org/traffic-safety/88-white-paper -compounding-anti-black-racial-disparities-in-police-stops/file?utm_source=press&utm _medium=release&utm_campaign=police-stops-disparities.

Grasso, Jordan, Stefan Vogler, Emily Greytak, Casey Kindall, and Valerie Jenness. *Policing Progress: Findings from a National Survey of LGBTQ+ People's Experiences with Law Enforcement.* New York: American Civil Liberties Union (ACLU), 2024.

Gregory, Ted. "The Original 'Me Too.': Tarana Burke Discusses the Movement She Made." The University of Chicago Harris School of Public Policy, 2023. https://harris.uchicago.edu /news-events/news/original-me-too-tarana-burke-discusses-movement-she-made.

Gross, Kali Nicole. "African American Women, Mass Incarceration, and the Politics of Protection." *Journal of American History* 102, no. 1 (2015): 25–33.

Grower, Petal, L. Monique Ward, and Stephanie Rowley. "Beyond Objectification: Understanding the Correlates and Consequences of Sexualization for Black and White Adolescent Girls." *Journal of Research on Adolescence* 31, no. 2 (2021): 253–481.

Grundy, Saida. *Respectable: Politics and Paradox in Making the Morehouse Man.* Oakland: University of California Press, 2022.

Gurusami, Susila, and Rahim Kurwa. "From Broken Windows to Broken Homes: Homebreaking as Racialized and Gendered Poverty Governance." *Feminist Formations* 33, no. 1 (2021): 1–32.

Hadden, Sally E. *Slave Patrols: Law and Violence in Virginia and the Carolinas.* Cambridge, MA: Harvard University Press, 2003.

Haley, Sarah. *No Mercy Here: Gender, Punishment, and the Making of Jim Crow Modernity.* Chapel Hill, NC: University of North Carolina Press, 2016.

Harcourt, Bernard E. *Illusion of Order: The False Promise of Broken Windows Policing.* Cambridge, MA: Harvard University Press, 2001.

Harding, Sandra. "Rethinking Standpoint Epistemology: What Is 'Strong Objectivity?'" *Centennial Review* 36, no. 3 (1992): 437–70.

Harris, Abril, and Ndidiamaka Amutah-Onukagha. "Under the Radar: Strategies Used by Black Mothers to Prepare Their Sons for Potential Police Interactions." *Journal of Black Psychology* 45, nos. 6–7 (2019): 439–53.

Harris, LaShawn. *Sex Workers, Psychics, and Numbers Runners: Black Women in New York City's Underground Economy*. Urbana/Chicago: University of Illinois Press, 2016.

Harris, LaShawn Denise. "'Women and Girls in Jeopardy by His False Testimony': Charles Dancy, Urban Policing, and Black Women in New York City During the 1920s." *Journal of Urban History* 44, no. 3 (2018): 457–75.

Harris-Perry, Melissa V. "Crooked Room." In *Sister Citizen: Shame, Stereotypes, and Black Women in America*, 28–50. New Haven, CT: Yale University Press, 2014.

Harris-Perry, Melissa V. *Sister Citizen: Shame, Stereotypes, and Black Women in America*. New Haven, CT: Yale University Press, 2014.

Henry, Tri Keah S., and Travis W. Franklin. "Police Legitimacy in the Context of Street Stops: The Effects of Race, Class, and Procedural Justice." *Criminal Justice Policy Review* 30, no. 3 (2019): 406–27.

Hickman, Matthew J. "Citizen Complaints About Police Use of Force." U.S. Department of Justice: Bureau of Justice Statistics, 2006. https://bjs.ojp.gov/content/pub/pdf/ccpuf.pdf.

Higginbotham, Evelyn Brooks. *Righteous Discontent: The Women's Movement in the Black Baptist Church, 1880–1920*. Cambridge, MA: Harvard University Press, 1993.

Hine, Darlene Clark. "Rape and the Inner Lives of Black Women in the Middle West." *Signs: Journal of Women in Culture and Society* 14, no. 4 (1989): 912–20.

Hinton, Elizabeth. *America on Fire: The Untold History of Police Violence and Black Rebellion Since the 1960s*. New York: Liveright Publishing, 2021.

Hinton, Elizabeth. *From the War on Poverty to the War on Crime: The Making of Mass Incarceration in America*. Cambridge: Harvard University Press, 2016.

Hitchens, Brooklynn K., Patrick J. Carr, and Susan Clampet-Lundquist. "The Context for Legal Cynicism: Urban Young Women's Experiences with Policing in Low-Income, High-Crime Neighborhoods." *Race and Justice* 8, no. 1 (2017): 27–50.

Hollander, Jocelyn A. "Vulnerability and Dangerousness: The Construction of Gender Through Conversation About Violence." *Gender and Society* 15, no. 1 (2001): 83–109.

hooks, bell. *All About Love: New Visions*. New York: Perennial, 2001.

hooks, bell. *Feminist Theory: From Margin to Center*. Cambridge, MA: South End Press, 2000.

hooks, bell. "Homeplace (a site of resistance)." In *Yearning: Race, Gender, and Cultural Politics*. Boston: South End Press, 1990.

hooks, bell. *Killing Rage: Ending Racism*. New York: H. Holt, 1996.

hooks, bell. *Teaching to Transgress*. New York: Routledge, 1994.

hooks, bell. *Yearning: Race, Gender, and Cultural Politics*. Boston: South End Press, 1990.

Horne, Christine, and Stefanie Mollborn. "Norms: An Integrated Framework." *Annual Review of Sociology* 46 (2020): 467–87.

INCITE! Women of Color Against Violence, ed. *Law Enforcement Violence Against Women of Color and Trans People of Color: A Critical Intersection of Gender Violence and State Violence*. 2008. https://incite-national.org/wp-content/uploads/2018/08/TOOLKIT-FINAL.pdf.

Interrupting Criminalization. "Sexualization Not Safety: Black Girls, Trans and Gender Non-conforming Youth's Experiences of Police Presence in Schools." Our Names Network, 2024. https://www.interruptingcriminalization.com/resources-all/sexualization-not-safety-black -girls-trans-and-gender-nonconforming-youths-experience-of-police-presence-in-schools -report.

Irizarry, Yasmiyn, Ellis P. Monk, and Ryon J. Cobb. "Race-Shifting in the United States: Latinxs, Skin Tone, and Ethnoracial Alignments." *Sociology of Race and Ethnicity* 9, no. 1 (2023): 37–55.

Itzigsohn, José, and Karida L. Brown. "The Sociology of W. E. B. Du Bois: Racialized Modernity and the Global Color Line." In *The Sociology of W. E. B. Du Bois*. New York: New York University Press, 2020.

Iwama, Janice, Yasmiyn Irizarry, Amy Ernstes, Melissa Ripepi, Anthony A. Peguero, Jennifer M. Bondy, and Jun Sung Hong. "Segregation, Securitization, and Bullying: Investigating the Connections Between Policing, Surveillance, Punishment, and Violence." *Race and Justice* 14, no. 3 (2024): 313–34.

Jacobs, Michelle S. "The Violent State: Black Women's Invisible Struggle Against Police Violence." *William and Mary Journal of Race, Gender, and Social Justice* 24, no. 1 (2017). https:// scholarship.law.wm.edu/wmjowl/vol24/iss1/4.

Jennings-Fitz-Gerald, Emma, Chris M. Smith, N. Zoe Hilton, Dana L. Radatz, Jimin Lee, Elke Ham, and Natalie Snow. "A Scoping Review of Policing and Coercive Control in Lesbian, Gay, Bisexual, Transgender, and Queer Plus Intimate Relationships." *Sociology Compass* 18, no. 7 (2024): e13239. https://doi.org/10.1111/soc4.13239.

Jones, Elizabeth. "Racism, Fines and Fees and the US Carceral State." *Race and Class* 59, no. 3 (2018): 38–50.

Jones, Nikki. *Between Good and Ghetto: African American Girls and Inner-City Violence*. New Brunswick, NJ: Rutgers University Press, 2010.

Kaba, Mariame, and Andrea J. Ritchie. *No More Police: A Case for Abolition*. New York: New Press, 2022.

Kendall, Mikki. *Hood Feminism: Notes from the Women That a Movement Forgot*. New York: Viking, 2020.

Kerner National Advisory Commission on Civil Disorders. *Report of the National Advisory Commission on Civil Disorders*. Washington, DC: Government Printing Office, 1968.

Kim, Mimi E. "The Carceral Creep: Gender-Based Violence, Race, and the Expansion of the Punitive State, 1973–1983." *Social Problems* 67, no. 2 (2020): 251–69.

King, Deborah K. "Multiple Jeopardy, Multiple Consciousness: The Context of a Black Feminist Ideology." *Signs: Journal of Women in Culture and Society* 14, no. 1 (1988): 42–72.

Kolysh, Simone. *Everyday Violence: The Public Harassment of Women and LGBTQ People*. New Brunswick, NJ: Rutgers University Press, 2021.

Koslicki, Wendy M. "'Rhetoric Without Reality' or Effective Policing Strategy? An Analysis of the Relationship Between Community Policing and Police Fatal Force." *Journal of Criminal Justice* 72 (2021): 101730. https://doi.org/10.1016/j.jcrimjus.2020.101730.

Kramer, Rory, and Brianna Remster. "The Slow Violence of Contemporary Policing." *Annual Review of Criminology* 5, no. 1 (2022): 43–66.

Lacy, Karyn R. *Blue-Chip Black: Race, Class, and Status in the New Black Middle Class*. Oakland: University of California Press, 2007.

LaMartine, Samantha, Nadine Nakamura, and James J. Garcia. "'Even the Officers Are in on It': Black Transgender Women's Experiences of Violence and Victimization in Los Angeles." *Women and Therapy* 46, no. 2 (2023): 103–29.

LeFlouria, Talitha L. *Chained in Silence: Black Women and Convict Labor in the New South.* Chapel Hill: University of North Carolina Press, 2015.

Lindsey, Treva B. *America Goddam: Violence, Black Women, and the Struggle for Justice.* Oakland: University of California Press, 2022.

Lorde, Audre. "Epilogue." In *A Burst of Light: Essays.* Ithaca, NY: Firebrand Books, 1988.

Lorde, Audre. "The Master's Tools Will Never Dismantle the Master's House." In *Sister Outsider: Essays and Speeches,* 110–13. Trumansburg, NY: Crossing Press, 1984.

Lorde, Audre. *Sister Outsider: Essays and Speeches.* Trumansburg, NY: Crossing Press, 1984.

Luna, Zakiya, and Whitney Pirtle. "Black Feminist Sociology Is the Past, Present and Future of Sociology. Period." In *Black Feminist Sociology: Perspectives and Praxis,* edited by Zakiya Luna and Whitney Pirtle, 1–15. New York: Routledge, 2022.

Luna, Zakiya, and Whitney Pirtle, eds. *Black Feminist Sociology: Perspectives and Praxis.* New York: Routledge, 2022.

Madriz, Esther I. "Images of Criminals and Victims: A Study on Women's Fear and Social Control." *Gender and Society* 11, no. 3 (1997): 342–56.

Mahbubani, Rhea. "As Police Violence Comes Under More Scrutiny, Black Parents Say They're Still Giving Their Kids 'the Talk' About Dealing with Cops," Business Insider, June 27, 2020. https://www.businessinsider.com/black-parents-the-talk-racism-kids-police-violence-2020-6.

Malone Gonzalez, Shannon. "Black Girls and the Talk? Policing, Parenting, and the Politics of Protection." *Social Problems* 69, no. 1 (2022): 22–38.

Malone Gonzalez, Shannon. "Making It Home: An Intersectional Analysis of the Police Talk." *Gender and Society* 33, no. 3 (2019): 363–86.

Malone Gonzalez, Shannon, and Faith M. Deckard. "'We Got Witnesses': Black Women's Counter-Surveillance for Navigating Police Violence and Legal Estrangement." *Social Problems* 71, no. 3 (2022): 894–911.

Malone Gonzalez, Shannon, Shantel Gabrieal Buggs, and J'Mauri Jackson. "Mourning for Strangers: Black Women, Sequelae, and the Digital Afterlife of Police Violence." *Feminist Criminology,* 2024. https://doi.org/10.1177/15570851241258316.

Malone Gonzalez, Shannon, Samantha J. Simon, and Katie Kaufman Rogers. "The Diversity Officer: Police Officers' and Black Women Civilians' Epistemologies on Race and Racism in Policing." *Law and Society Review* 56, no. 3 (2022): 477–99.

Mays, Kyle T. *An Afro-Indigenous History of the United States.* Vol. 6. Boston, MA: Beacon Press, 2021.

McCall, Leslie. "The Complexity of Intersectionality." *Signs: Journal of Women in Culture and Society* 30, no. 3 (2005): 1771–1800.

McDonald, Autumn. "The Talk: It's Time for White Parents to Take Over a Grim Ritual That Black Families Have Performed for Decades." *Slate,* June 15, 2020. https://slate.com/human-interest/2020/06/white-parents-the-talk-racism-police-brutality.html.

McGuffey, C. Shawn. "Rape and Racial Appraisals: Culture, Intersectionality, and Black Women's Accounts of Sexual Assault." *Du Bois Review: Social Science Research on Race* 10, no. 1 (2013): 109–30.

McHarris, Philip V. *Beyond Policing: What Better Way to Make the Case for a Police Free World Than to Show a World Where It's Possible.* New York: Hachette Book Group, 2024.

McKittrick, Katherine. *Dear Science and Other Stories.* Durham, NC: Duke University Press, 2021.

Menjívar, Cecilia. "State Categories, Bureaucracies of Displacement, and Possibilities from the Margins." *American Sociological Review* 88, no. 1 (2023): 1–23.

Merritt, Candice. "Lest We Forget Black Patriarchy; or, Why I'm Over Calling Out White Women." *South Atlantic Quarterly* 122, no. 3 (2023): 485–503.

Meyer, Doug. "'So Much for Protect and Serve': Queer Male Survivors' Perceptions of Negative Police Experiences." *Journal of Contemporary Criminal Justice* 36, no. 2 (2020): 228–50.

Mills, Charles W. "White Ignorance." In *Race and Epistemologies of Ignorance*, edited by Shannon Sullivan and Nancy Tuana, 13–38. Albany: State University of New York Press, 2007.

Montgomery, David, and Michael Wines. "Dispute over Sandra Bland's Mental State Follows Death in a Texas Jail." *New York Times*, July 22, 2015. https://www.nytimes.com/2015/07/23/us/sandra-blands-family-says-video-sheds-no-light-on-reason-for-her-arrest.html.

Morris, Aldon. *The Scholar Denied: W. E. B. Du Bois and the Birth of Modern Sociology.* Oakland: University of California Press, 2017.

Morris, Edward W. "'Ladies' or 'Loudies'? Perceptions and Experiences of Black Girls in Classrooms." *Youth and Society* 38, no. 4 (2007): 490–515.

Morris, Monique W. *Pushout: The Criminalization of Black Girls in Schools.* New York: New Press, 2016.

Moynihan, Daniel P. *The Negro Family: The Case for National Action.* Washington, DC: Office of Policy Planning and Research, US Department of Labor, 1965.

Mueller, Jennifer. "Racial Ideology or Racial Ignorance? An Alternative Theory of Racial Cognition." *Sociological Theory* 38, no. 2 (2020): 142–69.

Muhammad, Khalil Gibran. *The Condemnation of Blackness: Race, Crime, and the Making of Modern Urban America, with a New Preface.* Harvard University Press, 2019.

Nash, Jennifer C. "Black Feminine Enigmas, or Notes on the Politics of Black Feminist Theory." *Signs: Journal of Women in Culture and Society* 45, no. 3 (2020): 519–23.

Nash, Jennifer C. "Re-Thinking Intersectionality." *Feminist Review* 89, no. 1 (2008): 1–15.

National Coalition Against Domestic Violence. "Domestic Violence and the Black Community," 2020. https://assets.speakcdn.com/assets/2497/dv_in_the_black_community.pdf.

Neely, Cheryl L. *You're Dead—So What?: Media, Police, and the Invisibility of Black Women as Victims of Homicide.* Lansing: Michigan State University Press, 2015.

Nicholson-Crotty, Sean, Jill Nicholson-Crotty, and Sergio Fernandez. "Will More Black Cops Matter? Officer Race and Police-Involved Homicides of Black Citizens." *Public Administration Review* 77, no. 2 (2017): 206–16.

Norwood, Carolette. "Black Feminist Sociology and the Politics of Space and Place at the Intersection of Race, Class, Gender and Sexuality." In *Black Feminist Sociology: Perspectives and Praxis*, edited by Zakiya Luna and Whitney L. Laster Pirtle, 139–50. Routledge Press, 2021.

Nuamah, Sally A., and Quinn Mulroy. "'I Am a Child!': Public Perceptions of Black Girls and Their Punitive Consequences." *Journal of Race, Ethnicity, and Politics* 8, no. 2 (2023): 182–201.

Office for Civil Rights. *Student Discipline and School Climate in U.S. Public Schools, 2020–21 Civil Rights Data Collection.* Washington, DC: US Department of Education, 2023. https://www

.ed.gov/sites/ed/files/about/offices/list/ocr/docs/crdc-discipline-school-climate-report
.pdf.

Office of Public Affairs. "Six Former Mississippi Law Enforcement Officers Sentenced for Torturing and Abusing Two Black Men." United States Department of Justice, March 21, 2024.
https://www.justice.gov/opa/pr/six-former-mississippi-law-enforcement-officers
-sentenced-torturing-and-abusing-two-black.

Omi, Michael, and Howard Winant. *Racial Formation in the United States*. New York: Rout-
ledge/Taylor & Francis Group, 2015.

O'Quinn, Jamie, Erika Slaymaker, Jess Goldstein-Kral, and Kathleen Broussard. "Sociology
from a Distance: Remote Interviews and Feminist Methods." *Qualitative Sociology* 47
(2024): 43–67.

Parker, Kim, Jocelyn Kiley, Shannon Greenwood, and Kim Arias. "Trust in America: Do Americans Trust the Police?" Pew Research Center, January 5, 2022. https://www.pewresearch.org
/politics/2022/01/05/trust-in-america-do-americans-trust-the-police/.

Parker, Kim, Juliana Menasce Horowitz, and Monica Anderson. "Amid Protests, Majorities
Across Racial and Ethnic Groups Express Support for the Black Lives Matter Movement."
Pew Research Center, June 12, 2020. https://www.pewresearch.org/social-trends/2020/06
/12/amid-protests-majorities-across-racial-and-ethnic-groups-express-support-for-the
-black-lives-matter-movement/.

Pattillo, Mary. *Black Picket Fences: Privilege and Peril Among the Black Middle Class*. 2nd edition.
Chicago: University of Chicago Press.

Patton, Stacey. *Spare the Kids: Why Whupping Children Won't Save Black America*. Boston: Beacon Press, 2017.

Perillo, Jennifer T., Rochelle B. Sykes, Sean A. Bennett, and Margaret C. Readon. "Examining
the Consequences of Dehumanization and Adultification in Justification of Police Use of
Force Against Black Girls and Boys." *Law and Human Behavior* 47, no. 1 (2023): 36–52.

Pettit, Becky, and Carmen Gutierrez. "Mass Incarceration and Racial Inequality." *American
Journal of Economics and Sociology* 77, nos. 3–4 (2018): 1153–82.

The Pew Charitable Trusts. "Local Spending on Jails Tops $25 Billion in Latest Nationwide
Data," January 29, 2021. https://pew.org/39Zzn8g.

Phelps, Michelle S. *The Minneapolis Reckoning: Race, Violence, and the Politics of Policing in America*. Princeton, NJ: Princeton University Press, 2024.

Pierson, Emma, Camelia Simoiu, Jan Overgoor, Sam Corbett-Davies, Daniel Jenson, Amy Shoe-
maker, Vignesh Ramachandran, Phoebe Barghouty, Cheryl Phillips, Ravi Shroff, and Sharad
Goel. "A Large-Scale Analysis of Racial Disparities in Police Stops Across the United States."
Nature Human Behaviour 4, no. 7 (2020): 736–45.

Piser, Karina. "The Walking While Trans Bill Is 'Stop and Frisk 2.0,'." *The Nation*, February 19,
2020. https://www.thenation.com/article/activism/walking-while-trans-repeal/.

Pittman, LaShawnDa L. *Grandmothering While Black: A Twenty-First-Century Story of Love,
Coercion, and Survival*. Berkeley: University of California Press, 2023.

Plummer, Ken. *Documents of Life 2: An Invitation to a Critical Humanism*. London: Sage Publica-
tions, 2001.

Polletta, Francesca, Pang Ching Bobby Chen, Beth Gharrity Gardner, and Alice Motes. "The
Sociology of Storytelling." *Annual Review of Sociology* 37 (2011): 109–30.

Polletta, Francesca, and Nathan Redman. "When Do Stories Change Our Minds? Narrative Persuasion About Social Problems." *Sociology Compass* 14, no. 4 (2020). https://doi.org/10.1111/soc4.12778.

Potter, Gary. "The History of Policing in the United States." *EKU School of Justice Studies* 1 (2013): 16.

Potter, Hillary. "An Argument for Black Feminist Criminology: Understanding African American Women's Experiences with Intimate Partner Abuse Using an Integrated Approach." *Feminist Criminology* 1, no. 2 (2006): 106–24.

Potter, Hillary. *Battle Cries: Black Women and Intimate Partner Abuse.* New York: New York University Press, 2008.

Powell, Amber Joy, and Michelle S. Phelps. "Gendered Racial Vulnerability: How Women Confront Crime and Criminalization." *Law and Society Review* 55, no. 3 (2021): 429–51.

President's Task Force on 21st Century Policing. *Final Report of the President's Task Force on 21st Century Policing.* Washington, DC: Office of Community Oriented Policing Services, 2015.

Presser, Lois. *Unsaid: Analyzing Harmful Silences.* Oakland, CA: University of California Press, 2022.

Prieto-Hodge, Kayla, and Donald Tomaskovic-Devey. "A Tale of Force: Examining Policy Proposal to Address Police Violence." *Social Currents* 8, no. 5 (2021): 403–23.

Ransby, Barbara. *Making All Black Lives Matter: Reimagining Freedom in the Twenty-First Century.* Oakland: University of California Press, 2018.

Ray, Rashawn, Connor Powelson, Genesis Fuentes, and Long Doan. "The Sociology of Police Behavior." *Annual Review of Sociology* 50 (2024): 565–79.

Reichel, Philip L. "Southern Slave Patrols as a Transitional Police Type." *American Journal of Police* 7 (1988): 51.

Remster, Brianna, Chris M. Smith, and Rory Kramer. "Race, Gender, and Police Violence in the Shadow of Controlling Images." *Social Problems* 71, no. 2 (2024): 353–76.

Reyes, Victoria. *Academic Outsider: Stories of Exclusion and Hope.* Stanford, CA: Stanford University Press, 2022.

Rhimes, Shonda, Jase Miles-Perez, and Felicia Pride, writers. *Grey's Anatomy,* season 17, episode 12, "Sign O' the Times." Directed by Michael Medico. Aired April 21, 2021, on ABC.

Richie, Beth. "Battered Black Women a Challenge for the Black Community." *The Black Scholar* 16, no. 2 (1985): 40–45.

Richie, Beth E. *Arrested Justice: Black Women, Violence, and America's Prison Nation.* New York: New York University Press, 2012.

Richie, Beth E. "A Black Feminist Reflection on the Antiviolence Movement." *Signs: Journal of Women in Culture and Society* 2, no. 200 (2000): 1133–37.

Richie, Beth E. *Compelled to Crime: The Gender Entrapment of Battered Black Women.* New York: Routledge Press, 1996.

Rios, Victor M. *Punished: Policing the Lives of Black and Latino Boys.* New York: New York University Press, 2011.

Rios, Victor M., Greg Prieto, and Jonathan M. Ibarra. "*Mano Suave–Mano Dura*: Legitimacy Policing and Latino Stop-and-Frisk." *American Sociological Review* 85, no. 1 (2020): 58–75.

Ritchie, Andrea. *Invisible No More: Police Violence Against Black Women and Women of Color.* Boston: Beacon Press, 2017.

Ritchie, Andrea. "Law Enforcement Violence Against Women of Color." In *Color of Violence: The INCITE! Anthology*, edited by INCITE! Women of Color Against Violence, 138–56. Durham, NC: Duke University Press, 2016.

Ritchie, Andrea. "Say Her Name: What It Means to Center Black Women's Experiences of Police Violence." In *Who Do You Serve, Who Do You Protect? Police Violence and Resistance in the United States*, edited by Maya Schenwar, Joe Macaré, Alana Yu-Ian Price, and Alicia Garza, 79–89. Chicago: Haymarket Books, 2016.

Ritchie, Andrea. *Shrouded in Silence—Police Sexual Violence: What We Know and What We Can Do About It*. Interrupting Criminalization, 2021. https://static1.squarespace.com/static/5ee39ec764dbd7179cf1243c/t/6077769f7193356648d260fe/1618441890605/Shrouded+in+Silence.pdf.

Ritterhouse, Jennifer. *Growing up Jim Crow: How Black and White Southern Children Learned Race*. Chapel Hill: University of North Carolina Press, 2006.

Roberts, Dorothy E. *Killing the Black Body: Race, Reproduction, and the Meaning of Liberty*. New York: Vintage Books, 1997.

Roberts, Dorothy E. *Torn Apart: How the Child Welfare System Destroys Black Families—and How Abolition Can Build a Safer World*. New York: Basic Books, 2022.

Robinson, Brandon A. "The Lavender Scare in Homonormative Times: Policing, Hyper-Incarceration, and LGBTQ Youth Homelessness." *Gender and Society* 34, no. 2 (2020): 210–32.

Rocha Beardall, Theresa. "Police Legitimacy Regimes and the Suppression of Citizen Oversite in Response to Police Violence." *Criminology: An Interdisciplinary Journal* 60 (2022): 740–65.

Roehrkasse, Alexander F., and Christopher Wildeman. "Lifetime Risk of Imprisonment in the United States Remains High and Starkly Unequal." *Science Advances* 8, no. 48 (2022): https://pmc.ncbi.nlm.nih.gov/articles/PMC11636687/pdf/sciadv.abo3395.pdf.

Rojek, Jeff, Richard Rosenfeld, and Scott Decker. "Policing Race: The Racial Stratification of Searches in Police Traffic Stops." *Criminology* 50, no. 4 (2012): 993–1024.

Roy, Arundhati. "Peace and the New Corporate Liberation Theology." City of Sidney. Peace Prize Lecture *CPACS Occasional Paper* 4, no. 2 (2004): 1–9. https://sydneypeacefoundation.org.au/wp-content/uploads/2012/02/2004-SPP_-Arundhati-Roy.pdf.

Russell, Stephen T., Amanda M. Pollitt, Gu Li, and Arnold H. Grossman. "Chosen Name Use Is Linked to Reduced Depressive Symptoms, Suicidal Ideation and Behavior Among Transgender Youth." *Journal of Adolescent Health* 63, no. 4 (2018): 503–505.

Saar, Malka Saada, Rebecca Epstein, Lindsay Rosenthal, and Yasmin Vafa. "The Sexual Abuse to Prison Pipeline: The Girls' Story." Georgetown Law Center on Poverty and Inequality, 2015. https://genderjusticeandopportunity.georgetown.edu/wp-content/uploads/2020/06/The-Sexual-Abuse-To-Prison-Pipeline-The-Girls-Story.pdf.

Schwartz, Joanna C. "The Case Against Qualified Immunity." *Notre Dame Law Review* 93, no. 5 (2018): 1797–1852.

Selod, Saher. *Forever Suspect: Racialized Surveillance of Muslim Americans in the War on Terror*. New Brunswick, NJ: Rutgers University Press, 2018.

Serrano, Uriel. "Feeling Carcerality: How Carceral Seepage Shapes Racialized Emotions." *Social Problems* (2024): spae059. https://doi.org/10.1093/socpro/spae059.

Sewell, Alyasah Ali, Justin M. Feldman, Rashawn Ray, Keon L. Gilbert, Kevin A. Jefferson, and Hedwig Lee. "Illness Spillovers of Lethal Police Violence: The Significance of Gendered Marginalization." *Ethnic and Racial Studies* 44, no. 7 (2021): 1089–1114.

Sierra-Arévalo, Michael. *The Danger Imperative: Violence, Death, and the Soul of Policing.* New York: Columbia University Press, 2024.

Simon, Samantha J. *Before the Badge: How Academy Training Shapes Police Violence.* New York: New York University Press, 2024.

Simon, Samantha J. "Training for War: Academy Socialization and Warrior Policing." *Social Problems* 70, no. 4 (2023): 1021–43.

Skolnick, Jerome H. "Corruption and the Blue Code of Silence." *Police Practice and Research* 3, no. 1 (2002): 7–19.

Slatton, Brittany C., and April L. Richard. "Black Women's Experiences of Sexual Assault and Disclosure: Insights from the Margins." *Sociology Compass* 14, no. 6 (2020). https://doi.org/10.1111/soc4.12792.

Smith, Brad W. "The Impact of Police Officer Diversity on Police-Caused Homicides." *Policy Studies Journal* 32, no. 2 (2003): 147–62.

Smith, Brad W., and Malcolm D. Holmes. "Police Use of Excessive Force in Minority Communities: A Test of the Minority Threat, Place, and Community Accountability Hypothesis." *Social Problems* 61, no. 1 (2014): 83–104.

Smith, Christen A. "Facing the Dragon: Black Mothering, Sequelae, and Gendered Necropolitics in the Americas." *Transforming Anthropology* 24, no. 1 (2016): 31–48.

Smith, Christen A. "Impossible Privacy: Black Women and Police Terror." *Black Scholar* 51, no. 1 (2021): 20–29.

Smith, Dorothy E. *The Everyday World as Problematic: A Feminist Sociology.* Boston: Northeastern University Press, 1987.

Sojoyner, Damien M. *Against the Carceral Archive: The Art of Black Liberatory Practice.* New York: Fordham University Press, 2023.

Spillers, Hortense J. "Mama's Baby, Papa's Maybe: An American Grammar Book." In *The Transgender Studies Reader Remix*, edited by Susan Stryker and Dylan McCarthy Blackston, 93–104. Routledge, 2022.

Spira, Tamara Lea, Dayjha McMillian, Madi Stapelton, and Verónica N. Vélez. "ACAB Means Abolishing the Cop in Our Heads, Hearts, and Homes: An Intergenerational Demand for Family Abolition." In *Abolition Feminisms*, vol. 2 of *Feminist Ruptures Against the Carceral State*. Chicago: Haymarket Books, 2022.

Spivak, Gayatri C. "Can the Subaltern Speak?" In *Marxism and the Interpretation of Culture*, edited by C. Nelson and L. Grossberg, 271–316. Urbana/Chicago: University of Illinois Press, 1988.

Stack, Liam. "Tulsa Police Officer Who Killed Unarmed Black Man Won't Face Civil Rights Charges." *New York Times*, March 1, 2019. https://www.nytimes.com/2019/03/01/us/betty-shelby-terence-crutcher-tulsa.html.

Steinmetz, Kevin F., Brian P. Schaefer, and Howard Henderson. "Wicked Overseers: American Policing and Colonialism." *Sociology of Race and Ethnicity* 3, no. 1 (2017): 68–81.

Stern, Scott W. "Shadow Trials, or a History of Sexual Assault Trials in the Jim Crow South." *UCLA Journal of Gender and Law* 29, no. 2 (2022): 257–334.

Stinson, Philip Matthews, Sr. *Criminology Explains Police Violence.* 1st ed. Oakland: University of California Press, 2020.

Stinson, Philip, John Liederbach, Steven Brewer, and Brook E. Mathna. "Police Sexual Misconduct: A National Scale Study of Arrested Officers." *Criminal Justice Policy Review* 26, no. 7 (2015): 665–90.

Stuart, Forrest, and Ava Benezra. "Criminalized Masculinities: How Policing Shapes the Construction of Gender and Sexuality in Poor Black Communities." *Social Problems* 65, no. 2 (2018): 174–90.

Sweet, Paige. *The Politics of Surviving: How Women Navigate Domestic Violence and Its Aftermath.* Oakland: University of California Press, 2021.

Tapp, Susannah N., and Elizabeth Davis. *Contacts Between Police and the Public, 2020.* Bureau of Justice Statistics. Washington, DC: Department of Justice, 2022. https://bjs.ojp.gov/media/document/cbpp20.pdf.

Terrill, William, and Jason R. Ingram. "Citizen Complaints Against the Police: An Eight City Examination." *Police Quarterly* 19, no. 2 (2016): 150–79.

Thomas, Deja, and Juliana Menasce Horowitz. "Support for Black Lives Matter Has Decreased Since June but Remains Strong Among Black Americans." Pew Research Center. September 16, 2020. https://www.pewresearch.org/short-reads/2020/09/16/support-for-black-lives-matter-has-decreased-since-june-but-remains-strong-among-black-americans/.

Thompson-Miller, Ruth, and Leslie H. Picca. "'There Were Rapes!: Sexual Assaults of African American Women and Children in Jim Crow." *Violence Against Women* 23, no. 8 (2017): 934–50.

Threadcraft, Shatema. "Making Black Femicide Visible: Intersectional, Abolitionist People-Building Against Epistemic Oppression." *Philosophical Topics* 49, no. 1 (2021): 35–44.

Tillman, Korey. "Carceral Liberalism: The Coloniality and Antiblackness of Coercive Benevolence." *Social Problems* 70, no. 3 (2022): 635–49.

Toliver, S. R. *Recovering Black Storytelling in Qualitative Research: Endarkened Storywork.* New York: Routledge Press, 2022.

Travers, and Barbara J. Risman, eds. "Symposium: Say Her Name." *Gender and Society* 35, no. 4 (2021): 521–658.

Turney, Kristin. "Depressive Symptoms Among Adolescents Exposed to Personal and Vicarious Police Contact." *Society and Mental Health* 11, no. 2 (2021): 113–33.

Underhill, Megan R. "Parenting During Ferguson: Making Sense of White Parents' Silence." *Ethnic and Racial Studies* 41, no. 11 (2018): 1934–51.

Vitale, Alex S. *The End of Policing.* Verso Books, 2021.

Washington Post. "Police Shootings Database 2015–2024." Accessed October 25, 2024. https://www.washingtonpost.com/graphics/investigations/police-shootings-database/.

Weitzer, Ronald, and Rod K. Brunson. "Strategic Responses to Police Among Inner City Youth." *Sociological Quarterly* 50, no. 2 (2009): 235–56.

Wells-Barnett, Ida B. *The Red Record: Tabulated Statistics and Alleged Causes of Lynchings in the United States 1892–1893–1894.* Chicago: Donohue & Henneberry, 1895.

Westmarland, Louise. "Police Ethics and Integrity: Breaking the Blue Code of Silence." *Policing and Society* 15, no. 2 (2006): 145–65.

Whitaker, Tracy R., and Cudore L. Snell. "Parenting While Powerless: Consequences of 'the Talk.'" *Journal of Human Behavior in the Social Environment* 26, nos. 3–4 (2016): 303–309.

The White House. "Remarks of President Joe Biden—State of the Union Address as Prepared for Delivery," February 8, 2023. https://www.whitehouse.gov/briefing-room/speeches-remarks/2023/02/07/remarks-of-president-joe-biden-state-of-the-union-address-as-prepared-for-delivery/.

Williams, Apryl. "Black Memes Matter: #LivingWhileBlack with Becky and Karen." *Social Media + Society* 6, no. 4 (2020). https://doi.org/10.1177/2056305120981047.

Williams, Sherri. "Digital Defense: Black Feminists Resist Violence with Hashtag Activism." *Feminist Media Studies* 15, no. 2 (2015): 341–44.

Wilson, T. Anansi. "What is BlaQueer?" *BlaQueerFlow*. 2014. https://blaqueerflow.wordpress.com/about/what-is-blaqueer-2014/.

Wun, Connie. "Against Captivity: Black Girls and School Discipline Policies in the Afterlife of Slavery." *Educational Policy* 30, no. 1 (2016): 171–96.

Wun, Connie. "Unaccounted Foundations: Black Girls, Anti-Black Racism, and Punishment in Schools." *Critical Sociology* 42, nos. 4–5 (2016): 737–50.

Yazdiha, Hajar. "The Relational Dynamics of Racialised Policing: Community Policing for Counterterrorism, Suspect Communities, and Muslim Americans' Provisional Belonging." *Journal of Ethnic and Migration Studies* 49, no. 11 (2023): 2676–97.

Zuberi, Tukufu, and Eduardo Bonilla-Silva, eds. *White Logic, White Methods: Racism and Methodology.* Lanham, MD: Rowman & Littlefield Publishers, 2008.

INDEX

A NOTE ON THE TYPE

This book has been composed in Arno, an Old-style serif typeface in the classic Venetian tradition, designed by Robert Slimbach at Adobe.